T0328143

After Leadership

Leadership studies today resembles a bewildering diversity of theories, concepts, constructs and approaches, struggling in huge part for meaning, relevance and impact. As Dennis Tourish so eloquently puts it, much of the literature suffers from 'unrelenting triviality' and 'sterile preoccupations'. Seeking to create a clean break from this current state of leadership studies, *After Leadership* begins with the premise of a post-apocalyptic world where only fragments of 'leadership science' now remain, echoing Alisdair McIntyre's imagining of such a scene as the basis for re-establishing the foundations and focus of moral theory. From these fragments, the authors seek to construct a new leadership studies that challenges much of the established thinking on leadership, exposes its limitations and biases, and, most importantly, seeks to construct the foundations of a more inclusive, participatory, bold, relational and social platform for leadership in the future.

After Leadership thus imagines a brave new world where what leadership is and what we seek from it can be developed anew, rather than remaining bound up in the problematic traditions and preoccupations that characterise leadership studies today.

Offering both full length chapter explorations that explore new ways of understanding and practicing leadership, as well as shorter essays that aim to provoke further reflection on leadership and what we seek of it, *After Leadership* offers a uniquely critical and creative collection that will inspire students, scholars and leadership educators to reconsider their understanding and practice of leadership.

Brigid Carroll is Associate Professor in the Department of Management and International Business at the University of Auckland Business School, New Zealand.

Josh Firth is a PhD student at the University of Auckland Business School, New Zealand.

Suze Wilson is a Senior Lecturer at Massey University, New Zealand.

Routledge Studies in Leadership Research

After Leadership

Edited by Brigid Carroll, Josh Firth
and Suze Wilson

Routledge
Taylor & Francis Group

NEW YORK AND LONDON

First published 2019
by Routledge
605 Third Avenue, New York, NY 10017

and by Routledge
2 Park Square, Milton Park, Abingdon, Oxon, OX14 4RN

First issued in paperback 2020

Routledge is an imprint of the Taylor & Francis Group, an informa business

Copyright © 2019 Taylor & Francis

The right of Brigid Carroll, Josh Firth and Suze Wilson to be identified as the authors of the editorial material, and of the authors for their individual chapters, has been asserted in accordance with sections 77 and 78 of the Copyright, Designs and Patents Act 1988.

Library of Congress Cataloging-in-Publication Data
Names: Carroll, Brigid, editor. | Wilson, Suze, editor. | Firth, Josh.
Title: After leadership / edited by Brigid Carroll, Suze Wilson, and Josh Firth.
Description: New York, NY: Routledge, 2019. |
Series: Routledge studies in leadership research | Includes index.
Identifiers: LCCN 2018026776 | ISBN 9781138087811 (hardback) |
ISBN 9781315110196 (ebook)
Subjects: LCSH: Leadership.
Classification: LCC HD57.7 .A345 2019 | DDC 658.4/092–dc23
LC record available at https://lccn.loc.gov/2018026776

ISBN 13: 978-0-367-73319-3 (pbk)
ISBN 13: 978-1-138-08781-1 (hbk)

Typeset in Sabon
by Deanta Global Publishing Services, Chennai, India

Contents

List of Illustrations

Figures

Tables

List of Contributors

Brigid Carroll is Associate Professor at the University of Auckland Business School. She was drawn into leadership studies through investigating leadership as a possible alternative and emancipatory discourse, identity and practice. Currently, she is interested in leadership in a grassroots and transboundary context.

Peter Case is Professor of Organisation Studies at the University of the West of England and a member of the Bristol Leadership and Change Centre. He also holds a part-time chair in management at James Cook University, North Queensland, Australia. An irresistible offer of employment from Exeter University's Centre for Leadership Studies some 15 years ago enticed him into the leadership field and his current interest is in anthropological and linguistic understandings of leadership phenomena. Peter acts as a consultant to the Bill & Melinda Gates Foundation-funded research centre, Malaria Elimination Initiative, and has extensive experience of running rural development projects in Southeast Asia.

Stewart Clegg is Distinguished Professor at the University of Technology Sydney Business School and Visiting Professor at Nova School of Business, Lisboa, Portugal. His interest in leadership is an extension of his general interest in power relations and the result of having experienced extremes of occasionally good and mostly bad leadership in universities.

Josh Firth is Doctoral Researcher at the University of Auckland Business School. He is intrigued by the complexities of power that lie at the heart of leadership assumptions, and the question of whether or not leadership can and should be redeemed. His current research is an ethnographic exploration of the changing sociomaterial practices of leadership and management in the age of algorithms.

Jackie Ford is Professor of Leadership and Organisation Studies at Durham University Business School. She has long-standing frustrations with much research on leadership, especially the absent recognition of power and identities, and through her research she seeks to unsettle dominant understandings. Current interests include critical feminist, psychosocial and interdisciplinary approaches that recognise specific gender, wider diversity and ethical dimensions, and ways in which leadership research and practice impact on working lives.

Jonathan Gosling is an independent academic who is happily no longer managed. Emeritus at Exeter University and Visiting Professor at IIM-Ahmedabad & Renmin University, he is involved with several ventures aimed at more humane organisations (e.g. coachingourslves.com), the One Planet MBA and is also busy with Organisation Development in health care in Zimbabwe and the United Kingdom. He is interested in leadership where it might contribute to this.

Nancy Harding is Professor of Human Resource Management at the University of Bath School of Management, United Kingdom. She was drawn to studying leadership through finding herself, 22 years ago, allocated an office opposite Jackie Ford's. Over that first 'Hello, who are you?' cup of coffee, there was a meeting of minds and the start of a long and productive friendship during which Jackie introduced Nancy to critical leadership studies. Her current interests in leadership revolve around the notion of 'followership', which she finds deeply disturbing.

Vesa Huotari is Senior Researcher at the Police University College, Finland. An assignment in the evaluation of leadership competence in the police brought him originally into the field of leadership studies. Today, he finds the idea of leadership being stripped or naturalised, that is, approached and grasped rather from its effects than its presumed sources, most intriguing.

Marian Iszatt-White is Lecturer at the Lancaster University Management School, United Kingdom. She was drawn to studying leadership on the back of her experiences as a senior manager working in industry, and the desire to figure out whether leadership and management really are different. Her current interests revolve around leadership as emotional labour and the identity issues raised by the juxtaposing of emotional labour and authenticity in leadership.

Steve Kempster is Professor of Leadership Learning and Development at Lancaster University Management School, United Kingdom. He became interested in leadership learning through a frustration with the question 'are leaders born or made?' With an increasing need for leadership studies to make a useful contribution to humanity, Steve wonders whether humanity would be worse off if the billions spent on leadership studies and leadership development were spent elsewhere. To misquote Monty Python, 'what has [leadership studies] ever done for us?'

David Knights is Distinguished Scholar at Lancaster University Management School, United Kingdom. His research interests are broad within the area of work and organisation studies including gender, technology, higher education and the financial sector. His current research has been related to academics in business schools, the global financial crisis, leadership, the body and embodiment, and most recently, veterinary surgeons.

Donna Ladkin is Professor of Leadership and Ethics with Antioch University's PhD in Leadership and Change in the United States. She is drawn to exploring leadership as a lived phenomenon, particularly in terms of how it is experienced from aesthetic and embodied perspectives. Her current leadership fascination focuses on how Foucault's notion of discipline could inform the reality, versus the fantasy, of what it means to take up the leader role.

Helena Liu is Senior Lecturer at the University of Technology Sydney Business School. She chased leadership studies in fear of conforming to virulent stereotypes of Asian scholars, but now hopes her theorising may be activated towards decolonising leadership as well as decolonising her mind. She is currently writing her first book on anti-racist feminist resistance in leadership.

Sonia M. Ospina is Professor of Public Management and Policy at the R.F. Wagner School of Public Service, New York University. Her interest in the dynamics of social change drew her into leadership studies. She is currently exploring social change leaders' use of social identity as a leadership resource, and inquiring – with the leadership scholars' network Co-Lead Net – into the implications of a collective lens for leadership research and practice.

Martin Parker is Professor of Organisation Studies at the Management Department, University of Bristol. He is drawn to leadership studies only in order to puncture its smug pretensions. He is currently working on a book on anarchist thought and theories of organisation.

Ken Parry was Professor of Leadership Studies and Co-director of the Deakin Leadership Centre at Deakin University, in Melbourne. He sadly passed away in February 2018. Ken was an outstanding scholar (he wrote over 40 international journal articles, 28 chapters – including his chapter in this volume – and wrote and co-edited 7 books) and a wonderful teacher and supervisor. But more importantly, Ken never walked by an issue that needed attention, or indeed someone that needed help. Those who were fortunate to know Ken would all agree 'he was a great bloke': long may he run.

Miguel Pina e Cunha is Professor of Organisation Theory and Organisational Behavior at Nova School of Business and Economics, Universidade Nova de Lisboa Lisbon, Portugal. His research deals mostly with the surprising (paradox, improvisation, serendipity, zemblanity, vicious circles) and the extreme (positive organising, genocide). Miguel co-authored (with Arménio Rego and Stewart Clegg) *The Virtues of Leadership: Contemporary Challenge for Global Managers* (Oxford University Press, 2012) and received the 2015 Best Paper Award from the European Management Review.

xii   *List of Contributors*

Neil Sutherland spent his formative years touring across the world in DIY punk bands. Through this – playing in squats, social centres and radical bookshops – he became interested in how people were constructing practical and actionable alternatives to more traditional forms of organising. The theme of alternatives runs throughout his work, encompassing research on gender studies, industries and leadership. He still plays in punk bands.

Scott Taylor is Reader in Leadership and Organisation Studies at Birmingham Business School, United Kingdom. He started to research leadership and teach leadership studies to understand better why people follow. He is currently analysing data that provides insight into the embodiment of charismatic leadership.

Suze Wilson is Senior Lecturer in the School of Management at Massey University in New Zealand. Her ongoing fascination with leadership hinges on its complex and contested character and its potential to bring out both the best and worst in people. Her work seeks to foster new and different ways of thinking about leadership that better recognise these concerns.

1 Introduction

Brigid Carroll, Josh Firth and Suze Wilson

Leadership holds a paradoxical place in contemporary thought. On the one hand, ineffective and/or unethical leadership is commonly seen as a central, even causative, element of much that worries us, such as war, inequality, injustice and environmental degradation. Yet, on the other hand, it is to romantic notions of heroic leadership that attention so often turns when looking for some way through, past or around the challenges we face. As a consequence of these tendencies, understandings and expectation of leadership often fall prey to polarising extremes or wishful thinking. Indeed, it was as we were exploring these very concerns, at a seminar hosted by Brigid in 2016, that someone posed the provocative question: should we just do away with 'the L-word', given it has become over-burdened with a multiplicity of troubling, contradictory, limiting and yet impossible-to-fulfil expectations? This planted the seed in our minds that, eventually, became this book, in which we and our authors explore if there is something new and different that might come *after leadership*, or, at least, after leadership has been reimagined, reframed and rethought.

To take this intriguing possibility forward, this book takes inspiration from Alasdair McIntyre's *After Virtue* and in particular its opening chapter 'A Disquieting Suggestion'. In this chapter, MacIntyre describes a post-apocalyptic world where society has turned against the natural sciences for their perceived role in a series of environmental disasters and has abolished science, incarcerated scientists, and destroyed the majority of science books and artefacts. While such a regime doesn't last, all that remains with which to rebuild science are fragments of decontextualised, disconnected and sometimes illegible texts, theories, philosophies and artefacts. We quote MacIntyre's description of such a catastrophe here:

> Imagine that the natural sciences were to suffer the effects of a catastrophe. A series of environmental disasters are blamed by the general public on the scientists. Widespread riots occur, laboratories are burned down, physicists are lynched, books and instruments are destroyed. Finally a Know-Nothing political movement takes power and successfully abolishes science teaching in schools and universities, imprisoning

and executing the remaining scientists. Later still there is a reaction against this destructive movement and enlightened people seek to revive science, although they have largely forgotten what it was. But all that they possess are fragments.[1]

After Virtue is a true classic and landmark work in ethics and morality and we certainly make no claim to be anywhere near its exalted company. We merely seek to borrow the premise above for leadership studies and follow to some extent MacIntyre's key aims of deconstructing the current state of such studies in order to build a different future for those moving forward. We agree that we do live in a time of a number of catastrophes that can clearly be laid at leadership's door – global warming, polarisation of wealth and poverty, unresolved and often generational conflicts and wars, racism, sexism and fear and mistrust of 'the other' – to name but a few. We can't be sure whether leadership scholars and scholarship would be held to account for these and confess that we doubt that leadership scholars are in fact considered influential and significant to any degree at all. That, of course, might be the bitterest truth of all for us in such a scenario. However, let's proceed as if we are in fact a key player in such a scenario and we have something to offer a new epoch of leadership studies – and in so doing we might find relevance and value if indeed we lack it now.

Arising from this, the overall intent of *After Leadership* is to step readers into an imaginative recreation of leadership and its theories and practices that will offer bold, creative and compelling ideas for how leadership might evolve into the future. By creating a 'mythic and metaphoric' break with the past and present of leadership research, we hope to enable ourselves and our authors to be less fettered by the constraints and limitations of the field, so that readers will find here genuinely new and exciting ways to work with leadership as a theory and set of practices. Put simply, we want this book to go further than any has before in projecting leadership firmly into the future.

While our debt is to MacIntyre and our inspiration is a future world where someone – an academic, practitioner, activist, critic, youth – will collect and sift through leadership fragments of a bygone era on the off chance of finding something of value, the driver for this book lies in a sense of current leadership scholarship, practice and development as being stuck in a holding pattern. We see a field bounded by old or well-established ways of thinking and doing, engaging in limited critical assessment of its assumptions and making few excursions into new or exciting terrains. We want to test this sense with readers right at the start of this book.

We know that leadership studies today resembles a bewildering diversity of theories, concepts, constructs and approaches, struggling in huge part for meaning, relevance and impact. Much of the literature suffers from 'unrelenting triviality' and 'sterile preoccupations'.[2] Yet nor are we tempted by any forlorn desire to converge on any one definition of leadership or to privilege any particular school of theory. In short, ontological, epistemo-logical and methodological polyphony delight us and attest to the energy of a conceptual terrain. We are wary, however, of a concept that can come to mean everything and therefore end up meaning nothing.[3] Leadership is attributed to CEOs earning more than 250 times the average wage;[4] lone entrepreneurs; celebrities; the unexpected heroic individual who achieves 'success'; collaborative networks engaging in one of society's wicked problems; high school students chosen as prefects; and team, division and site managers trying to get through their 'to do' list. If leadership can be applied to all of the above, then to whom can't it be applied? If leadership encompasses exceptional success, the relentless slog through everyday work activity, the discovery of some breakthrough idea and the multiple small ordinary moments that connect people and groups in larger endeavours, then is there anything that can't be called leadership? If we return to MacIntyre's post-apocalyptic scenario presented earlier, then one fear is that surviving fragments show no traces of anything conceptually coherent at all but, instead, merely offer a bricolage of phenomena at the intersection of authority, position, management and influence.

We need to not stop our scrutiny at the scholarship and studies of leadership, for we are aware of complicities and confusions at the level of practice and development equally. Many of us, academics and practitioners alike, pay attention to leadership in the first place because we experience poor, bad, toxic and inadequate leadership in our places of work, in our communities and nations, and in the international and global arenas of which we are all a part. There is no solace or solution to be found in a reductionist blame game here, however. While there are certainly individuals who lack the skills to be part of effective leadership processes, there are deeper material and epistemic structures and challenges that make it formidable for even those with immense human, social and cultural capital to achieve what our world needs. Vast sums of money are being poured into leadership development efforts in schools, universities, businesses, social enterprises and in every community and social context one could think of to build leadership capability and capacity, as if that is the sole or obvious solution to our leadership 'problem'. This book invites us to step back from this frenzied effort to interrogate the nature of leadership itself, consider its deep ties to assumptions that are problematic or limiting, and to focus on the imaginative possibilities with which it can be reconstructed.

Foremost we offer this book as a work of conceptual theorising and the authors, alongside us editors, take the role of conceptual theorist in this context and in this instance. We are not foolish enough, however, to believe intrinsically in such typologies and instead merely wish to point out that the nature of this book has invited and given permission for the conceptual theorist to emerge from us all.

We take our definition of conceptual theory, and the conceptual theorist, from Ian Mitroff and Ralph Kilmann's 'The Four-Fold Way of Knowing'.

Consequently, conceptual theory is oriented towards *interesting* theory, as opposed to demonstratively true theory. Theory can be considered interesting if it: 1) makes the underlying assumptions of a field or conceptual terrain visible; 2) if it exposes such assumptions 'for critical and public scrutiny'; and 3) offers and argues for counter-assumptions.[5] We need to note that Mitroff and Kilmann argue that conceptual theory is a tricky process and runs the risk of being called obvious, irrelevant or absurd. Those are risks we are prepared to take in efforts to 'shake us from our dogmatic slumbers' and 'mount the strongest possible challenge to our most sacred, cherished, and commonly accepted ideas'.[6]

We therefore invite the reader to encounter a range of authors who fit the following description:

> Apparently, the Conceptual Theorist is a speculative theorist who deeply values broad-ranging novel ideas, and who does not demand that these ideas be tied down to 'reality' in the sense of being verified by accepted theories or facts. Indeed, the CT often prefers to challenge known facts and ideas, if only for the sake of speculative argument. Above all, the CT values the creation of novel conceptual possibilities, schemata and hypotheses which allow us to revise, rethink, and challenge even the most firmly entrenched and accepted ideas.[7]

This book will be successful if no entrenched plank of leadership studies is left entirely unturned and if a proliferation of new thinking can be sparked from its pages. So, let's turn to who this book is for and how it should be read.

This book is primarily aimed at leadership scholars. Its provocative nature, along with the professional standing and influence of many of its contributors, means it will potentially attract the attention of both critical and mainstream scholars, offering what we hope will be a unique and important source of inspiration. It should also be of interest to management scholars more generally who recognise that leadership plays an important role in contemporary workplace relationships and decision making, even if they do not directly study it.

Despite our scholarly focus, many of the chapters are written in ways that a practitioner and lay audience will find accessible, so we hope the book will also find a wider readership from those with a general interest in the topic who, in an era of unsettling change, are looking for fresh thinking about leadership. Equally, this book should be of interest to a senior undergraduate and postgraduate student audience, particularly as a resource to showcase the latest and most creative and critically inspired thinking in respect of leadership.

Extensive prior knowledge is not assumed, as each chapter is a standalone contribution that examines some aspect of the leadership phenomenon. We hope readers will come to this book to find a counter-argument to thinking they find in other leadership books. It stands, we hope, as an antidote to a terrain that is too often elite, rarefied, abstracted, masculine, Western and overly rational. We would love this to be the book that prospective research students pick up to spark a thesis topic or new inquiry, as they look to move to the cusp and edges of the current discipline. Yet no matter who picks up this book, we hope they *feel* something as a result of having read it, be that shock, surprise, relief to see something in words that legitimises their instincts, outrage, excitement, disbelief or hope. In a sense, it doesn't matter what the reaction is, for our ambition is that these pages exhibit a rare scholarship that speaks to a reader's emotional and imaginative repertoire.

Regardless of background, then, we want to invite you as a reader to playfully engage with the scenario posed in this book, just as the contributors have. Each chapter presents a possible response to the central question it raises, which is whether or how leadership theory ought to be rebuilt. Authors vary in the degree and manner in which they have brought this imaginative scenario to life in each chapter, just as they vary immensely in the extent to which they seek to hold to, reclaim, redefine, or outright abandon the contours of the leadership canon. The structure of the book reflects this variation, with each section increasing the degree of radical departure. As such, each chapter can be read as a conversation partner that invites you also to step into the role of a conceptual theorist and lay aside momentarily whatever learning, theoretical frameworks or assumptions you may have about leadership in order to find fresh insights and possibilities.

We are going to state that this is a book worth reading from cover to cover, but not necessarily in one sitting and not necessarily in linear fashion. This is a book that is worth a prolonged swim from shore to shore, a deep dive into one or more of its spaces, or a playful paddle on its fringes. The chapters reflect such different approaches. Some are scholarly, serious and dense; some are polemics – direct, impassioned and persuasive; others blend fiction, media and commentary in creative and provocative ways. We haven't standardised or restrained the length, tone, voice or genre of the chapters: if this is a book that works off fragments towards a new scholarly future, then an expansive range of authorial and scholarly styles and techniques are to be encouraged. We can safely say there is nothing dehydrated about the academic or scholarly here – and that would be one of our hopes for a new leadership epoch.

Overview of the Book

We set out the three parts of our book and give a summary of each of the chapters here to frame your encounter with this book, enable you to pinpoint a jumping-in point, or guide you in how to wander across its many delights and differences.

Part I: Revealing, Reframing, Reimagining

Part I of this book brings together chapters that hone in directly, deeply and intently on one core fragment of the leadership studies world. Such fragments – competencies, scientism, emotionality, leaders and bodies – unlock some of the key boundaries in the field to date and make visible many of the contours of the leadership landscape that can appear concreted in. The book begins with them as they provide entry points into the reframing, refining and reimagining of the leadership future that we aim to help advance. We note that none of the chapters stop at merely revealing a lack or a deficit. Rather, all offer radical, transformational alternatives for a world hopefully poised to put together such fragments in new ways, combinations and wholes. In order, we now introduce each of these.

Chapter Two

Vesa Huotari and Brigid Carroll's 'An Archaeological Dig into Leadership Competencies in the Twenty-First Century' takes a literal and direct approach to the leadership apocalypse scenario posed by the book and title and for that reason it opens the book. Two motifs – archaeology and cartography – underpin this chapter as the authors lament the fact that the bulk of leadership research and artefact fragments that might survive the apocalypse are likely to be competency-based lists, assessments and descriptions. These they liken to maps, using which they embark on an archaeological-style 'dig' to prove their importance to their creators and adherents, and the research and practice cultures of the era from which they emerged. They then turn to alternative cartography to generate new and alternative mapping possibilities, settling on new reference points of an organised social whole (latitude) and contestability (longitude). These, they argue, will ensure any new post-apocalyptic mapping ventures honour leadership as an emergent, collective, dynamic and fluid concept and set of practices that are best represented in processually aware, aesthetically provocative, conversational and contextual ways. In short, this chapter gives competencies the full post-apocalyptic makeover.

Chapter Three

Scott Taylor's 'Reviving the Moral Meaning of Leading and Following: The Lost Metaphysics of Leadership' references MacIntyre and *After Virtue* in a sustained and direct way and begins by locating us in our lecture halls and classrooms with students. For both these reasons – the link to MacIntyre and the evoking of teaching and students as central to the leadership's future enterprise – we wanted to position this chapter close to the beginning of the book. The chapter borrows MacIntyre's concept of a 'lost metaphysics' as a central issue for the leadership research and education of our times.

Any moral or metaphysical dimension of leadership gets lost in the perva-siveness of scientism, which privileges abstract, empirical, evidential and 'tidy' thought. Readers – past and present students, teachers and lectur-ers – will recognise the example of working with a class and co-creating an exploratory, participatory, discovery-oriented interaction and thinking space, only to watch all traces of it recede back into scientism at assessment and examination time. Taylor again borrows from MacIntyre in seeking to ground leadership studies in philosophical and conceptual debate, which is strongly embodied and embedded in enactment and equally open to revision and ongoing dialogue.

Chapter Four

Marian Iszatt-White's 'I, Leader: Becoming Human Through the Emotional Grounding of Leadership Practice' offers a provocative analysis reveal-ing the limited, problematic manner in which emotions are routinely dealt with in leadership studies – as potentially irksome or useful 'add-ons' to an assumed core of rationality which can be measured, rendered 'objective', deployed for instrumental purposes and made amenable to dispassionate discussion. She then experiments with a reversal of this state of affairs, in which she imagines reason being rendered subservient to emotion, but finds this is also wanting. However, the experiment serves to reveal a further alternative, one which embraces both reason and emotions as central fea-tures of human nature and, thus, as central features of leadership. Through making this shift in our thinking, she argues, the criticality of emotions to questions of purpose, to leader identity and to the role of leader as a source of guidance becomes evident. The proposition advanced is that this entwine-ment of both emotion and reason, in which each tempers the limitations of the other, is vital if leadership studies is to help stave off an actual, rather than imaginary, apocalypse. Indeed, the extent to which leadership studies is at present routinely neglectful of or distanced from the place of emotions in human existence is further exposed through Iszatt-White's discussion of interactions between robots and humans, drawn from Isaac Asimov novels, throughout the chapter. From these, we are left with the clear message that leadership studies is itself currently all too robotic when it comes to grap-pling with the centrality of emotions to what it is to be a human involved in leadership.

Chapter Five

Steve Kempster and Ken Parry's 'After Leaders: A World of Leading and Leadership ... with no Leaders' literally waves goodbye to leaders and investigates how leading becomes leadership without the need to enshrine individuals as leaders. Nouns need to give way to verbs. Banishing leaders means banishing entity concerns such as charisma, ego and personality and placing purpose front, right and centre, which they argue the bulk of leadership studies to date has failed to do. This chapter is structured as a critically reflexive dialogue between Steve and Ken where Steve offers and details a new language – a language of inputs, processes and outputs – while Ken tests how this might work particularly through words, talk and speeches. Their dialogue is playful, provocative, irreverent, bold and warm. They put themselves firmly on the page and bring their formidable flair, passion, energy and commitment to this chapter. This was finished just before Ken's death, in February 2018, and as you read this chapter remember a scholar who in many ways forged a path that this book has tried to tread in pushing back the boundaries of the discipline and being unafraid to bring a strong, personal, lively and ethical voice to a field of studies in which he was, and will remain, a key figure. Ken writes in this chapter that he wasn't sure if he was a leader or not – something he calls a 'narrow pass leader' – and gives himself a one out of four. While we don't want to give him a title (leader) he argues us out of, we must acknowledge his extraordinary sustained leading and contribution to leadership in this space.

Chapter Six

David Knights' 'Leadership Lives? Affective Leaders in a Neo-humanist World' fittingly concludes this section in the scholarly, erudite, expansive manner we expect from him and, without realising it a priori, speaks to all the chapters in this section in one way or the other. His title 'Leadership Lives?' needs to be read as both a question and an invitation into a neo-humanism that acknowledges the affective, embodied and ethical in leadership. Like all the chapters in this section, he rues what he terms a 'proprietary individualistic, psychologistic, reductionist, and deterministic' legacy of leadership scholarship. He brings power necessarily into dialogue with this legacy, but it pops up in perhaps a rather expected place in directing us to the body, embodiment and affect as one way to subvert and transform both leadership scholarship and practice. He argues that while the body is often minimally present, that presence is not often made visible reflexively or critically. This he calls the 'absence presence' of the body. His chapter looks for an inter-corporeality not just with other humans but with the material world as well. From such inter-corporeality comes an ethical identity and responsibility that is as far from instrumental as one can get.

Part II: Unravelling, Disentangling, Refashioning

In the second part of the book, our authors adopt a determinedly sceptical, perhaps even hostile, attitude towards conventional understandings of leadership, seeking to unravel what has been normalised, disentangle what is typically only implied rather than spelt out, and highlight ways in which we might now refashion how leadership is conceptualised, researched and practised. What these contributions share in common is a mode of analysis which exposes assumptions that are routinely hidden from conscious attention or are presumed to be rational, ethical or desirable, revealing instead their problematic nature or effects. In shaking the very foundations on which conventional understandings of leadership rely, however, new possibilities begin to emerge as to how leadership could be constituted differently. What is on offer here, then, is a critique designed to liberate and empower, along with an exploration of how things might be otherwise.

Chapter Seven

Helena Liu's 'Redoing and Abolishing Whiteness in Leadership' addresses the underlying 'whiteness' that has permeated leadership studies, leadership practice and leadership development right from the onset. Whiteness can be defined as a set of interdependent assumptions and conceptual propositions that create, maintain and normalise white supremacy and privilege. The invisibility of such a pervasiveness has been almost total over the history of leadership studies and this chapter sets out a way of reading, recognising and breaking through its pervasiveness. Liu draws on critical race theory in a mission to both redo and abolish whiteness that draws on discursive strategies of renaming and re-languaging, counterstorying, political listening and rejecting any complicity with any aspect of a whiteness ideology. This chapter is central in our endeavour to rethink leadership studies at the point of its hypothetical demise, as this chapter lifts the veil on the degree to which leadership has always been indebted and complicit to white privilege. Pull the threads of whiteness, as this chapter does, and leadership begins to unravel at multiple points creating glimpses of the spaces where something else might grow, if we can do this redoing and abolishing work well enough.

Chapter Eight

Nancy Harding offers us a delightfully novel take on a cult classic in 'Films as Archives of Leadership Theories: The Terminator Film Franchise'. In this chapter, she considers what we might learn about leadership theory if the only artefacts that remained to us were films. Marshalling a diverse array of literature from media studies and feminist critique to organisation theory, Harding argues that, perhaps against our first impressions, films go beyond mere representation and actually '*perform* the social and cultural mind'. Harding therefore sets about deconstructing the Terminator franchise in order to offer an insightful exposition of its implicit leadership theory. This, she argues, reveals an intriguing uneasiness between the power and powerlessness of leadership and an associated collective terror at the faceless, inhuman corporation. The net effect of this analysis leaves a lingering sense that the fantasy of leadership has a murky depth to it, with much that lies beneath the surface.

Chapter Nine

Jonathan Gosling and Peter Case's 'Choosing a Life: (Re)incarnating after Leadership' engages with Platonic and Buddhist myths, psychodynamic theory and Jungian thought in relation to issues of forgetting/knowing the truth, choice, death and rebirth, exploring their relevance for an understanding of the psychological, moral and existential implications that arise in respect to transitioning into and out of a leadership role. Roles, they contend, carry with them unforeseen demands and opportunities that act to reshape the subjectivity of the role-holder. They suggest that the choice to take on a leadership role should be founded in what they call the 'moral craft of self-management', whilst highlighting that mythic knowledge implies that in many instances aspiring leaders are instead governed by 'impatience, grandiose ambition and avarice' when choosing to take on a leadership role. While they understand leadership as involving choice, knowledge and the exercise of agency, power and influence, moving into a stage of life after leadership, as it were, will nonetheless bring with it a new set of possibilities. Forgetting the obligations that came with leadership, they argue, can free us from anxiety and regret, shift our attention 'toward hope and the possibility of insight' and engage us in a process of rebirth that occurs on a 'moment-to-moment basis'. One wider implication of their chapter, we suggest, is that leadership scholars ought not fear or avoid contemplation of the death of leadership, at least in terms of how it is currently known, whilst also recognising that the ongoing process of reincarnating a new understanding of leadership will demand philosophically informed wisdom (*phronesis*) as we face up to existential, psychological and moral choices as to what we forget and how we exercise choice, agency, power and influence in ways that offer hope and insight.

Chapter Ten

Sonia M. Ospina's 'Toward Inclusive Leadership Scholarship: Inviting the Excluded to Theorize Collective Leadership' offers a frank and thoughtful thought experiment that considers how leadership theory might have or could be different if it 'took seriously the plurality of voices, perspectives and experiences that have been mostly excluded from prior research and knowledge development'. To make this argument, Ospina skilfully weaves together her own story as a researcher, a robust critique of the status quo in the leadership canon, and vivid vignettes from her research, creating a narrative that inspires hope as much as it provokes questions. She argues that once leadership theory expands beyond its monocultural monopoly, a richly broader lens awaits. She cites example after example of the ways in which the inclusion of presently excluded voices would offer insights into the heterogeneous, collective, emergent and constructed practices of leadership in places that are often overlooked or misinterpreted. Like many of the authors in this book, however, she concludes by entreating us not to think of this as a mere thought experiment, but as a very real option already waiting for us.

Chapter Eleven

Jackie Ford's 'Rethinking Relational Leadership: Recognising the Mutual Dynamic Between Leaders and Led' draws our attention to the interdependence of leader and led where recognition of the self and other is an essential dynamic to leadership. This chapter takes a radical and at times shocking stance in alerting us to the intertwined complexities of dependence, independence and interdependence by juxtaposing two stories – a sadomasochist fantasy called the *Story of O* and a public sector manager's career story. Both stories show that, regardless of the perceived attachment between someone leading and someone led, the denial of power, whether that denial is embraced (due to the admiration of someone leading) or resisted (due to the lack of regard for someone leading), vulnerability, insecurity and often damage will result. The suggestion is that loss of subjectivity will result in compliance or submission as the only identity position made available. Jackie draws on Jessica Benjamin's psychodynamic thinking to reorientate leadership studies away from discrete entity assumptions to an awareness of an intersubjectivity that inevitably sits between leader and led. Inability to acknowledge the latter sustains a persistence of dominance, control and asymmetry right at the heart of leadership.

Chapter Twelve

Stewart Clegg and Miguel Pina e Cunha's 'Post-leadership Leadership: Mastering the New Liquidity' draws on Zygmunt Bauman's notion of liquid modernity as the basis for highlighting changes occurring in the form, focus and effects of organising practices, contemporary subjectivity and, thus, leadership, which are rarely discussed in leadership studies. In this partially imagined, partially already real world, in which that which was previously solid, certain and stable is increasingly liquid, uncertain and dynamic, the expectation that leaders are capable of creating strategies, structures and processes that will ensure the achievement of their intended outcomes is exposed as naive, inadequate and out of touch with new realities. Rather than top-down control by leaders situated in clearly defined roles within organisations with definitive boundaries, they highlight how the distinction between leader and follower is being increasingly blurred through networked, distributed and technologically mediated ways of working. Consequently, liquid leadership, serving no fixed or enduring purpose and not founded in any sustained commitment to a particular set of values, is undertaken by liquid selves, who are constantly adapting themselves to be, or appear to be, whatever it takes to remain employable.

These dynamics play out in liquid organisations characterised most markedly by the absence of moral concern combined with an intense attention to matters of aesthetics. Key questions that arise from their analysis is how, in the face of such trends, might we encourage leadership that is not grounded in 'indifference to the fate of others' or where matters of style trump substance.

Part III: Discarding, Deconstructing, Starting Again

Part III of this book pushes against the boundaries of the scenario we have posed, and attempts to take a good, hard look at whether or not we might be able to do without leadership altogether, rather than assume that it must be rebuilt. The authors in this section vary with respect to this question: some argue that leadership is akin to a poisoned chalice and consider how we might reconstruct organisations without the meddlesome assumption that leadership is an essential ingredient. Other authors maintain hope in the power and purpose of leadership and work instead to reclaim the territory of the concept itself. The tension these authors wrestle with is if critical leadership scholarship succeeds in radically redefining what we mean by leadership, in what sense does it continue to still be leadership – and indeed why would we persist in calling it so? This is a thorny issue that threads through the final section of this book and each chapter in its own way invites the reader to hold at bay their own assumptions about leadership long enough to consider a markedly different possible reality.

Chapter Thirteen

Suze Wilson sets the scene in this section by dethroning the taken-for-granted timelessness of leadership truth in 'Imagining Organisation With and Without Leadership'. Drawing inspiration from Foucault, Wilson firstly tackles head on the unique specialness claimed for leadership, such as its ability to inspire loyalty, generate inspirational visions and overcome wicked problems. One by one she dismantles the idea of special functions claimed as the sole province of leadership, suggesting instead that the one thing leadership may alone offer organisations is the misguided glorification of ordinary managerial practice by presumed rare and special leaders. Then from amidst the rubble and ruins of modern leadership theory, Wilson turns to the medieval literature on leadership for a radical redefinition based on the duty to serve the community. This leads Wilson to the intriguing conclusion that such a rebuilt concept of leadership suggests an important tension against, rather than the assumption of subservience to, the interests of business. Ultimately, this short provocation opens up rather than nails down possibilities and leaves us with the ineffable conviction that the form and function of leadership is far from a stable and enduring timeless truth.

Chapter Fourteen

Martin Parker's 'Can We be Done with Leadership' cuts straight to the point in suggesting that leadership is, in fact, a rather dangerous idea. Provocative, witty and incisive, Parker teases apart the fundamental assumptions of leadership, notably the 'necessary subordination of the many to the will of a few'. While such an assumption betrays its own considerable moral and ethical issues, Parker hones in especially on the troublesome consequence of leadership for organisation theory. He notes how leadership has brought about the misconceived 'truth' that organisations naturally require it, at peril of their otherwise imminent implosion. Not so, argues Parker, as he sets about debunking the necessity of leadership myth and dares us to consider a world that is done with leadership.

Chapter Fifteen

Neil Sutherland takes up the spirit of this book with laudable verve in 'After Hierarchy: Building a New World in the Shell of the Old'. In this highly original and vividly imaginative chapter, Sutherland brings the great anarchist philosophers to life as ghostly apparitions in a tale worthy of a bedtime story. The chapter fleshes out a common, if often unadmitted, anxiety at the thought of a world without leadership, and through dialogue with real and imagined characters, Sutherland offers a plausible picture of a world that has truly left hierarchy behind. Perhaps most chilling is the idea that in such a world, people might actively *refrain* from leadership, rather than attempt to take up or step into its practices. As such, this chapter offers a noteworthy counterpoint to the taken-for-granted assumption that leadership is an unqualified good for which we all ought to automatically strive.

Chapter Sixteen

Donna Ladkin offers the final contribution in this volume for good reason. In 'The Last Leaders', she paints the picture of a grim post-apocalyptic future in which we have laid waste to our planet, exploiting her to the hilt and violently destroying one another in the process. This scene may be familiar to lovers of science fiction, but Ladkin confronts us with a haunting twist: her provocation is written in tones redolent of a rueful confession as we acknowledge our complicity in humanity's downfall – that is, complicity secured through docile faith in our leaders. Yet there is more than a hint of hope in Ladkin's chapter as we begin to realise that 'in order to survive, we need one another, rather than a "leader"' and like the rest of the chapters in this section, the possibility of life 'without the fantasy of leadership' is awakened. This provocative little chapter ends both the section and the contributions because it reminds us of what is potentially at stake for leadership and its theories and reminds us that the call to action is never more needed than now.

After Leadership?

What should be clear from these previews of our author's chapters is that *After Leadership* is a far from typical exploration of the subject. If 'conceptual theorizing' is what we are doing, our motivation for adopting this stance lies in a real sense of unease about leadership itself, which our authors share. Many of us are concerned to foster leadership practice that is both ethical and effective and believe that doing so could aid in enhancing human and planetary well-being. And, our hope is that leadership research and theorizing ought to reveal its complex, multifaceted and often ambiguous nature. However, we also recognise that the hype surrounding the 'L' word is now such that in just using that term we risk compounding the very problem we wish to confront, namely the idolization and glorification of leaders and leadership which problematically functions to imply a select, elite few know best what others need.

To try to break free from this dominant way of thinking about leadership, which is both anti-egalitarian and anti-democratic in nature, our authors have engaged in the kind of speculative exploration of new ideas that is the hallmark of the 'conceptual theorist'. For that reason, we expect readers will find in this collection many ideas that disturb, confront, challenge and possibly even infuriate. Our authors, individually and collectively, are seeking to shake up established ways of understanding and practicing leadership, even, at times, to the very point of questioning its fundamental desirability and utility. Yet leadership, as a concept and a practice, warrants this kind of critical interrogation and creative reappraisal if it is to be remade into something that is responsive and aligned to the needs of a changing world and if it is to better serve the interests of all. If leaders are to avoid being positioned as secular, corporate gods, and if our ideas about leadership are to be freed from the rose-coloured tinting with which they are so often affected, then *After Leadership* offers inspiration for such aims.

Notes

1 MacIntyre, 1981, 1.
2 Tourish, 2015, 137.
3 Alvesson, 2017.
4 http://fortune.com/2017/07/20/ceo-pay-ratio-2016/
5 Mitroff & Kilmann, 1981, 238.
6 Mitroff & Kilmann, 1981, 242.
7 Weick 1992, 175.

References

Alvesson, M. (2017). Waiting for Godot: Eight major problems in the odd field of leadership studies. *Leadership*. doi:10.1177/1742715017736707.
MacIntyre, A. C. (1981). *After Virtue: A Study in Moral Theory*. Notre Dame, IN: University of Notre Dame Press.

Mitroff, I. I. & Kilmann, R. H. (1981). The four-fold way of knowing. *Theory and Society*, 10(2), 227–248.

Tourish, D. (2015). Some announcements, reaffirming the critical ethos of Leadership, and what we look for in submissions. *Leadership*, 11(2), 135–141.

Weick, K. E. (1992). Agenda setting in organizational behavior: A theory-focused approach. *Journal of Management Inquiry*, 1(3), 171–182.

Part I
Revealing, Reframing, Reimagining

2 An Archaeological Dig into Leadership Competencies in the Twenty-First Century

Vesa Huotari and Brigid Carroll

Below are fragments from a veritable mountain of leadership texts, artefacts and documents from the era we understand as the pinnacle of leadership studies – the twenty-first century. We include them here to illustrate the nature of the fragments that have survived the leadership studies apocalypse, but also to remind any reader of the myriad of ways that leadership inserted itself into that epoch and most of all that we have an opportunity now to decide how it can be reasserted into the future.

> Presumably then, when the historical circumstances change along with the criteria for this relevance, a new truth will have to be found that captures the new essence of leadership. This is the ideological at work – the replacement of truth and fact with the need for beliefs that fit with the sociopolitical and economic demands of the day.
>
> (Kelly 2014, 913)

Introduction

- Provides opportunities for people to learn to work together as a team.
- Enlists the active participation of everyone.
- Promotes cooperation with other work units.
- Ensures that all team members are treated fairly.
- Recognizes and encourages the behaviors that contribute to teamwork.
  [surviving fragment of leadership competency list]

This is an era reportedly obsessed, as you can see from the bulk of fragments surviving the apocalypse, on nailing down leadership, chunking out its component parts, creating models, frameworks and assessments, and above all designing a plethora of representations and maps for the so-called leaders of those times to follow. From such fragments we, as the archaeologists and custodians of leadership knowledge, can retrospectively explore a largely lost form of social process, as well as doctrinal trajectory, points of agreement, fields of dispute and sites of conflict, both internal and external to organisations, and both real and imagined to its adherents. Given the scale and scope of this lost leadership world, we will draw on the science and art of cartography to not just assemble an understanding of the past leadership mapping obsession, but also to experiment with new mapping technologies and paradigms to help us avoid the pitfalls our predecessors fell into so we can benefit from their leadership pursuit for the good of our own new society.

From the first sight, most of the fragments appear in the guise of 'shopping lists' of features, skills and behaviours that we suspect are somehow meant to characterise leadership, the character of a true leader and successful or effective leader behaviour. The vast number of such defining properties, ranging from the practical and pragmatic to the conceptually complex, have perplexed us for a long time. How do we even read these? What were they for? How did anything resembling leadership result? Our first task, as with any unknown terrain, is to assemble fragments into a terrain and investigate its topographical features, hence our incursion into cartography. Our second step is to construct alternative maps and mapping methodologies. It is well-known that mapping territory that no longer exists (like the mythical land of Atlantis) can best be evaluated against alternative mappings and not by comparing a map with the actual object it is attempting to map (in this case leadership). Furthermore, we must acknowledge that all such endeavours are conceptually mediated. The choice of terms and symbols and the relations they purport to capture reflect the very purpose of their makers. The latter, we need to acknowledge, are always immersed in or given legitimacy by the prevailing interests and the respective structures of power. No cartographic account or map after all can be objective, value-neutral or benign. This applies not just to our fragments either as all theoretical accounts should be taken as maps or processes akin to mapping. As such, we include some recovered commentaries from leadership scholars that are insightful for the assumptions and intent they reveal about these fragments.

The notion of an alternative map is an important one in this chapter. Our concept of an alternative map is one that structurally corresponds with the original one (in the sense that both have the very same form) but offers an alternative interpretation or meaning, caters for ideological critique, has the capacity for systematic reflection of its internal and external relations, pinpoints possible sites of contestation, and opens up possibilities for new syntheses and ongoing development. In fact, we envisage that an alternative map for our own era should remain essentially contestable. An essentially contestable map means a map with the capacity to continually change as contexts and conditions change, or new learnings and insights are shared and is driven by divergent perspectives and dialogue. We propose that an alternative map for the leadership terrain can be rigorously achieved as well as advanced systematically by figuring out alternative, formally equivalent, conceptually coherent and thus credible maps, putting the two side by side, and assessing the similarities and differences between them.

This chapter follows the aforementioned method. We shall use recently discovered fragments of texts to give empirical substance to the archaeological work we are undertaking and to help the reader discover and engage with a past leadership era. Our movement forward will need to partly derive from the lessons put forward by the historical case at hand. We suspect our progress will be heavily in debt to the specific fragments of texts we have recovered and feature here. We suspect that the survival of such fragments reflects their sheer prevalence at that time and, in all likelihood, they probably gave character to a whole era in leadership studies. Therefore, we claim them as truly representative of what was significant about leadership over the time. It is thus not only possible but also vital to reconstruct a new era of leadership scholarship from careful consideration and critique of these very cues.

Leadership Competencies: Reconstructing a ByGone Scholarship

Archaeological forays invite us into a different relationship with maps, categories and lists of things. Given much of the surviving leadership fragments are maps, categories and lists, we note that we have to pay a particular kind of attention to their composition and assumptions.

> A map says to you, "Read me carefully, follow me closely, doubt me not." It says, "I am the earth in the palm of your hand. Without me, you are alone and lost."
>
> (Beryl Markham 1983, cited in Harley 1989, 1)

- Provides opportunities for people to learn to work together as a team.
- Enlists the active participation of everyone.
- Promotes cooperation with other work units.
- Ensures that all team members are treated fairly.
- Recognizes and encourages the behaviors that contribute to teamwork.

[surviving fragment of leadership competency list]

From a shopping list, one can reconstruct numerous different dishes. Likewise, a list of leader competencies gives a glimpse of what we take to be a range of leadership ingredients. While we are very familiar with the function of a shopping list (essentially a reminder of what we need to have at hand for the days ahead), we have to ask ourselves what a similar list of leadership skills and behaviours could be good for and perhaps more importantly why someone thought they needed such a list in the first place.

The fragment above suggests that such leadership lists might have reminded leaders of their duties or tasks for their leadership responsibility. In that sense, at least some of these fragments seem more like behavioural recipes than simple lists of properties, characteristics and features. They suggest lines of action to anyone who wondered what he or she was supposed to do, look after or accomplish as a leader, particularly in order to make leadership happen. Put succinctly, they appear to offer pointers on what to busy oneself with as one undertakes being a leader or displaying leadership.

However, there is evidence from other fragments that such prescriptions could be turned around and used as a form of leadership inventory to evaluate the degree to which the respondent's behaviours or doings meet these criteria in his or her daily practice. We wonder if evaluation, measurement and appraisal are the real subtext behind this competency movement. Our next text fragment appears as part of such an evaluative questionnaire.

- 4. I lead my people by example.*
  - o   A
  - o   F
  - o   S
  - o   R

- 5. I have the leadership skills and resources necessary to perform my tasks effectively.*
  - o   A
  - o   F
  - o   S
  - o   R

[surviving fragment of leadership competency assessment]

If this evaluative intent is a significant one, then at this point we need to ask where all the different competencies come from and how they might relate to each other. In asking this, we are really inquiring how the different competency descriptors came to have a place in the leadership map and even beyond that the overall leadership landscape. We assume, but don't actually fully know, that researchers played some role in this partnership, perhaps with leadership practitioners and 'mapping' experts who we understand were generally called consultants. If our assumption is correct, then how do combinations of researchers, consultants and practitioners succeed in identifying the features that made a difference in and only in leadership, but not say in management or, more generally, processes of work? Furthermore, how are the different features (ingredients) meant to combine with each other? How were such dynamics and relationships verified empirically, derived conceptually and embedded across collective endeavour? There are so many questions that the passage of time thoroughly complicates.

The lists of competencies of course do not reveal their origins. However, their widespread use over the twenty-first century suggests a widespread trust in them and their analytical potential to function as maps for navigating the terrain of leadership. They seem to have been valued in numerous ways: as a means to pinpoint prized behaviours, choose between prospective leaders, and develop the art of leadership in new adherents, to name just a few. As archaeologists we feel there must be more to them, in particular a theoretical framework or theory we can't yet find that points to genuine insight underneath their very surface. Sadly, we meet the limits of our archaeology here. We have to give the benefit of the doubt to the era's leadership scholars; they surely knew their trade and were aware of the dangers of naming competencies haphazardly and compiling lists of them indiscriminately. The following fragment, which we believe is part of an instruction on how to use such theoretically sophisticated instruments, is telling however in the way it blends potentially deep self-reflection with a simplistic and formulaic assessment system:

> Whether you seem to be a "born leader" or are uneasy with the role of leader and need to develop leadership skills methodically, you will discover valuable insights through a self-assessment. You will want to examine your skills, traits, competencies, abilities, and experience. Since the days of the ancient Eastern and Western philosophers, such a rigorous self-assessment has been seen as the starting point for success. "Know thyself" is a key lesson of life. Give yourself an "S" for strength or "D" for a trait that needs development.
>
> [surviving fragment of instruction for
> leadership competency assessment]

'Know yourself' points to an assumption perhaps that leadership resides 'within' a persona and hence introversion is required to draw out an individual's self-construction and delineate his or her surfaces, boundaries and even abysses. 'Know yourself' also appears to assume that any traits named and identified are presumably clear if not self-evident for any person doing the self-evaluation. Perhaps the inhabitants of such an era thought selves were knowable with some degree of certainty and that selves remained relatively settled. Of course the existence of such quantities of these competency fragments might indicate that they self-examined with great regularity given we know now that selves are precarious, mutable, fluid and ceaselessly changing. We remain intrigued, however, by how any identified trait could be categorised as a strength or development point in itself. Our own era understands that the same dimension of self can be a source of potential strength and development given different relationships and contexts. We clearly live in a far less categorisation-secure era!

It is most likely that the inhabitants of the twenty-first century thought that strengths made someone a better leader, while those pointed out as needing further development were perceived as undermining leadership. This could only be assumed, we think, if the criteria for a true leader were presumed to be universal and equally valid across time, context, gender and purpose. From this we extrapolate that 'knowing yourself' means knowing your relative position comparative to others so developmental trajectories can be built and then subsequently evaluated and measured. The inventory gives a clear direction for anyone who engages in measuring his or her leadership competence against its scale and in its terms. The result is that one can feel reassured that one can become a better leader because the potential for growth in relation to leadership is without a limit. Such a discovery feels like a breakthrough, as if we are getting closer to the ubiquity and appeal of such maps.

We now think we understand that the leadership community of the twenty-first century was pursuing the very constitution of excellence in leadership and wanted to craft tools that made it possible for anyone to put him or herself on the leadership map, and that the competencies are akin to values and variables or the equivalent of navigational markers such as latitude and longitude. Let's pause for a moment at this insight into the ghost of a past. What we seem to have discovered is that these competency fragments point to an underlying developmental architecture. We cannot know at this point whether such an architecture is genuine scientific pursuit or a giant marketing exercise underpinning an organisational selection and promotion strategy and/or a leadership development industry. We are slightly sceptical that taking a competency inventory could be nothing more than a prelude for buying the remedy. In this case, 'know yourself' would be reduced to knowing what to purchase next under the banner of self-improvement.

We think we are at a point where we could propose that twenty-first century leadership researchers, when it comes to leadership competencies, successfully explicated and promoted a view of leadership in which everyone was portrayed as a carrier of leadership potentiality in an objective sense and to a measurable extent. Moreover, they also propagated a view that it was possible to develop that potential further. Even at the most advanced level, it was possible to become better and better without any natural limit. The proof of such an advanced status seemed to be diplomas from leadership development programmes and engagement in continuous self-development. Leadership is for adults what reading, writing and arithmetic are for the children. Consequently, the answer to the question of why leadership matters was most likely as obvious then as the reply to the question of why literacy matters today.

Furthermore, it appears to be a system of leadership that was built purely upon individual and personal merits. Those who invested more in the development of their leadership competencies would have led those who had not had the opportunity, due to age, gender or profile, to invest in the development of their own competencies. Perhaps it is not an overstatement to claim the twenty-first century as the golden age, not of leadership, but of leadership development and evaluation in the history of humanity. Leadership, in other words, was permeated by a measurement logic, embedded in a likely development industry and enveloped by organisational objectives and aims. In short, it was this the era of making artistic, but marketable maps for the hopeful yearning for individual/personal growth in leadership or transformation as a leader.

The cartographers are talking about their maps and not landscapes. That is why what they say frequently becomes so paradoxical when translated into ordinary language. When they forget the difference between map and landscape – and when they permit or persuade us to forget the difference – all sorts of liabilities ensue.

(Roszak 1972, 410)

Alternative Maps and Imagined Landscapes

In the archaeology of scholarship, alternative maps stand out as a method for figuring out the possible relationships between fragments and empirical bits and pieces.

The heresy we propose is that the enchanting song of the competency sirens has lured us into dangerous rocks. It is time to put wax in our ears and seek a better route.

(Hollenbeck et al. 2006, 399)

They explore whether such bits and pieces can be successfully put together into a larger whole, such as a reconstructed building, way of life or system of thought. This kind of approach serves several different purposes.

First, it asks us to put together the fragments into a new, coherent whole. What is required, thus, is a theoretical account that displays or points out how the discovered bits and pieces could become true parts, that, once placed, fit perfectly with one another and form a credible, fully integrated system. Such an archaeological account or map should appear trustworthy and, once rigorously compiled, become loaded with persuasive power. Naturally, we are presuming that our scholarly predecessors were very much like we are as rational thinkers, writers and discussants. However, having the advantage of hindsight, we are able to safeguard ourselves and liberate our thoughts from competency's once irresistible charm by methodically bracketing it as just one system of thought and possible map from a group of numerous, but equally possible, others. As our picture of the past grows, we become increasingly capable of delineating the epistemological, theoretical, organisational, social and even personal factors that favour some novel constructions while destining others to the dustbin of ideas.

Second, alternative maps effectively draw attention to the very limits of any theoretical doctrine, its possibly outdated or unwarranted presumptions, vague theoretical concepts, gaps in logic and incoherencies between the theory and claims of practices. In this sense, an alternative map is an essential vehicle for systematic, well-warranted and accurately pointed critical reflection and systematic analysis that might avoid the pitfall of purely political or ideological critique. Furthermore, as an inherently dialectic move, it paves way for theoretical synthesis and original ways of thinking, and thus expands the horizon of thought, that is, what is deemed possible to say, conceivable and arguable.

Alternative maps need to be maps of something that they share or have in common with original maps. In our case, the first candidate is the very landscape inhabited or given shape by leadership competencies. It could be generative to see such a view, not in opposition, but as a head start to our alternative reconstruction. After all, we are not setting up a contest here or an elimination round, but more a point of reflexivity, dialogue and excursion into new territory that as of yet has not been mapped. Therefore, it is necessary to take one step further in order to find a more neutral ground to put forward alternative and genuinely novel interpretations. Naturally, this methodical step stands out as a leap into the dark. Any claim to it will be fully retrospective, that is, it will reveal itself as the analysis unfolds and, ultimately, its value or worth will depend on the vista it reveals.

We suggest the following as a joint or common territory: a theory of leadership as a rigorous attempt to make sense of the differences that *organised social wholes* display in their survival, success and quality of life of their members. The very quest, first to identify leadership competencies and second to find ways to increase them, needs to be founded on the social and holistic. We agree with those from our archaeological era that leadership matters in society and hence receives its character and potentiality from constituents such as competencies.

The analysis proceeds diagrammatically from such joint ground. We have created a diagram that encompasses the past competency path that was actually trodden alongside an alternative path that some fragments attest was theorised but did not fully materialise; it never had a chance to prove its practical worth and theoretical merits, and therefore was not in place to change history or even to ultimately prevent the leadership studies apocalypse that is the subject of our archaeology. Learning from past tragedies is substantially facilitated by knowledge of positive historical alternatives that remained unarticulated, were silenced or were simply neglected and thereby contributed to a smaller or larger degree to the unfolding of events leading to the catastrophe. Our analytical diagram is depicted in Figure 2.1.

The two maps offer mutually alternative ways to conceptualise leadership, understand it, define the focus in it, organise tasks, define the responsibility derived from it and carry it out. Traditionally, when leadership has been grasped in terms of competencies, the level of analysis is set to the individual where the success of any organised action as a whole derives from the level of performance of individual leaders. Respective competencies, or combined competencies, are thus linked to individual performance. The challenge then becomes identifying them, putting them on the map, measuring them and designing programmes for strengthening them. This is all underpinned by an

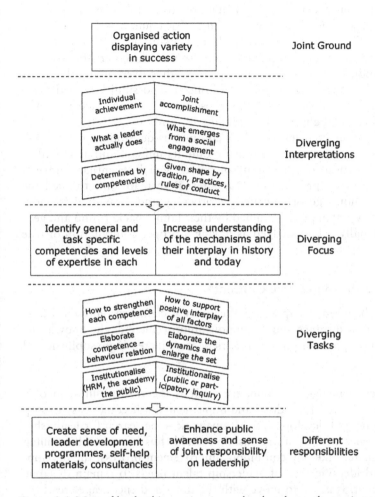

Figure 2.1 Map of leadership competence school and our alternative to it.

understanding of the relationship between what is measured and how someone is actually able to perform. The public responsibility consists of making people aware of the relation between individual competencies and leadership behaviour, how to make a change in terms of them and why striving for such a change in their competencies actually matters. Thus, leadership is essentially a more or less skilful personal accomplishment. It exists because those behaviours, along with acts and deeds that are integral to it, have been and are continuously done.

Our alternative map interprets the very same differences as a result of an interplay of various dynamics that include the historical situation, often conflicting rules and duties, and interdependent practices from which a shared route is negotiated and over time continually renegotiated.

Leadership becomes a question of being able to mobilise, bring together and articulate what is already present and what could come within reach if systematically and jointly pursued. Leadership is now a collective accomplishment. At its best, leadership centres on the co-creation of new resources, finding a way to activate them and thus overcoming the limits of any and all individuals towards new collective possibilities. Leadership then energises, revitalises and fulfils those who are embedded in it and living/working through it both individually and collectively. To focus on individual competencies and their continuous development is to miss the real power of leadership, to pursue only its mirage, and above all to provide legitimation to a hierarchy of power, which, eventually, invests mostly in its own reproduction. Our alternative map aims to shed the ideological camouflage of so-called meritocracy and individual freedom where only few, often predetermined by their family background and gender, were actually acknowledged as having a proper combination of true leadership competencies.

Leadership as a Contestable Concept

The relation between a map and the territory it claims to represent leaves room for endless disputes and continuous improvement as the knowledge, interests and purposes of potential users become increasingly sophisticated and diverse.

> A further challenge also remains: what is the realistic lifespan of a framework? Once formalised and implemented it becomes easy to stop challenging and developing the framework – the search for leadership competencies within an organisation could thus become self-fulfilling and stagnate. Like any continuous improvement process, the development and identification of leadership talent needs to remain dynamic and current. It needs to move with the times and encourage creativity and diversification.
>
> (Bolden et al. 2003, 38)

A map is simply unable to cater for all purposes, operations on every possible scale or users characterised by different tastes, skill sets and amount of experience. Perhaps then the most significant purpose of a map lies in its precariousness, its temporariness, its eternal contestability and the continuous presence of such contestation. Without the latter, maps would stagnate and lose their usefulness for human purposes and, consequently, we would end up lost in relation to our environment and our ability to push on into unknown territories would be at risk. Our very progress in this world is thus tied to maps, an understanding of their contestability, and the development of new and alternative maps. Every new map potentially stands for a new group of users, new uses and unforeseen purposes. No map is impartial and without social consequences; therefore, it needs to be always contestable from social or human points of view.

If making sense and being able to navigate leadership is a terrain that depends upon being continuously contested, the lack of the latter, whether by suppression, lack of imagination, misplaced trust for paradigmatic consensus, or misuse of power, may well explain not just competency's own demise but also the apocalypse of leadership studies. While claiming the latter would go beyond our evidence, our analysis does suggest that the very idea of leadership competence is inherently an essentially contestable concept and its usefulness in a larger social world depends upon such contestation. Without the latter, it is destined to stagnate and bring to a halt a

Table 2.1 Leadership competence as essentially contestable

Features of essentially contestable concept	*Leadership competence*
I Appraisiveness, i.e. 'signifies or accredits some kind of valued achievement', the term for the concept stands for an achievement and generally implies a positive normative value.	Socially valuable, individually rewarding, publicly acknowledged, educationally attainable, widely pursued through several paths, various forms and kinds (seen as naturally diverse, but evolving too, historically contingent, but also necessary to change that history).
II–III Internal complexity and diversity. Describability, i.e. different facets or features may be weighted differently.	Tied to the times, mores and objective possibilities (sphere of proximal development, horizon of understanding, state of technology) and, simultaneously, continuously seeking new, real possibilities that emerge and evolve along with its own progress as well as progress in general.
IV Openness, i.e. subject to unpredictable change of meaning. V Reciprocal recognition, i.e. awareness of the definitions of others with attacking and defending conceptual positions (aggressiveness/defensiveness).	Actively kept open by allowing all kinds of pursuit for closure, but preventing none of them acquiring a privileged position, for instance, by funding its rivalries, discussion forums, continuous challenging appraisals, etc.
VI Exemplars, i.e. paradigmatic cases or uses, the authority of which are acknowledged by all (also a membership in a [progressive] tradition including a number of exemplars?).	Finding exemplars and refutation of exemplars found by applying more encompassing frameworks, better standards and justified new expectations; bringing up cases where similar practice appears insufficient or otherwise lacking.
VII Progressive competition, i.e. resulting in an evolution of level of understanding and quality of arguments.	Leadership that is deserved by everyone, that is beneficial to increasing the number of those involved in it, and which all are capable or competent of contributing to or taking responsibility for.

whole form of endeavour that was named as leadership. Our archaeology of leadership scholarship and practice should thus seek future evidence of whether true contestation existed, not between scholars promoting this or that list of competencies as the right one, but between scholars who offered alternative maps of the phenomenal field itself and those who relied on the standard account.

Table 2.1 displays criteria for a contestable concept and suggests a platform of contestability that future scholars can protect and enliven.

Conclusions

Our final two fragments point to the precariousness of competency and competencies. What seems competent, strong and in place one moment can fleetingly turn to problematic, vulnerable and questionable the next. One forgets that where there is competence, ultimately there is incompetence not far away.

> competence hovers undetected over the perception of situations until incompetence appears.
>
> (Holahan 2014, 478)

> In a past company, we had a small team that worked remotely. We got together a few times a month, but otherwise relied on email and calls to stay on the same page. This was great to allow everyone to be efficient and focused on their work. Unfortunately, it also created management blind spots. Over time, another leader and I noticed one of our best team members seemed to be disengaging
>
> [surviving fragment of leadership narrative]

While we may never know fully what brought about the leadership studies apocalypse and wiped out the old leadership maps and competency school and practice, there are arguably multiple pathways into disaster (and out of it). Our analysis here shows one possible narrative for why leadership went astray. There are, however, clear lessons to be drawn from our archaeological analysis. Effective counter-cartography foregrounds the processes of co-construction of mapping that competency frameworks tended to veil. Therefore, the first dimension of a new leadership map ought to be the very visibility of mapping processes in relation to the map. This could look like leadership mapping forums where different organisational stakeholders discuss leadership, share leadership stories and unpack leadership mindsets and assumptions together. In a sense, the map then becomes the text of an ongoing conversation on leadership throughout an organisation or collective. That would mean any map needs to be approached as malleable, fluid, dynamic and partial. It is a mapping in progress: never finished and never complete.

That means it can 'travel' in different forms to its various stakeholders: as text if appropriate but equally as diagram, podcast, interactive display, oral feedback session or discussion board, to name a few. Where a polished, seamless and official interpretation is required, then different representatives can produce one for whatever the event or context requires, but where possible, conflictual, divergent, contradictory and counter-perspectives can and should be included given graphic design processes can easily incorporate them. There are fabulous examples of counter and alternative cartography processes that reflect a genuine landscape or terrain of difference.

Finally, we live in a day and age where there is no excuse for text lists rendered without context, nuance, authorship and meaning. Incorporating performance and play means simply using the resources of our times that abound beyond organisational life and managerial horizons. Such resources can be aesthetic, embodied, affective, narrative and holistic and are particularly resonant with leadership. The fragment that begins this section is a story and storytelling has a particularly long pedigree in terms of leadership and its development given stories are understood as a vehicle for complexity. Storytelling sessions, artefacts, texts and mediums tend to capture multiple dimensions of phenomena and are a compelling and meaningful medium for most. We can also see rehearsed and improvisational theatre; photo, film and art competitions; unconferences; dialogue and open conversational fora; and virtual, online and blended design innovations. Such practices can be framed as 'the ways maps can work otherwise'. We are looking to a world where organisations find their creativity and sense of possibility to explore ways that leadership maps might 'work otherwise'.

We believe that leadership is a terrain where narrow and managerially orientated competency thinking has turned out to be misplaced and, if left unguarded, unchallenged and blindly followed, is indeed dangerous. Therefore, we need to rethink and rework alternative sets of assumptions for any maps that attempt a leadership 'capture'. Construction of a new theory of leadership competence must purport to bridge a gap between individualistic, discrete behaviour and collective interdependent action. While competencies variously labelled to individuals have become second nature to us, competencies as collective, emerging, constitutive, organic and boundary setting remain very much unmapped territory – a promising peninsula of vocabulary, tradition, systematic thinking and organised effort. Identifying leadership as something shared between collectives of individuals and the relations between them, networks, organisations or even societies, seems possibly far-fetched and futile when seen from the conventional psychological point of view. However, the latter should rather encourage than discourage us. Failing to do so may simply mean another future leadership studies apocalypse. Let history help us learn while we can before any vestige of this phenomenon called leadership becomes truly extinct.

Endnote

Our very attempt to view our own time as it might appear to our successors in the future has relied on the very scholarship we aim to reconstruct here. Naming the most obvious sources of ideas in the text itself would have created a breach of logic – how can we simultaneously have all the sources at hand and claim to possess just bits and pieces from the whole scholarship? Therefore, the sources of ideas are not duly mentioned where they should be. To give credit to those to whom it belongs, we want to express our debt to them here.

The idea of essentially contestable concepts has been developed by Walter Gallie and others (e.g. Gallie 1956; Boromisza-Habashi 2010; Clarke 1979; Gray 1977; MacIntyre 1973; Ruben-Hillel 2010; Swanton 1985). The idea of scientific theories as maps belongs in our reading to John Ziman (2002). On the nature of maps in general, we are in debt to Sismondo and Christian (2000), Harley (1989), Roszak (1972) and Stallman (2012). The very idea of maps applied to leadership studies stands out in the texts of Richard Bolden and his associates (see Bolden et al. 2003; Bolden et al. 2011; Bolden & Gosling 2006). While they have also provided a comprehensive critique on the very idea of leadership competencies both as an approach and concept, they are not the only ones (e.g. Brundrett 2000; Carroll et al. 2008; Grzeda 2005; Hager 2006; Holahan 2014, Hollenbeck et al. 2006; Lum 2013; McClelland 1973; Sparrow 2002, Stevens 2012; Westera 2001; Pikkarainen 2014). In the field of leadership scholarship, the sources that need to be mentioned here are Barker (2001), Kelly (2008; 2014) and Ladkin (2010).

Of course, numerous other scholars not mentioned here may well see traces of their thinking in the text too, especially all of us putting forward alternative conceptualisations of competency thinking in the field of leadership. However, the ones named and not named above, are not responsible for any possible misunderstanding of their valuable insights and ideas here.

References

Barker, Richard (2001). The nature of leadership. *Human Relations* 544, 469–494.
Bolden, R. & Gosling, J. (2006). Leadership competencies: Time to change the tune? *Leadership* 2(2), 147–163.
Bolden, R., Gosling, J., Marturano, A. & Dennison, P. (2003). A review of leadership theory and competency frameworks. University of Exeter. Centre for Leadership Studies. https://ore.exeter.ac.uk/repository/bitstream/handle/10036/17494/mgmt_standards.pdf?sequence=1.
Bolden, R., Hawkins, B., Gosling, J. & Taylor, S. (2011). *Exploring Leadership. Individual, Organizational, and Societal Perspectives.* Oxford: Oxford University Press.
Boromisza-Habashi, David (2010). How are political concepts 'essentially contested'? *Language & Communication* 30, 276–284.

Brundrett, M. (2000). The question of competence: The origins, strengths and inadequacies of a leadership training paradigm. School Leadership & Management; August. www.researchgate.net/profile/Mark_Brundrett2/publication/232875071_ The_Question_of_Competence_the_origins_strengths_and_inadequacies_of_a_ leadership_training_paradigm/links/00463525ceb133944e000000.pdf.

Carroll, B., Levy, L. & Richmond, D. (2008). Leadership as practice: Challenging the competency paradigm. *Leadership* 4(4), 363–379.

Clarke, Barry (1979). Eccentrically contested concepts. *British Journal of Political Science* 9(1), 122–126.

Gallie, Walter Bryce (1956). Essentially contested concepts. *Proceedings of the Aristotelian Society* 56, 167–198.

Gray, John (1977). On the contestability of social and political concepts. *Political Theory* 5(3), 331–348.

Grzeda, Maurice (2005). In competence we trust? Addressing conceptual ambiguity. *Journal of Management Development* 24(6), 530–545.

Hager, Paul (2006). Competency standards – a help or hindrance? An Australian perspective. *The Vocational Aspects of Education* 47(2), 141–151.

Harley, J. B. (1989). Deconstructing the map. *Cartographica* 26(2), 1–20.

Holahan, Lauren (2014). Quality-in-doing: Competence and occupation. *Journal of Occupational Science* 21(4), 473–487.

Hollenbeck, George P., McCall, Morgan W. & Silzer, Robert F. (2006). Leadership competency models. *The Leadership Quarterly* 17(4), 398–413.

Kelly, Simon (2008). Leadership: A categorical mistake? *Human Relations* 61(6), 763–782.

Kelly, Simon (2014). Towards a negative ontology of leadership. *Human Relations* 67(8), 905–922.

Ladkin, Donna (2010). *Rethinking Leadership. A New Look at Old Leadership Questions*. Cheltenham: Edward Elgar.

Lum, Gerard (2013). Competence: A tale of two constructs. *Educational Philosophy and Theory* 45(12), 1193–1204.

McClelland, D. (1973). Testing for competence rather than for intelligence. *American Psychologist* 28(1), 1–14.

MacIntyre, Alasdair (1973). The essential contestability of some social concepts. *Ethics* 84(1), 1–9.

Pikkarainen, Eetu (2014). Competence as a key concept of educational theory: A semiotic point of view. *Journal of Philosophy of Education* 48(4), 621–636.

Roszak, Theodore (1972). *Where the Wasteland Ends*. Garden City, NY: Doubleday.

Ruben-Hillel, David (2010). W.B. Gallie and essentially contested concepts. *Philosophical Papers* 39(2), 257–270.

Sismondo, Sergio & Chrisman, Nicholas (2000). Deflationary metaphysics and the natures of maps. *Philosophy of Science* 68(3), 38–49.

Sparrow, P. (2002). To use competencies or not to use competencies? That is the question. In M. Pearn (Ed.) *Individual Differences and Development in Organisations*. Chichester: John Wiley & Sons, pp. 112–130.

Stallman, Timothy (2012). *Alternative Cartographies: Building Collective Power*. Thesis. University of North Carolina, Chapel Hill.

Stevens, Gregory (2012). A critical review of the science and practice of competency modeling. *Human Resource Development Review* 12(1), 86–107.

Swanton, Christine (1985). On the 'essential contestedness' of political concepts. *Ethics* 95(4), 811–827.

Westera, Wim (2001). Competences in education: A confusion of tongues. *Journal of Curriculum Studies* 33(1), 75–88.

Ziman, John (2002). *Real Science. What it is and What it Means.* Cambridge: Cambridge University Press.

3 Reviving the Moral Meaning of Leading and Following

The Lost Metaphysics of Leadership

Scott Taylor

The False Promise of Scientism in Leadership Studies

How do educators decide what to include in a course on leadership studies? There are so many theories, so much data, so many books and journal articles, and so many different approaches to teaching and learning. Many of us seem to fall back on the 'usual suspects', those theories that are generally accepted as forming the 'canon' – the theories that most of us accept have some conceptual validity or empirical support. As you can see from most leadership textbooks, these canonical theories of leading and following tend to emphasise the functions of practice, causal links between present or absent variables, and performance outcomes. But leadership studies is increasingly polyvocal, with symbolic and linguistic social theories in particular contributing to our understanding of what it means to lead and follow. Nonetheless, just on the basis of probability, what would survive of leadership studies if we found ourselves in a world 'after leadership' are the most widely represented approaches in our journals and books – the functionalist, positivist and performance oriented.

Unfortunately, as I argue here, these approaches are scientistic and metaphysically empty. They emphasise evidence, in the form of data – usually interview or questionnaire data – with a strong tendency to empiricism, assuming that such data can tell us how the world works. That in turn means that abstract concepts, such as space, time, identity, knowing or being, are ignored. At best, the more metaphysical aspects of leadership are reduced to simplistic questions for an interview, or variables that can be tested in questionnaires. This approach to understanding leadership ignores the immaterial and its place within our understanding of leadership, in the pursuit of an empiricist normal science that generates one universal leadership theory.

There is another way of thinking about leadership. Leadership and its study could look and feel very different: clearly defined, strongly contextualised, culturally specific and morally rooted. This is a challenge, but it could be relatively easily done, by returning to what MacIntyre calls the 'lost metaphysics' of philosophically informed critical thinking. If we were to do this, as I explain here, it would provide us with much more meaningful ideas and accounts of practice to work with in research and education as we attempt to build something that resembles MacIntyre's community of virtuous leaders and followers. And if we talked more in these terms, it would also increase the possibility of morally driven ideas about leadership surviving MacIntyre's bonfire of leadership studies' scientific vanities.

From Critical Thinking to Uncritical Writing

Every year I stand up in front of around 200 final year undergraduate students taking an elective course on leadership development in their autumn term,[1] and ask them to think about a range of leadership-related issues. We talk and think about identity, alienation, whistleblowing, feminism and neuroscience. Of course, I know very little about neuroscience – more than the students, I think, but not much more. We're only talking about it because it has become significant, fashionable even, in leadership studies. We spend about an hour contextualising this latest project to identify 'leadership potential' by conducting allegedly scientific experiments on people – starting as usual with Thomas Carlyle's 'Great Man' theory, followed through the twentieth century as it transformed into trait theories, to make the case that the attempt to develop a biology of leadership has a long and not-very-proud history based on the desire to exclude groups from even attempting to engage in leadership.

Then we spend an hour looking closely at published peer-reviewed research, consultancy activity and organisational practice in this area. After that, we ask and answer some questions, such as: Is this ethical? How would you feel if you were neurologically tested as part of a selection process for a job or for some leadership training? Is the brain really the best predictor of good leadership? How would you feel if you were identified as having a 'brain profile deficiency' during a test for your leadership qualities?

The conversations are fun and interesting, for me and I think for the students. Published critiques of this kind of neuroscientific leadership research are many, sometimes obvious and sometimes surprising, and the students often articulate them spontaneously before reading them. As a session, it gives me faith that we're developing critically reflexive students of management knowledge and education. I go home happy, and I imagine the students going home to tell their housemates or family horror stories about this particularly weird branch of leadership studies and how we're on to it as a critical community.

Then a strange thing happens, predictably, every year. A significant number choose to write about 'neuro-leadership studies' when they develop their assessed work. The vast majority of those that do this write in enthusiastic terms about the promise of neuro-techniques, for the identification of leadership qualities in organisations and individuals. Some acknowledge the ethical counterarguments, some don't. Either way, the message is clear – they believe this is a good, useful, helpful technique in identifying and developing leaders. What on earth happens in between the evident critical reflection in the classroom and the essay writing?

The Power of Scientism

I'm used to, and happy with, students arguing against ideas I like that are presented to them during lectures, seminars or in texts. What I'm not used to is such a complete turn away from the key purpose of a learning opportunity, away from what is clearly the central purpose of the time spent on the topic, towards the completely contrary outcome of uncritical acceptance of some highly problematic premises. It's worth revisiting these premises here to try to understand why this happens.

Neuroscientific approaches to understanding leadership are based on researcher claims to be able to identify what constitutes leadership through brainwaves and patterns. From this evidence, some researchers claim to be able to identify people who are not, and will not be able to become, leaders. Alongside this, others claim to have identified means of 'rearranging' the neural pathways they take images of during their empirical work – in other words, being able to develop leaders through neurological training. Still others promote neurological selection methods for expensive, time-consuming leadership development programmes, sorting those who would benefit from those who wouldn't on the basis of those patterns of biological reaction to specific tests.

Direct quotes from this research can be horrifying, emphasising that the ontological and epistemological position on what it is to be human in the world is, to say the least, reductionist. Critiques, especially from Dirk Lindebaum and colleagues,[2] have repeatedly pointed out the almost complete absence of an ethical aspect to neuroscientific research and its potential consequences for individuals or communities. It is, as a perspective, also founded on somewhat shaky datasets, contravening even its own norms, in an echo of a similar fundamental critique of evolutionary psychology.[3]

I read and celebrate these carefully crafted critiques of what I interpret as amoral evidence-based theories of leadership. Theories are scientistic, in the sense that they are unreflectively positivist and empiricist, applying natural science methodologies to a social scientific phenomenon.[4] I encourage students to read this kind of leadership research as part of engaging with the ideas that researchers working within this paradigm develop about the social activity we call leadership. But I'm always left with the uncomfortable feeling, based on experience with those large groups of undergraduate students, that critiques are ineffective, and scientism asserts a powerful attraction for people looking for answers to the challenges that understanding leadership presents. I fear that the critiques are ignored, ignorable and more ephemeral than the research they critique – more likely, in short, to disappear during the bonfire of leadership studies when the attack comes on the records of our knowledge. The objectivism, the naive realism in appeals to 'facts', and seductively clear statistical relationships protect this kind of knowledge from methodological or philosophical critique.

So why is this? I suspect, in an unscientific way, that it's related to normative expectations of what good research is, and an associated desire for certainty in knowing something. Where I work, we spend a lot of time telling students things – introducing or revisiting theory, working through empirical evidence, suggesting ways of thinking, checking to make sure that ideas and techniques have been absorbed, and encouraging students to be confident that they can engage in a 'leadership conversation' with work colleagues and academics. We spend a lot less time finding out what students think and believe – the only real access I have to that is when I read their assessed work. Based on that, most of the people in student groups I work with have a desire for clarity, tidiness and guides to action. It helps to construct a plausible essay if there is a beginning, middle and end that tell a tidy story. That means the questions or issues I want them to think about, in parallel to getting to know the established knowledges of leadership studies, are at best in the background – critiques may be acknowledged but are not central. The grand narratives and claims to generalisable law-like knowledge that scientism promotes are strangely attractive in a messy, complex subject area like leadership studies. That brings us back to wondering how this comes to be – something that the historical development of leadership studies may help understand.

Narrating Leadership Studies: Challenging Scientism by Returning to Metaphysical Meaning

If we think of the leadership studies 'canon' of knowledge, the kind of thing that students and scholars sometimes reproduce without critical reflection,[5] we find a neat story – first one theory, then another, then another, always improving methodologically and becoming increasingly sophisticated. That is, to some extent, true – biographical analysis, for example, has developed methodologically from the nineteenth century to today.[6] However, these theories also run in parallel. Trait theory continues to be very influential in scholarship and in practice; behavioural theories show no signs of being abandoned. This can be productively critiqued through Foucauldian social theoretical methods.[7] As Suze Wilson elegantly demonstrates, asking 'why this idea?' and 'why this point in time?' are both very productive questions to ask of theory. Foucauldian social theory provides the necessary critical distance, by positioning theory as discourse. Here, I try another method – following MacIntyre's way of thinking, I suggest thinking about how and why the desire for clarity and tidiness comes about through ideology.

In his early work, MacIntyre examined the interplay of Marxism and Christianity during the 1950s and 1960s, updating and developing his arguments as the sociopolitical context changed.[8] Despite the revisions he made to the argument, its base is always clear: Marxism and Christianity can coexist as metaphysical and moral belief systems. Both can be read as ways of understanding human nature, history and capitalism. MacIntyre chooses to analyse Marxism as a political philosophy because he sees it as the only socioeconomic theory with the scope of a religious belief system, and also because, practically, aspects of Marx's thought developed from the early eighteenth century dialogue between religion and philosophy on humanity and society.

MacIntyre's substantive argument about the continued utility and meaning of Marxism beyond the sociopolitical changes of the 1980s is framed by the idea that it was politically appropriated by both Communist and anti-Communist groups to provide material for ideological battles. This meant that the complex realities of Marx's thought, especially its metaphysics, were lost, as theories were rearticulated for specific purposes. What Marx's social and political philosophy meant ethically was lost, as the social and historical conditions of its development were lost or ignored. Its ideological appropriation also reduced the people who were so prominent in Marx's original writing to instruments or abstract forms or politics, philosophy and economy.

If the complexity was lost, a reductionist sort of clarity was achieved. Marx's political philosophy was uprooted from its socio-historical complexity, disembedded from cultural time, place and context of practice. The ideas and arguments were stripped of their metaphysical and moral scope, and the people subject to the ideas were treated as less human and less agentic.

MacIntyre aims to recover some of that humanity and its metaphysics. His observations about Marxism and Christianity are the basis of an argument on the grandest scale possible. He is analysing the development of the two most socially, culturally and politically significant philosophical schemes of the nineteenth and twentieth centuries. In comparison, leadership studies as a research and educational endeavour feels, and is, much smaller in scale. Notwithstanding, I think the arguments presented in *Marxism and Christianity* are relevant to the argument I'm developing here. If we, as MacIntyre recommends, attempt to recover the metaphysical meaning of social and economic theories, we will think in a quite different way. The reductionism of a scientistic approach that positions social life as a set of variables, and people as a set of physical responses to stimuli, is impossible to sustain if we ask the simple question of what actions such as leading or following mean for us as moral agents with an interest in being, identity, knowing, time or space. Hopes and aspirations are recovered because a metaphysical way of thinking provides a very different narrative and vocabulary.

After the Bonfire: Reasons to be Cheerful

There are many critical, in a negative sense, observations that can be made about leadership studies as a field. Nick Butler and his colleagues summarise them well: leadership studies and its practitioners lack 'rigour' in their research work, lack 'relevance' to practitioners, lack academic status and credibility on campus, encourage arcane theoretical and methodological debate, and are prone to giving in to the temptation of generating additional personal income through dubious consultancy.[9] Some of these critiques are applicable to other areas of management and organisation studies, but leadership studies seems to be especially prone to corruption as an academic endeavour. The attractiveness of studying and talking about leadership is thus double-edged – students and practitioners are more likely to attend to theories but are more demanding of 'good' theory. The definition of what good theory is can easily be reduced to helpful but reductionist scientistic guidance on how to identify leaders, how to become a leader and how to practise leadership successfully. Critical reflection on the discourse, ideology or existence of leadership may not be an expectation that many bring to the business school.

In this context, when there are researchers willing to satisfy a desire for simplistic amoral answers to complex ethical questions such as 'how should I lead or follow?', I'm suggesting that metaphysics offers hope. MacIntyre's arguments in *After Virtue*, and in related work such as *Marxism and Christianity*, provide three areas in which we might be optimistic, first in the fact that the issues explored through philosophical and conceptual debate can only be found 'embodied in the historical lives of particular social groups'.[10] There is variety in practice over time and across places; all activity can only be understood as located, embedded in societies that vary according to place and time. For me, that is hopeful because it means the practices associated with leading, leaders and leadership are always open to change and difference, in the moment of their embodied enactment, and in analysis.

Second, following from this, MacIntyre suggests that moral inquiry is always an articulation of the society that the speaker or writer inhabits. There is no transcendent or socially abstract argument or position, and different claims are therefore incommensurable solely in terms of rationality. Truth or falsehood cannot be established, except through sensitive empirical research – asking questions such as how the theory came to be, how its social context helps us understand it and what is different now. In relation to the substantive topic of this book, this again feels optimistic to me – it enables us to approach the theories that currently constitute leadership and leading with a view to both extracting them from and embedding them in the context of their development.

Finally, paradoxically, all of MacIntyre's ideas are always presented as work in progress. This can be seen in the revisions he makes to books such as the two referenced here, which make their way in the world in multiple editions, each with an additional preface or afterword, and generous acknowledgement of critiques and criticisms of the previous edition. This is for me the most hopeful and thought-provoking aspect of MacIntyre's work, how he stewards it when published – the arguments and the evidence are located as part of a continuing dialogue as to the nature of the thing he is writing about. If we could adopt a similar approach to the topic of leadership, rather than uncritically accepting situated data and knowledge as universally true, then we would present a much more interesting, insightful, thoughtful, scholarly and educational face to those who engage with it as students and practitioners. To do that, we can do nothing more hopeful than emphasise the metaphysics of leadership, and in doing so, examine the morality of its practice and research.

Notes

1 Teaching in a business school in English higher education is currently characterised by bizarre statements like this, statements that juxtapose apparently contradictory terms such as 'final year elective' and '200 students'. A colleague working in another English Midlands university school speaks every year with horror about teaching a final year undergraduate module called 'Introduction to Human Resource Management' to 350 students. As he says, it's difficult to know where to start with the contradictions built into that one ...
2 See Lindebaum 2013 and 2015, and Lindebaum & Zundel 2015.
3 See Sewell 2004.
4 See O'Mahony 2016.
5 For example, the periodisation of leadership studies along the following lines: first there was the 'Great Man' theory, then trait theories, then behavioural theories, then contingency theories, then 'New Leadership' theories focusing on transformation and charisma, and now there is the pinnacle of our understanding, ethical/neuroscientific/relational leadership theory. The linear representation of knowledge development suggests evolution and progress. It is sometimes challenged by historians attempting to recover the complexity of ideas that have become packaged and marketed in simplistic ways (e.g. Cummings et al., 2016; Hassard, 2012). This important recovery work emphasises the social contexts of theory alongside the inherent subtlety of argument, both usually lost in textbook representations and therefore in student learning.
6 Compare Carlyle's (1841) methods to more recent proposals (Shamir et al., 2005) in this area.
7 See Wilson 2013.
8 See Macintyre 1995[1968].
9 See Butler et al. 2015.
10 MacIntyre, 2007[1981]: 265.

References

Butler, N., Delaney, H. & Spoelstra, S. (2015) Problematizing 'relevance' in the Business School: The case of leadership studies. *International Journal of Management Reviews*, 26(4): 731–744.

Carlyle, T. (1841) *On Heroes, Hero-Worship, and the Heroic in History*. London: James Fraser.

Cummings, S., Brigdman, T. & Brown, K. (2016) Unfreezing change as three steps: Rethinking Kurt Lewin's legacy for change management. *Human Relations*, 69(1): 33–60.

Hassard, J. (2012) Rethinking the Hawthorne Studies: The Western Electric research in its social, political and historical context. *Human Relations*, 65(11): 1431–1461.

Lindebaum, D. (2013) Pathologizing the healthy but ineffective: Some ethical reflections on using neuroscience in leadership research. *Journal of Management Inquiry*, 22(3): 295–305.

Lindebaum, D. (2015) Critical essay – Building new management theories on sound data: The case of neuroscience. *Human Relations*, 69(3): 537–550.

Lindebaum, D. & Zundel, M. (2015) Not quite a revolution: Scrutinizing organizational neuroscience in leadership studies. *Human Relations*, 66(6): 857–877.

MacIntyre, A. (1995[1968]) *Marxism and Christianity*. London: Duckworth.

MacIntyre, A. (2007[1981]) *After Virtue*, third edition. London: Duckworth.

O'Mahony, J. (2016) Archetypes of translation: Recommendations for dialogue. *International Journal of Management Reviews*, 18: 333–350.

Sewell, G. (2004) Yabba-dabba-doo! Evolutionary psychology and the rise of Flintstone psychological thinking in organization and management studies. *Human Relations*, 57(8): 923–955.

Shamir, B., Dayan-Horesh, H. & Adler, D. (2005) Leading by biography: Towards a life-story approach to the study of leadership. *Leadership*, 1(1): 13–29.

Wilson, S. (2013) Situated knowledge: A Foucauldian analysis of ancient and modern classics of leadership thought. *Leadership*, 9(1): 43–61.

4   I, Leader[1]

Becoming Human through the Emotional Grounding of Leadership Practice

Marian Iszatt-White

Introduction

As the world turns, the possibility of a modern, knowledge-based 'bonfire of the vanities'[2] seems not unlikely. The advances in knowledge and understanding that began with the Age of Enlightenment seem set to be once again subsumed in religious turmoil with possibly disastrous consequences. If, like the burning of the Library at Alexandria,[3] huge swathes of written treasures were to be lost in this return to the Dark Ages,[4] what would survive of our attempts to understand the role of emotions in leadership? And what would we lose – and gain – by having to undertake this journey of learning a second time? In the event of such a wholesale loss of the academic bedrock of leadership writing, it seems likely that the many different attempts to measure emotions in the workplace (emotional labour scales, emotional intelligence scales and a range of psychometric tests including aspects of emotion management) might be some of the fragments of knowledge to survive in dusty filing cabinets and outmoded ring-binders on the shelves of human resource departments and leadership development organisations and in the muddled half-memories of past leadership learning intervention participants. Like a puzzle with no instructions, this chapter speculates on the potential for 'emotions in leadership – mark II' and how we might reassemble the pieces differently the second time around.[5]

Drawing from our rescued fragments, it will first consider the affordances of current perspectives, which have tended to treat emotions as an 'add-on' for otherwise rational leaders and managers. From this perspective, we have tended to view emotions as a resource and a tool, using which effective leaders can better achieve their goals. At the same time, the notion of workplaces and organisations as largely rational places, where emotions are to be banished – or at least managed – has shaped our expectations of leaders as operating as emotional 'containers' for those around them. And the organisational and cultural 'display rules'[6] attending this emotional adjunct have been rooted in gender and professional stereotypes and enacted in gendered performances. These have been useful approaches to help us get to grips with this most wayward and messy of topics, but treating emotions as 'add-ons' has simultaneously saddled us with some constraints. Thinking of emotions as something to be 'reinserted' into the workplace, something to be 'performed' rather than just felt or listened to, or as a 'component' of practice rather than something integral and holistic has often resulted in a mechanical or reductionist research stance. Emotions are to be 'measured', their consequences and effects are to be 'correlated' and their expression is reduced to an instrumental task.

There are also practitioner implications of this presumption that rationality should prevail. There is something calculating and manipulative about the 'use' of emotions as a 'tool' of leadership, something to be layered on top of a rational decision-making process or interactional stance. The ethics of choosing between a deontological (worthy ends are never sufficient to justify unethical means) versus teleological (unethical actions can be justified where the benefits outweigh the costs) stance in how we enact leadership has a significant role to play in how we view this emotional adjunct. Whether we are talking about the little white lie of the 'of course your bum doesn't look big in that' variety – designed to avoid giving offence or to align with cultural norms of courtesy – or the more strategic 'of course there won't be any redundancies' style of deception practised in business, how we reason about deliberate acts of emotion management *should* be an inherently ethical affair, but our current models of leadership seem to have leached such considerations from our consciousness. Instead, our instrumental stance towards emotions focuses concern largely on the effectiveness of such performances, with any consequent 'emotional dissonance'[7] being of largely academic interest: it is viewed as all part of the job of the professional manager, rather than an equal – if sometimes troubling – partner in the accomplishment of leadership work.

In an attempt to turn our current 'rational' world on its head, this chapter explores the potential to see emotions as more fundamentally connected to the leadership purpose; as more definitive of leadership identity; and as a well-spring of guidance and direction. After an intellectual experiment that tries (and broadly fails!) to put emotionality *before* rationality, it goes on to suggest a new kind of authenticity and a new kind of emotion-led, 'affective' leadership which might offer a more genuine intertwining of emotion and reason in the conception and practice of leadership. In exploring this possibility, I draw upon what seems to me to be a curious phenomenon: the high proportion of science fiction writing that uses robots to explore what it means to be human. Some personal favourites include Data and his 'emotions chip' in *Star Trek*, the Terminator coming to understand why humans cry, Marvin, the Paranoid Android and – of course – Sonny in Asimov's *I, Robot* stories. Sonny's journey towards being an individual – rather than just another characterless robotic servant – and Detective Spooner's journey to viewing him as 'someone' rather than 'something' – provides a number of poignant touchstones for my own journey to recast the role of emotions in the practice of leadership, and to explore both the potential and the risks of this radical 'rebooting' of our understanding of leadership.

Emotions in the Workplace – Interpreting the Fragments

As someone who has been both a trainer and developer and a training participant before becoming an academic, I have a significant collection of folders,
ring-binders and practitioner manuals on my shelves relating to psychometric
instruments. Many of these instruments – if you like, the 'technology' of emotions – include attempts to measure emotions or emotional competencies in
one form or another, such as emotional intelligence,[8] emotional labour[9] and
specific 'emotions' such as curiosity[10] and work passion.[11] A particularly apt
example of the latter strand of work is the psychometric evaluation of the
propensity to worry[12] entitled 'why worry II', or WWII for short! They are,
I suspect, representative of the documentary traces of our understanding of
emotions in the workplace likely to be found in any human resource department, training and development function or – consciously or not – in the
heads of most managers. Whilst highly technical and statistical in their development, they present what appears to be a clear and accessible model of 'how
emotions work' that anyone can pick up and apply (albeit the application is
sometimes *over*-simplified and the potential for personal insight reduced to a
self-categorisation exercise). More academic in their readership – and potentially better candidates for the bonfire – are our near obsession with measuring
and validating anything that emotion touches: from how we regulate (or not)
our emotions[13] to whether they are learned or innate,[14] it seems our emotions
have been dissected, catalogued, correlated and constructed from every possible angle. Ironically, of course, this activity is undertaken in a determinedly
non-emotional manner, producing the paradox of talking about emotions
unemotionally, and talking about them but not expressing them! Like
Dr Calvin in *I, Robot* – who describes her job as being to make the robots seem
more human – we seem to be trying to 'anthropomorphise' leaders by adding
emotions, completely oblivious of the fact that in our case the emotions are
already there. It is (for me, at least) a rather depressing premise of this genre
of research that emotions – so lately invited to join the management party –
remain a hanger-on, lucky to get a look-in to our thinking at all and definitely
'handmaidens'[15] of the more central construct of rationality. Our understanding of emotions is as a resource or tool (with affordances, to be performed)
or as an encumbrance or liability (with risks, to be managed), rather than
integral and holistic to us as human beings (to be felt or listened to). What
does it say for us as academics that we have promulgated this perspective of
'robotic' leadership sans emotions – or of emotions as a 'software upgrade'
which managers need to install or an 'app' they can tap into when necessary –
as a normative ideal for practitioners despite our undoubted awareness of the
inherently emotional (i.e. human) nature of organisational workplaces? This
rather sad perspective is ably captured, and critiqued, in Debra Meyerson's[16]
contribution – 'If emotions were honoured' – to Fineman's[17] seminal work on
emotion in organisations: here, Meyerson makes a call for genuine engagement with emotions in the workplace that has yet to be answered. At the

same time, she articulates the near-universally understood stance of research when she says:

> Researchers are supposed to be objective, dispassionate observers outside the systems we observe. Thus, empathy is not supposed to be employed as a source of understanding, and connections with those we are observing threaten the integrity of the data.[18]

Anyone who has tried to have, say, an autoethnographic paper accepted by a 4* journal will feel the truth of this statement. Speaking personally, I can travel through disappointment, anger, resentment and even hopelessness before eventually achieving resignation and then determination on receipt of the almost inevitable rejections such attempts occasion – so how, and why, should I be expected to undertake work that I am passionate about in an entirely mechanical, robotic way? And the scorn heaped upon anthropologists who 'go native' is, as Meyerson notes, an indication of how little room the social sciences make for emotions – surely a nonsense when empathy is such a natural bedfellow of the sensemaking upon which much social science depends.

This perspective is a good fit with our broader worldview, in which the environment – human, social, economic and geographical – is largely seen as a habitat for *homo economicus*, there to supply his needs and serve his purposes. In economics, *homo economicus*, or economic man, is the concept underpinning many theories portraying humans as consistently rational and narrowly self-interested agents who usually pursue their subjectively defined ends optimally. I think we can all see how inadequate – and inaccurate – a view of man's doings that is. (Surely this is science fiction in reverse – humans trying to be robots instead of robots trying to be human.) Whilst this theory has been contrasted by the concepts of, for example, behavioural economics (which examines actual economic behaviour, including widespread cognitive biases and other irrationalities) and human co-operation, even here the starting point is one of rationality. Closer to home for leadership scholars has been the development from 'scientific management'[19] and 'command and control'[20] leadership to 'emotional intelligence'[21] and 'leadership as emotional labour',[22] but even here the progress has been slow and has yet to break the bounds of its rational ancestry. It is interesting to note that this ancestry has not been evenly distributed (or at least perceived), with rationality tending to be viewed as masculine[23] and emotionality as feminine:[24] as with many supposedly gendered aspects[25] of leadership, the perception of these characteristics (as positive or negative) has shifted somewhat over the years.

The Limitations of *homo economicus*

As the story of *I, Robot* plays out around the relationship between robot Sonny and human Detective Spooner, a commentary on the state of humanity is provided by VIKI[26], the computer at the heart (no pun intended) of the robot-producing company. Speaking as a rational being, VIKI uses a twisted understanding of the Three Laws of Robotics[27] to justify the decision to take control of human affairs: according to her logic, our propensity for waging wars and toxifying the planet makes us unfit to be trusted with safeguarding our own survival. Whilst this logic is irrefutable, Detective Spooner – and later Sonny – still see human frailty as preferable to robotic 'perfection'. A sentiment we would all agree with, I suspect.

So where have *homo economicus* and his bosom buddy the rational leader got us as a species? Is VIKI right to suggest that we can't be trusted with our own future? Ironically, I think it is the statement of our goals for that future that present the starkest statement of our failings from the past. Consider the 'millennium development goals'[28] and – more specifically business-focused – the Global Compact. Developed at the UN Millennium Summit in 2000 with a deadline for achievement of 2015, the millennium development goals focused on such major issues as eradicating extreme poverty and hunger, ensuring environmental sustainability and reducing child mortality. Other goals related to the promotion of gender equality and the empowerment of women; combating HIV/AIDS, malaria and other diseases; and achieving universal primary education, with the recognition that a spirit of global partnership would be needed for these goals to be met. It seems inconceivable that with all the 'progress' we have made in science, technology, medicine and knowledge, generally these most funda-mental of goals still evade our grasp – and with 2015 long gone, we are still only infinitesimally nearer to achieving them than we were when they were set. So, for example, according to a 2016 UNICEF[29] study, 385 mil-lion children still live in poverty worldwide, and infant mortality (classi-fied as babies dying within one year of birth) just one year earlier stood at 4.5 million.[30] Worldwide, 36.6 million people are living with HIV/AIDS[31] and half the world's population are still at risk from malaria with 429,000 deaths in 2015.[32] At the same time, other potentially catastrophe-generating challenges are rearing their ugly heads: in particular, the rise of religiously inspired terrorism (a daily worry for us all as I am writing) is testament to how limited our rationality actually is and how inadequate is our ability (or desire?) to quietly listen to and understand our fellow human beings. Surely, we have arrived at the worst of all possible worlds.

So much for world leadership based on supposedly rational princi-ples. What of business? This is the territory of the UN Global Compact. Convened as a policy platform and practical framework for companies committed to sustainability and responsible business practices, the princi-ples of the UN Global Compact[33] fall into four categories covering human rights, labour standards, the environment and anti-corruption. Under the banner of human rights, the Compact states that businesses should support and respect the protection of internationally proclaimed human rights and make sure that they are not complicit in human rights abuses. The labour standards category requires businesses to uphold the freedom of association and the effective recognition of the right to collective bargaining; eliminate all forms of forced and compulsory labour; bring about the effective abolition of child labour; and eliminate discrimination in respect of employment and occupation. In safeguarding the environment, businesses are called upon to support a precautionary approach to environmental challenges; undertake initiatives to promote greater environmental responsibility; and encourage the development and diffusion of environmentally friendly technologies. And finally, businesses should work against corruption in all its forms, including extortion and bribery. Once again, one would have thought that these were 'no-brainers' for advanced and advancing societies, but the many shortcomings in our working world suggest that here, too, leading with the head rather than the heart leaves much to be desired. Again, some examples will serve to illustrate the point. There are an estimated 200 million child labourers worldwide, with 120 million working in hazardous jobs and 73 million under ten year's old.[34] Around 21 million people are victims of forced labour, modern slavery or human trafficking.[35] We seem to have made only limited progress with the introduction of clean/green technologies (we do now have more places to plug in electric cars but the NIMBYs[36] are still battling against wind farms and other forms of sustainable energy) and the Paris Climate Accord has suffered a serious blow with President Trump's decision to withdraw America from it. And even such positive initiatives as there are (such as advances in corporate social responsibility) seem prone to the manipulation and instrumentalism of greenwashing and worse.[37] Surely, we should all feel ashamed and angry that we allow these horrors to persist in a supposedly civilised world, and yet don't seem to see the need for a new way of conceptualising leadership – leadership that will actually address the serious problems we and our planet now face.

At an individual level, too, the demigod that is rationality seems to have constrained our understanding of leadership at the same time as its enactment has produced less than optimal results. We are taught to keep our emotions under control in the name of professionalism and appropriateness[38] rather than celebrating them as the essence of our humanity. Like Data, we switch our 'emotion chips' off when we walk through our employer's doors – or like Sonny, we 'simulate' emotions as tools of enacting leadership. Our leadership duties include acting as emotional 'containers'[39] and 'toxic emotion handlers'[40] rather than conductors/conduits and responsive interpreters: emotions are 'systems malfunctions' to be corrected and prevented. From workplace stress[41] to worker alienation,[42] from toxic leadership[43] to toxic followers,[44] there seem to be so many ways in which we have lost our way, with the 'wetware' of emotions coming a poor third to the 'hardware' of physical bodies and the 'software' of intellectual acumen. And hanging over all is the sense that commercial success and humanism are to be understood as competing values in a crowded world where embracing one entails suppressing the other. We have made our choice: emotions are rationality's 'handmaiden' – the nice-to-have add-on, but not the driving force. Perhaps, rather than using our psychometric 'fragments' as scaffolding for a new leadership edifice, we should tear them up completely and start again! Perhaps we should consider what it would mean to acknowledge that emotions are a fundamental part of what it is to be human and to treat them with respect and inclusivity.

Finding a Future for I, Leader

In *I, Robot*, Dr Alfred Lanning, Director of Research at US Robots and Mechanical Men, talks about the notion of 'ghosts in the machine', suggesting that machines created and programmed by humans have always had the potential to develop beyond their programming, to learn and evolve in ways that engender questions of free will and consciousness. He asks the question of where the boundaries lie between a 'difference engine' and the 'search for truth', between a 'personality simulation' and something (someone) that can be said to have a 'soul'. Such speculations are the very essence of intelligent science fiction, placing in sharp relief as they do our own search for the essence of our own humanity. In the context of the current chapter, they provide the jumping-off point for my own attempts to speculate on what a shift from 'robotic' to 'human' leadership might look like – how things might be if we put emotions on top, as both its heart and its soul. But first, it is worth considering what 'ghosts' we might find in current leadership theories that could show us the way towards a more human leadership stance. One promising place for such ghost hunting is the recent development of responsible leadership. The call for responsible leadership to move us 'from value to values, from shareholders to stakeholders, and from balance sheets to balanced development'[45] still echoes through our lives long after it was first made, but can it deliver? Is it enough? Responsible leadership has been defined as:

> a values-based and thoroughly ethical principles-driven relationship between leaders and stakeholders who are connected through a shared sense of meaning and purpose through which they raise one another to higher levels of motivation and commitment for achieving sustainable values creation and social change.[46]

Can leaders, in seeking to enact responsibility, re-inscribe their understanding of themselves[47] and reinvent business in order to deliver the 'restorative economy'[48] required in response to the current ecological and humanitarian crises? Maybe – but it may also be that 'responsibility', however laudable, is just another add-on, another app, and that a more fundamental upgrade is required. As mentioned above, the often flawed nature of corporate social responsibility initiatives is witness to the instrumental overtones responsible leadership has acquired to date, which suggests it doesn't go far enough in overthrowing its supposedly 'rational' predecessors. So, what might leadership look like if emotions were truly put at the heart of it, with rationality relegated to the role of junior partner, rather than the other way around? And would it be any better than what we have now? So, let us speculate what leadership might be like if we grounded it on emotionality before rationality: what would happen if the whole of business (and research – although I'm choosing to steer clear of politics!) was based on emotional judgements (e.g. of right and wrong, of how decisions feel) rather than rational ones (e.g. measures of profit and loss or competitive advantage). In what follows, I offer some thoughts on how the canon of leadership knowledge and practice might be reconstructed on this premise.

If we start at the top, what would strategy and strategizing look like if our emotions were given free rein? Strategic leadership has been defined by Johnson, Scholes and Whittington[49] as 'the *direction* and *scope* of an organisation over the *long term*, which achieves *advantage* in a changing *environment* through its configuration of *resources and competences* with the aim of fulfilling *stakeholder* expectations. It thus relates to the responsibility for managing the resources and capabilities of the organisation such as to create and maintain competitive advantage',[50] and is 'marked by a concern for the evolution of the organisation as a whole, including its changing aims and capabilities'.[51] In relation to employees, the role of strategic leaders has also been couched in terms of the creation of meaning and purpose.[52] So would the goals our organisations strive for – their direction and scope – and the meaning senior leaders offer to their organisations change for the better if we put emotions at their heart?

At first blush, it is tempting to suggest that such goals would be radically better – that drawing on positive emotions as a source of inspiration would produce more sustainable, responsible visions for the future with consequent moderation in consumerism and growth, and more user-friendly workplaces. But why should this be? We have 'bad' emotions too and could just as easily be led towards greater greed and destruction, or greater employee exploitation, if they aren't kept in check. Nor would bringing emotions to bear on strategic decision making eliminate the bounded rationality[53] of senior leaders that is said to constrain the manner in which strategic choices are made and which can be traced through to specific organisational outcomes. Based upon their values and beliefs as well as their past experience, CEOs would continue to bring their own 'givens' to any new situation, limiting their field of vision and how their attention is directed, causing selectivity in perception of events and their significance, and thus resulting in a filtering of the ways in which information is evaluated. These values and beliefs would be just what they always had been – but less constrained by rational counterweights. It is also to be expected that a 'bounded emotionality' – the emotional 'givens' we carry with us that make us optimists or pessimists, empathetic or resentful, and so on – will constrain our decisions in equally traceable and flawed directions.

So far, our speculative reconstructions seem less than compelling. Are things any clearer if we ask what kind of workplaces emotion-led leaders would create? Notwithstanding the ever-present human failings of leaders (just as much as the rest of us) is this where we might find more purchase for the emotional ideal? It has been suggested that the dynamic and uncertain environment of the twenty-first century requires a new kind of leadership if organisations are to successfully negotiate a path to competitive advantage,[54] and that it is the role of strategic leaders to instil challenge and purpose, break through perceived barriers and encourage potential in order to effectively leverage the resources at their disposal. In delivering on this essential task of leadership, Hitt and Ireland[55] see leaders as requiring astute interpersonal skills and relational competence in order to operate as 'human modems' in an increasingly networked environment. This suggests the importance of the 'emotional skills' we are already familiar with, such as emotional intelligence and emotional labour, but how would things change if these were placed centre stage rather than as added extras: would workplaces be better places to be or just different?

This is where the academic literature and 'real life' appear to part company – or rather, where they have long since parted company. In our everyday lives, we are all too aware of our emotions as an essential part of ourselves. We live them – feel them – minute by minute, day by day, as an integral part of what we do, what we say, how we make decisions, how we interact with others – and most certainly as part of how we lead. This is a 'natural' way for us to be. It is only through the development of acquired 'knowledge' – academic research feeding into journal papers feeding into leadership textbooks feeding into shared understanding feeding into practice – that we are taught to think of our emotions as something almost separate from ourselves.

This is not to say that we aren't taught to manage our emotions – through cultural and social mores and practice – as part of our 'natural' way of being, or that the free expression of emotion would be permissible in society if not for those pesky academics! But it is, I think, *academic* knowledge that has created the sense of separation between what is rational and what is emotional as such an all-encompassing paradigm within which we are so effectively caged. One only has to look at the roots of the Age of Enlightenment to see the strength of this opposition in the very heart of academic thinking. Heavily influenced by thinkers such as Descartes and Locke, the Enlightenment was a European intellectual movement of the late seventeenth and early eighteenth centuries emphasising reason and individualism rather than tradition and faith. Marked by an emphasis on the scientific method and reductionism along with increased questioning of religious orthodoxy, the driving force here was the overthrow of faith-based (aka non-rational) forms of authority and knowledge in favour of science-based (aka rational) alternatives. In its most radical form, inspired by the philosophy of Spinoza, the Enlightenment advocated the complete eradication of religious authority, whilst other more moderate strands envisaged a mere rebalancing of power.

The important role of science – or 'natural philosophy' as it was initially known – in Enlightenment discourse and thought saw the development of many ideas with which we are all familiar today. Scientific methods (the nature of knowledge, evidence, experience and causation) were largely developed by David Hume and Adam Smith during this period. And we should not underestimate the advances accruing to scientific progress during the Enlightenment period. These included the discovery of carbon dioxide (fixed air) by the chemist Joseph Black, the argument for deep time by the geologist James Hutton, the invention of the steam engine by James Watt, the experiments of Lavoisier that led to the first modern chemical plants in Paris, and the experiments of the Montgolfier brothers that led to the first manned flight in 1783. But now it is payback time. Listen to any news broadcast today and you are likely to hear that 'scientists' are telling us about something we should do or not do to be healthier, wealthier or (very occasionally) wiser. The ubiquitous and hopelessly generic term 'scientist' is an accepted shorthand for 'something we should accept as true because it has been researched in a rational way and is supported by empirical evidence'. The Enlightenment has done its work well and the power of the rational has, in many spheres of our lives, long since overthrown the power of the non-rational as the source of all that is good and desirable. At the very least, it has created a bifurcated structure whereby reason and faith are largely separated from each other and we, the people, are left to try to integrate their differing edicts in our complex and often messy everyday lives. (It is, perhaps, worth speculating whether the current growth in religious terrorism has as one of its drivers an instinctive backlash against this forced separation.)

So what if we turn the tables on the Enlightenment: what would an emotion-led research paradigm look like and what would it mean for our understanding of leadership? What topics would leadership academics be researching and what methods would we be using? Perhaps how leaders motivate employees would be taken for granted in much the way rational decision making is now. We wouldn't need job enrichment theories[56] or positive reinforcement theories,[57] because it would be a foundational premise of other research topics that leaders are motivational and effortlessly inspire their employees. We would, instead, investigate how leaders could add elements of rationality to their natural feeling for what was right and good for their organisation and for their workers, and how this rationality impacts on a range of outcomes. We might measure rationality as a tool or resource of emotion-led leadership and evaluate its benefits in terms of more empathetic interactions. There would be a whole genre of work around how leaders support their emotions with rationality instead of how they soften their rationality with emotions. Organisations would be constructed as holistic, person-centred collectives operating as centres of fulfilment and self-actualisation, with outputs and profits as secondary adjuncts. Leaders would be portrayed as 'keepers of the faith' of humanistic and compassionate organisational goals, instead of harbingers of productivity and performance. Their practice would reflect this hierarchy through relational transparency, passionate advocacy for humanitarian goals and a day-by-day attention to employee well-being. They would rank worker self-actualisation above profit generation and feel comfortable in showing their true selves to colleagues rather than wearing professional masks. And they would bring generosity and kindness to managerial decision making.

Methodologically, the social science of leadership would, perhaps, give up the aims of measuring, calibrating and predicting and be satisfied with a more empathetic attempt at understanding. Our 'fragments' of psychometrics – rescued from the bonfire – would not be revered as ancient wisdom to be reinstated and emulated, but would be set aside as hopelessly reductionist and partial attempts to quantify the essentially unquantifiable. New methods of data collection would develop based on compassionate observation and empathetic imagination. Data analysis would derive from an empathetic interpretation of events and their meanings, based on researcher feelings of what was important rather than on weight of evidence. Intuitive processes would be utilised to generate themes and clusters within the data and to capture the … (at this point I headed to my online dictionary to search out an antonym for 'logic', wanting to capture some counterpoint that we might be aiming for in envisioning patterns within our data. It is disappointing, but telling, that all my dictionary had to offer in this regard was 'unreasonableness') … aesthetic of our argument.

In all honesty, I would have to concede that these proposals seem as alien to me as they probably will to most of you reading them. They sound, even to my ears, like a too-loud echo of the supremacy of religious doctrine and superstition over any form of evidence-based knowledge. But they can perhaps offer a provocation to the taken-for-granted-ness of our assumptions about the 'rightness' of the ways of science: about their inherent fitness for purpose in the development of useful knowledge. If we can even partially dislodge the grip that logic and rationality has over our research processes, we can perhaps develop a richer tradition of investigation and knowledge generation – one that has room for both the rational and the intuitive, for our feelings as well as our thoughts, and which acknowledges their intertwined-ness and mutual dependence. What we need, perhaps, is a research equivalent of Aristotle's phronesis or practical wisdom: not just techné (craft or skill) or episteme (knowledge), but some synthesis of both.

Finding our way to leadership purpose

As *I, Robot* concludes and Sonny has completed his programmed purpose of helping Detective Spooner solve the crime of Dr Lanning's death, he is left contemplating what his future – unprogrammed – purpose might be.

Spooner's response to this question is to suggest that he will just have to find his way like 'the rest of us': this, he says, is what it means to be free. So if we were 'free' of past programming in relation to what constitutes effective leadership – or any kind of leadership – what would we do? Where would we go? And could we find, or create, a middle ground between rationality and emotions?

In the previous sections, I have deliberately overstated the case against rational leadership. It is wrong, however, to suggest that current leadership is entirely without passion, or that all companies operate entirely from motives of profit. There are clearly many companies that are passionately creative (Steve Jobs' Apple always comes to mind here, but I prefer to think of its 'kid brother' Pixar) or fiercely ethical (Anita Roddick's Body Shop is a well-known example here but Patagonia outdoor clothing company is a personal favourite). And great ideas that arise from curiosity and passion can often be the start of hugely successful businesses. Richard Branson's vast empire is said to have started in a telephone box because he envisaged a better way of selling and making records: he is supposed to have once said, 'There is no point in starting your own business unless you do it out of a sense of frustration'. And the Polaroid camera, revolutionary in its day, was only invented because Edwin Land's three-year-old daughter asked why she could not immediately see the picture he had just taken of her. That it would go on to transform his company and how we think of photographic media was almost certainly not on his mind as he set to work figuring out how to grant his daughter's wish. These ideas may have required reasoned thought in their implementation, but they would never have got off the ground without the very worthy human qualities of curiosity, faith and determination.

Similarly, leadership research has not been without its virtues and there are other, less reductionist 'fragments' of this work that we might take as a starting point for a more realistically woven fabric of reason and emotion within our understanding of leadership. An obvious starting point would be forms of positive leadership[58] and authentic leadership[59] as their self-proclaimed 'root construct'. Authentic leadership has been summarised as:

> a pattern of leader behaviour that draws upon and promotes both positive psychological capacities and a positive ethical climate, to foster greater self-awareness, an internalized moral perspective, balanced processing of information, and relational transparency on the part of leaders working with followers, fostering positive self-development.[60]

Although this definition has a moral (that is, relating to principles of ethical/right conduct) component and includes the need for relational transparency (which implies that it is ok to show our feelings?), thus offering us the potential of an emotion-led leadership, it arguably goes too far the other way in not acknowledging the 'hard-edged', commercial realities of most leadership roles and the need for reasoned, evidence-based decision making.

Even – or perhaps especially – those in the not-for-profit sector must be cognizant of these realities, where every penny has to be made to do the work of two and passionate goals require reasoned implementation.

Before seeking to articulate the warp and weft of an interwoven emotional–rational leadership, however, let's push the pendulum a little further towards a 'stronger' form of authenticity: an authenticity that is directly driven by a felt sense of purpose and which explicitly draws on such feelings of 'rightness' and 'fidelity to purpose'[61] as a well-spring of decision-making ability, direction and guidance. By definition, this requires leaders to draw on positive emotions and to underpin them with positive principles/purpose – which, as already noted, is not unproblematic, but which does hold promise. Perhaps research currently devoted to optimising the recruitment, selection and development of effective leaders (based on rational criteria relating to largely economic organisational outcomes) might instead be devoted to the development of alternative frameworks relating to possession of a strong moral compass, purposeful motivation and the honest expression of feelings. In turn, workplaces would become places where feelings were accepted, respected and engaged with as an integral part of how work was undertaken – a call first made by Meyerson[62] but which has yet to be taken up in any truly integral, holistic sense. This change of culture would be role modelled by leaders, whose identities would be defined by their emotional qualities (empathy, compassion, enthusiasm) rather than by their rational ones (strategic mindset, professionalism).

Taking this idea a little further, what would be the components of an emotion-led, 'affective' model of leadership practice? According to the internet[63] (which inevitably has a list for everything), the 20 most positive emotions – in no particular order – are joy, interest, serenity, hope, gratitude, kindness, surprise (pleasant), cheerfulness, confidence, admiration, enthusiasm, euphoria, satisfaction, pride, contentment, inspiration, amusement, enjoyment, awe and love. Some of these strike me as more useful leadership qualities than others. Kindness, enthusiasm and cheerfulness could make workplaces less stressful and more rewarding places to work; contentment could result in more modest, planet-friendly organisational goals; inspiration and gratitude could make leaders themselves feel more rewarded; and a little bit of amusement never did any of us any harm. We might structure our organisations around working with people we like and respect, and collectively decide on goals to which we can feel committed.

It all sounds very cosy, but I suspect that self-actualising humans might want more. A desire for challenge and achievement, a sense of ambition and a need for progress are also natural, human qualities. Just as a knife is neither inherently good nor inherently bad (it depends on whether it is in the hands of a surgeon or a murderer), so our more 'hard-edged' emotions are only as good (or bad) as the purpose to which we put them. For example, as a society, we are currently ambitious for material growth and consumerism, but substituting this for ambitious targets for reducing, reusing and recycling could satisfy the same emotions at the same time as having very different consequences for both people and the planet. This observation brings me back to the idea of phronesis. We undoubtedly have a vast array of techné (craft skills, technological development, innovativeness, and the like) and we also have underpinnings of episteme (knowledge, rational thought, scientific process, etc.): what we need to do better is to bring them together in a spirit of phronesis (the practical wisdom to make the right choices about how they are applied and to what purpose). Dr Lanning predicted a time when robots would have secrets and dreams: perhaps re-evolved human leaders might bring their secret dreams to the forefront as a force for good in their leadership practice.

In attempting to think through the notion of an alternative leadership paradigm, we don't need to imagine a post-apocalyptic future. We need only consider the contrast between Western ideas of individualism, masculinity, hierarchy and performativity[64] and Confucian notions of collectivist, feudal/family-based ties and loyalties to reflect on how things might be different. Quite telling here is the practice of guanxi – and the West's mistaken belief that it would make Chinese partner organisations receptive to Western team-working initiatives.[65] Guanxi is an important concept in China, both in terms of its practical impact on people's lives and as a mechanism of social control. It holds individuals within a relational network governed by *wu lun*, or the five fundamental relationships: individual to government, father to son, husband to wife, elder to younger siblings and friend to friend. One's position within each of these relationships provides order and stability to the social system and denotes specific roles the individual is required to play in any given situation. Importantly, it is also the basis of cultural collectivism, which is thus viewed as network first, country second and culture third – for those trying to instigate teamwork in China, the absence of organisational collectivism within that list is an important omission.

Based on extensive research with Sino-American joint ventures located on mainland China, Hui and Graen[66] noted how the Chinese relational system of guanxi can render Western leadership relations compromised. Confucianist notions of exclusive, deterministic feudal/family-based ties – with those within this network automatically being granted trust, respect and performance of obligations – sit uneasily with Western leader–follower relations where the choice of a personal network is likely to be based on competence and liking. The six influences of guanxi on Chinese management, listed below, have considerable resonance with the current attempt to develop a more affective or emotion-led model of leadership:

1   Loyalty and commitment are to the guanxi 'in-group' not to the organisation or leader.
2   Job satisfaction and involvement will be moderated by the strength of the guanxi network in the workplace – and whether one is in the right network.

3 Role reinforcement and fulfilment of obligations are more important than fairness and equity.
4 Chinese management values loyalty more than competence.
5 Maintaining guanxi and the obligations it calls forth can be more important than morality.
6 Guanxi produces a tendency to be person-oriented rather than solution-oriented in the face of organisational problems.

Hui and Graen suggest that the success of Sino-American joint ventures will be based on building 'third cultures' that synthesise the important features of each system. To do this, they propose that foreign leaders trying to build partnerships on Chinese soil need to:

a Cultivate long-term, holistic relationships with their Chinese partners.
b Build quality, long-term Leader-Member Exchange relationships with competent individuals within partner organisations.
c Develop functional relationships – that is, relationships aimed at organisational and individual growth – with the joint venture partners.

These principles of integration could also add value more broadly, and give us a clue as to what might be called 'matrix leadership'. Taking the idea of interweaving suggested above, matrix leadership would combine the warp of emotions and the weft of reason/rationality in an integrated web, where neither has priority and each draws strength from the other.

Conclusion – A question of balance?[67]

In practice, it is unlikely that we could sustain perfect parity between these two modes of operating without one or the other taking the lead in guiding our lives. But perhaps we could attain a kind of balance. John Adair's action-centred leadership[68] posited the need for a balance of focus between task, team and individual, at the same time as recognising that specific situations might require a leader to deliberately skew that balance in a specific direction for a limited period of time. In a similar vein, perhaps matrix leadership would in practice consist of a more mutual symbiosis between the emotional and rational aspects of our nature, alongside the recognition that each element would be likely to come to the fore as naturally prompted by the needs of the situation. Each would be recognised as adding to our abilities and as having value in shaping the world, and a form of 'tempered' leadership – where both our emotions and our rationality are made less intense or violent by the influence of something good or benign from the other – would result. Like justice tempered with mercy, we can think of performativity tempered with empathy, competitiveness tempered with loyalty and individual achievement tempered with collective support. Given that this is not, in fact, a radical reconstruction of current understandings, it should be within our grasp to achieve tempered leadership without the need for a wholesale sweeping away of current knowledge. Which leaves us with the question, how can we as academics contribute to a more balanced, tempered construction of 'matrix' leadership in the way we pursue our craft – both as researcher and as teachers? To use Meyerson's[69] phrase, we need to 'honour' emotions at a more deeply cultural and holistic level: in our research methods, in our models and theories, and in our practice. That means moving away from the current deficit model and giving emotions equal footing with their rational counterparts in both our thinking and – importantly – our feeling about leadership. Detective Spooner explains the meaning of a wink to Sonny as being a sign of trust, an essentially human thing: a shift towards balanced, matrix leadership requires a giant leap of faith by the leader, but an equally giant amount of trust in followers to do the rest.

Notes

1 With apologies to Isaac Asimov. This paraphrase is based on the film *I, Robot* (2004). starring Will Smith, directed by Alex Proyas and based on *The Complete Robot* (1983) short stories written by Asimov. The 'touchstones' referred to in this chapter are based on script extracts from the film, as accessed on www.imdb. com on 2 April 2017.
2 A 'bonfire of the vanities' is a burning of objects condemned by authorities as occasions of sin. The phrase usually refers to the Florence bonfire of 7 February 1497, when thousands of objects including art and books were publicly burned.
3 The Ancient Library of Alexandria was one of the largest libraries of the ancient world, and a major center of scholarship from its construction in the third century bc until the Roman conquest of Egypt in 30 bc. Its burning in 48 bc with the loss of many scrolls and books has become a symbol for the loss of cultural knowledge.
4 The Dark Ages is a term used to refer to the demographic, cultural and economic deterioration that supposedly occurred in Western Europe during the Middle Ages and following the decline of the Roman Empire.
5 Ensuring, of course, that we aren't just preserving and embellishing shopping lists and instruction manuals, mistaking them for philosophical treatises in some long forgotten jargon – See Walter M. Miller Jr's 'A Canticle for Leibowitz', first published in 1964.
6 Ekman (1992).
7 Brotheridge and Grandey (2002).
8 Bar-On (1997); Schutte et al. (1998); Mayer, Caruso and Salovey (1999).
9 Brotheridge and Lee (2003).
10 Kashdan et al. (2009).
11 Zigarmi et al. (2011).
12 Hebert et al. (2014).
13 Zelowitz et al. (2016).
14 Sohn and Lee (2012).
15 This idea of a 'handmaiden' as the lesser partner in any knowledge pairing began in the Middle Ages with philosophy as the handmaiden to theology. It later became the handmaiden to science...or the other way around depending on who you listen to.

16 Meyerson (2000).
17 Fineman (2000).
18 Meyerson (2000, p.179).
19 Taylor (1903, 1911).
20 Wheatley (1997).
21 Goleman, Boyatzis and McKee (2001).
22 Iszatt-White (2009, 2012).
23 Berg, Barry and Chandler (2012).
24 Brescoll (2016).
25 McCabe and Knights (2016); Muhr (2011); Taylor and Hood (2011); Thory (2013).
26 Virtual Interactive Kinaesthetic Interface – US Robotics' managing computer
27 The Three Laws of Robotics, quoted as being from the 'Handbook of Robotics, 56th Edition, 2058 a.d.', are:

1 A robot may not injure a human being or, through inaction, allow a human being to come to harm.
2 A robot must obey the orders given to it by human beings except where such orders would conflict with the First Law.
3 A robot must protect its own existence as long as such protection does not conflict with the First or Second Laws.

28 www.mdgfund.org/node/922 – accessed 6 June 2017.
29 www.worldbank.org/en/news/press-release/2016/10/03/nearly-385-million-children-living-extreme-poverty-joint-world-bank-group-unicef-study – accessed 28 June 2017.
30 www.womenandchildrenfirst.org.uk/infant-mortality-newborn-health – accessed 28 June 2017.
31 www.cdc.gov/hiv/basics/statistics.html – accessed 28 June 2017.
32 www.who.int/features/factfiles/malaria/en/ – accessed 28 June 2017.
33 www.unglobalcompact.org/what-is-gc/mission/principles – accessed 6 June 2017.
34 www.theworldcounts.com/stories/Child-Labor-Facts-and-Statistics – accessed 28 June 2017.
35 www.ilo.org/global/topics/forced-labour/lang--en/index.htm – accessed 28 June 2017.
36 Not In My Back Yard.
37 Cherry and Sneirson (1999); Furlow (2009).
38 Iszatt-White (2012); Bolton and Boyd (2003); Hochschild (1983); Ekman (1992).
39 Iszatt-White and Ralph (2016).
40 Gallos (2008).
41 Buckley (2016); van Gelderen, Konijn and Bakker (2017).
42 Gemmill and Oakley (1992).
43 Goldman (2008); Pelletier (2012); Kets de Vries (2014).
44 Gallos (2008).
45 Kofi Annan (14 October 2002).
46 Pless (2007, p.438).
47 Du Toit and Woermann (2012).
48 Hawken (1992).
49 Johnson, Scholes and Whittington (2008, p.3, original italics).
50 Hitt and Ireland (2002).
51 Selznick (1984, p.5).
52 House and Aditya (1997).

53 Hambrick and Masons (1984).
54 Hitt and Ireland (2002).
55 Hitt and Ireland (2002).
56 Hackman et el (1975); Hackman and Oldman (1976).
57 Daniels (2000).
58 Cameron (2008).
59 Avolio and Gardner (2005).
60 Walumbwa et al (2008, p.94).
61 Kempster, Iszatt-White and Brown (2018).
62 Meyerson (2000).
63 http://positivewordsresearch.com/list-of-top-20-positive-feelings-and-emotions/
    – accessed 14 August 2017.
64 Hofstede (1980).
65 Hui and Graen (1997).
66 Hui and Graen (1997).
67 Apologies to Pink Floyd and their classic album of the same title.
68 Adair (1979).
69 Meyerson (2000).

References

Adair, John (1979) *Action Centred Leadership*. Aldershot, UK: Gower Publishing Ltd.

Annan, Kofi (2002) Speech made at the MIT Sloan School of Management, Cambridge, Massachusetts on 14 October 2002. As cited in Global Responsible Leadership Initiative [no specific author stated – report said to be the 'shared thoughts and beliefs of all founding members of the GRLI'] (2005) Globally responsible leadership: A call for engagement. EFMD.

Avolio, B and Gardner, W (2005) Authentic leadership development: Getting to the root of positive forms of leadership. *The Leadership Quarterly*, 16(3), 315–338.

Bar-On, R (1997) *Development of the BarOn EQ-i: A measure of emotional and social intelligence*. Paper presented at the 105th Annual Convention of the American Psychological Association in Chicago.

Berg, E, Barry, J and Chandler, J (2012) Changing leadership and gender in public sector organizations. *British Journal of Management*, 23(3), 402–414.

Bolton, SC and Boyd, C (2003) Trolley dolly or skilled emotion manager? Moving on from Hochschild's Managed Heart. *Work, Employment and Society*, 17(2), 289–308.

Brescoll, VL (2016) Leading with their hearts? How gender stereotypes of emotion lead to biased evaluations of female leaders. *The Leadership Quarterly*, 27(3), 415–428.

Brotheridge, CM and Grandey, AA (2002) Emotional labour and burnout: Comparing two perspectives of 'people work'. *Journal of Vocational Behaviour*, 60, 17–39.

Brotheridge, CM and Lee, RT (2003) Development and validation of the emotional labour scale. *Journal of Occupational and Organizational Psychology*, 76, 365–379.

Buckley, Paul (2016) *Work related stress, anxiety and depression statistics in Great Britain 2016*. Health and Safety Executive (www.hse.gov.uk/statistics/).

Cameron, KS (2008) *Positive Leadership: Strategies for Extraordinary Performance*. San Francisco, CA: Berrett-Koehler Publishers.

Cherry, MA and Sneirson, JF (1999) Beyond profit: Rethinking corporate social responsibility and greenwashing after the BP oil disaster. *Tulane Law Review*, 85(4), 983–1038.

Daniels, AC (2000) *Bringing Out the Best in People: How to Apply the Astonishing Power of Positive Reinforcement*. New York: McGraw-Hill, Inc.

Du Toit, Louise and Woermann, Minka (2012) When economy becomes ecology: Implications for understanding leadership. Reflections on Responsible Leadership: 2nd International Conference in Responsible Leadership. Pretoria. 18–21 November 2012.

Ekman, P (1992) Facial expressions of emotion: New findings, new questions. *Psychological Science*, 3(1), 34–38.

Fineman, Stephen (1993) *Emotion in Organisations*. London: Sage.

Furlow, Nancy (2009) Greenwashing in the new Millennium. *Journal of Applied Business and Economics*, 10(6), 22–25.

Gallos, JV (2008) Learning from the toxic trenches: The winding road to healthier organisations – and to healthy everyday leaders. *Journal of Management Inquiry*, 17(4), 354–367.

Gemmill, G and Oakley, J (1992) Leadership: An alienating social myth? *Human Relations*, 45(2), 113–130.

Goldman, A (2008) Company on the couch: Unveiling toxic behaviour in dysfunctional organizations. *Journal of Management Inquiry*, 17(3), 226–238.

Goleman, D, Boyatzis, R and McKee, A (2001) Primal leadership – The hidden driver of great performance. *Harvard Business Review*, 79(11), 42–51.

Hackman, JR and Oldham, GR (1976) Motivation through the design of work: Test of a theory. *Organizational Behaviour and Human Performance*, 16, 250–279.

Hackman, JR, Oldham, GR, Janson, R and Purdy, K (1975) A new strategy for job enrichment. *California Management Review*, 17(4), 57–71.

Hambrick, DC and Mason, PA (1984) Upper echelons: The organisation as a reflection of its top management. *Academy of Management Review*, 9(2), 193–206.

Hebert, EA, Dugas, MJ, Tulloch, TG and Holowka, DW (2014) Positive beliefs about worry: A psychometric evaluation of the Why Worry-II. *Personality and Individual Differences*, 56, 3–8.

Hitt, MA and Ireland, RD (2002) The essence of strategic leadership: Managing human and social capital. *The Journal of Leadership and Organizational Studies*, 9(1), 3–14.

Hochschild, A (1983) *The Managed Heart: Commercialization of Human Feeling*. Berkeley, CA: University of California Press.

Hofstede, G (1980) *Culture's Consequences: International Differences in Work-Related Values* (abridged edition). Newbury Park, CA: Sage.

House, RJ and Aditya, R (1997) The social scientific study of leadership: Quo vadis? *Journal of Management*, 23, 409–474.

Hui, Chun and Graen, George (1997) Gaunxi and professional leadership in contemporary Sino-American joint ventures in mainland China. *The Leadership Quarterly*, 8(4), 451–465.

Iszatt-White, M (2012) *Leadership as Emotional Labour: Management and the 'Managed Heart'*. London: Routledge.

Iszatt-White, M (2009) Leadership as emotional labour: The effortful accomplishment of valuing practices. *Leadership*, 5(4), 447–467.

Iszatt-White, M and Ralph, N (2016) Who contains the container? Creating a holding environment for practicing leaders. *British Academy of Management Conference*. Newcastle, 6–8 September 2016.

Johnson, G, Scholes, K and Whittington, R (2008) *Fundamentals of Strategy*. Upper Saddle River, NY: FT Prentice Hall.

Kashdan, TB, Gallagher, MW, Silvia, PJ, Winterstein, BP, Breen, WE, Terhar, D, et al. (2009) The Curiosity and Exploration Inventory-II: Development, factor structure, and initial psychometrics. *Journal of Research in Personality*, 43, 987–998.

Kempster, S, Iszatt-White, M and Brown, M (2018) Authenticity in leadership: Reframing relational transparency through the lens of emotional labour. *Leadership*, first published online 3 April 2018.

Kets de Vries, MFR (2014) Coaching the toxic leader. *Harvard Business Review*, 92(4), 100–109.

Mayer, JD, Caruso, DR and Salovey, P (1999) Emotional intelligence meets traditional standards for an intelligence. *Intelligence*, 27(4), 267–298.

McCabe, D and Knights, D (2016) Learning to listen? Exploring discourses and images of masculine leadership through corporate videos. *Management Learning*, 47(2), 179–198.

Meyerson, Debra E (2000) If emotions were honoured: A cultural analysis. In Stephen Fineman (editor) (1993) *Emotion in Organisations*. London: Sage, pp.167–183.

Muhr, SL (2011) Caught in the gendered machine: On the masculine and feminine in Cyborg leadership. *Gender, Work and Organization*, 18(3), 337–357.

Pelletier KL (2012) Perceptions of and reactions to leader toxicity: Do leader-follower relationships and identification with victim matter? *The Leadership Quarterly*, 23(3), 412–424.

Pless, NM (2007) Understanding responsible leadership: Role identity and motivational drivers. *Journal of Business Ethics*, 74(4), 437–456.

Schutte, NS, Malouff, JM, Hall, LE, Haggerty, DJ, Cooper, JT, Golden, CJ and Dornheim, L (1998) Development and validation of a measure of emotional intelligence. *Personality and Individual Differences*, 25, 167–177.

Selznick, P (1984) *Leadership in administration: A sociological interpretation*. Berkeley, CA: University of California Press (originally published in 1957).

Sohn, HK and Lee, TJ (2012) Relationship between HEXACO personality factors and emotional labour of service providers in the tourism industry. *Tourism Management*, 33(1), 116–125.

Taylor, FW (1903) *Shop management*. New York, Harper & Brothers.

Taylor, FW (1911) *The principles of Scientific Management*. New York, Harper & Row.

Taylor, SN and Hood, JN (2011) It may not be what you think: Gender differences in predicting emotional and social competence. *Human Relations*, 64(5), 627–652.

Thory, K (2013) A gendered analysis of emotional intelligence in the workplace: Issues and concerns for human resource development. *Human Resource Development Review*, 12(2), 221–244.

Van Gelderen, BR, Konijn, EA and Bakker, AB (2017) Emotional labour among police officers: A diary study relating strain, emotional labour, and service performance. *International Journal of Human Resource Management*, 28(6), 852–879.

Walumbwa, FO, Avolio, BJ, Gardner, WL, Wernsing, TS and Peterson, SJ (2008) Authentic leadership: Development and validation of a theory-based measure, *Journal of Management*, 34(1), 89–126.

Wheatley, Margaret (1997) Goodbye, command and control. *Leader to Leader*, 1997(5), 21–28.

Zelowitz, RL and Cole, DA (2016) Measures of emotion reactivity and emotion regulation: Convergent and discriminant validity. *Personality and Individual Differences*, 102, 123–132.

Zigarmi, D, Nimon, K, Houson, D, Witt, D and Diehl, J (2011) A preliminary field test of an employee work passion model. *Human Resource Development Quarterly*, 22(2), 195–221.

5 After Leaders
A World of Leading and Leadership ... With No Leaders

Steve Kempster and Ken Parry

We have for such a long time tied ourselves up in knots with the word *leader*. We argue in this chapter[1] that the field of leadership would make its greatest contribution thus far by jettisoning the word *leader* and giving prominence to leading and leadership. The preoccupation with, on the one hand, seeking the entitative traits, style, authenticity, and charisma of *leaders*, and, on the other hand, endlessly problematizing the existence of such heroic mythical creatures, has consumed so much resource for such little gain. This view is not new. Drath and colleagues[2] expressed this well in their pitch for repositioning leadership toward outcomes and process. Yet despite the eloquence and authority of their reasoned argument, they could still not let go of *leader*. In a parallel way, there is a growing group of researchers seeking to push forward with the notion of leadership-as-practice[3]—where *leader* is problematic, and notions of agency are rightfully given much greater attention.

This chapter seeks to connect the arguments of Drath et al. and emerging work on leadership-as-practice through the analogous use of an operations management lexicon—the notion of context, inputs, process, and outputs: *leadership effect* as the output—are people more or less motivated, inspired, committed, confident, aligned, and directed; *practices of leading* (that generate the leadership effect) as the process—such as sense framing, directing, caring, and visioning; and three forms of inputs (using Archer's[4] notion of agents and structures)—*primary agents* as people in a condition prior to being influenced, *corporate agents* in positions of influence, and an array of *structural antecedent influences*. Aspects such as servant leadership, distributed leadership, authentic leadership, and transformational leadership become realigned and are viewed very differently through the lens of inputs, process, and outputs—certainly, very differently when the *leader* aspect no longer exists. The sacred and romantic notion of *leaders* has been long forgotten. Critical leadership scholars' work has borne fruit, and their work has been done. The world has moved on. The agenda is to perhaps understand the purposes and responsibilities of the leadership effect and a greater alignment of inputs and processes to achieve necessary action to the wicked problems that face humanity.

In this way, the orientation of the chapter seeks to offer up an unapologetic vision of a world that has a much more deliberate appreciation of "leading" and "leadership." With these two words much more clearly understood and enacted in everyday activity, we suggest that the much-overlooked sense of purpose—including societal purpose—will become salient and palpable to such everyday acts of leading and emergent leadership. This is because those leading are most conscious of the purposes for which they are leading, and they are not caught up in entity orientations associated with the *leader*. The distracting and anachronistic ontological fixation to a *leader* concept as a categorical mistake[5] has led discourses on leading and leadership into a wasteful cul-de-sac. Wasteful in the sense of expenditure on leadership development, wasteful regarding academic attention, and so wasteful in terms of contributing to society. We position the chapter as a reflexive dialogue between ourselves, examining our hopes for the demise of the *leader* concept and debating the argument for a different lexicon for leadership and leading.

We draw on a research approach Steve has used elsewhere[6] described as *testimonio*,[7] where letters are exchanged that allow a particular phenomenon to be examined in a critically reflective manner. In this way, we offer up our letters between ourselves as the basis of the chapter. As a consequence, the chapter is structured by Ken first examining the futile search for the *leader*. Steve responds to this provocative opening letter by offering up an alternative way of conceiving leadership—he draws on the language of operation management and the notion of inputs, process, and outputs. Ken's response is to imagine how this would become operationalized (excuse the pun), with emphasis on leading through speeches. Steve concludes the chapter by exploring how leadership without the *leader* might address the enormous challenges our societies face.

Incidentally, we shall persist with italicizing *leader* in order to make this word salient and to irritate so people similarly take to hating the word!

Letter #1: Ken on Futility and Fixation of the Leader

Dear Steve,

You asked me a few days ago, can we imagine a world without people using the word *leader*? I have chosen to take up that question, challenge indeed, and pen some thoughts to you. I do this as a researcher and writer of leadership, and it is in this context my letter is situated.

Perhaps if we get rid of the word *leader*, indeed if we get rid of the whole concept of *leader*, then leading and leadership immediately fill the gap. For researchers, if we do not have to write about the *leader*, then we must write about what is causing and doing the leading and the leadership effect that follows. It might be about the person engaged in leadership in some way. But there's more, it is not just the person doing these things—indeed it might not even involve a person; for example, Microsoft Word and the red that underscores spelling errors leads to changes! We will have to examine the structures that allow for the wielding of power in order to influence other people. We will have to look for the ways in which power is generated and allocated within the organization or society. Then, we look at leadership. Suddenly, it all becomes fun and purposeful for researchers.

I have had a bee in my bonnet for some time about the overuse of the word *leader*. In fact, if I had my way, I would have it removed from our lexicon. If I did not say this in the second edition of our book,[8] I will be making this point in the third edition. I think that too many people use the word *leader* as a cop out when they cannot be bothered explaining the position of the person whom they are discussing. I see it all the time in journal submissions. I see it everywhere.

I have a case in point.

I am on the editorial board of *The Leadership Quarterly* journal; although that might be in doubt after this book comes out. I have reminded authors and editorial colleagues many, many times that this is a leadership journal, and not a *leader* journal. Under the cloak of researching leadership, and with an article title that invariably says "leadership" the discourse falls almost immediately into that of *leader* and *leaders*. Usually, the author is researching the leadership of a manager or some other role in an organization. However, without further ado, these managers get called *leaders*. No-one even bothers to explain the difference between *leader* and leadership, or who this rogue *leader* is who always seems to appear immediately, often in the abstract no less. This blunder comes from "big" names who at least should be open to questioning the ontological premise that is assumed. It is slovenly at best and unprofessional at worst.

This matter is a bit like the American Presidential election in 2016, when people should have known better. They just go with the crowd, because "everyone else is doing it," and because "I don't want to get a bad name" by making it difficult for everyone else. So, they just go along with the sham. Eventually, as we now know, people don't even realize that there is a problem let alone a solution to the problem. There's a sense of what Alvesson and Spicer describe so beautifully as the "Stupidity Paradox." People accept the dubious or the absurd, for short-term result, and then continue doing it without questioning or challenging why. They conform thoughtlessly. Thoughtless conformity is stupid. People who raise the alarm become demonized and become the victims of what Giacalone and Promislo[9] call the stigmatization of goodness. The population becomes socialized into notions that honesty actually means undermining the organization's interests, or that courage is actually disloyalty, or that "social responsibility" is actually losing interest in the welfare of the institute. I have become demonized by raising the alarm about the indiscriminate use of *leader*. Subtle threats have been made about being removed from the editorial board. Perhaps my windows will get smashed. Perhaps I will be put on an agrarian steam train and taken somewhere. I should be so lucky.

But what do we really mean when we write or talk about *leader*? Invariably people are referring to the CEO, or the person in charge, or the manager, or the senior Parliamentary member of the political party, or whatever. The problem is that I don't know who the devil they are referring to is because they just take the easy option and call them *leader*. If one is to refer to the manager and then talk about the leadership challenges that they face (or the management challenges of course), then we would also know what they are on about. As it is at the moment, the situation is more confused rather than less so by calling people *leader*. Instead of clarifying the knowledge and understanding of the reader, authors are making the whole argument more confusing. Sense-making is not being achieved. Ironically, within a body of knowledge that is all about sense-making,[10] those very authors are sense-destroying.

Also, there is a sexiness or populism about the use of the term *leader*. Partly it is a cop out and partly it is a form of bullying, wherein power is vested with the *leader*. Others have to play the weaker role of follower. This asymmetry of power flies directly in the face of leadership, let alone the popular notion of distributed leadership that, apparently, we all should be trying to achieve. If anyone is going to be in charge and have the power, then that person should be the manager who has control as one of their responsibilities. Generating leadership among the workforce is another of his/her responsibilities. Many people eschew the notion of having multiple *leaders*. They usually say that we have only one *leader*. Therein lies the problem. Leadership is partly about generating and developing leadership (not *leaders* of course) right through the organization. As a respected colleague said, management is the toughest gig of them all, and we enfeeble "the manager" by frivolously calling them *leader*.

Calling someone *leader* seems so permanent. Along with its associated quasi-bullying acquisition of power, it suggests that no-one can become leader, and that leadership is restricted to one person. Now, that person usually has the better job title, salary, expense account, and budget. But yet, still, more is expected and given—the title of "leader" and a sense of exclusivity and hegemony around such a title.

For years Steve, you and I have asked people of all ages, "What does a *leader* do?"

The answer always is, "Leadership."

I looked up quite a few dictionary definitions of *leader* and they all say "person who leads."

... Hello ...

Bing!!

Yes, it is all about leading and leadership! After we all get that worked out with the notion of *leader*, THEN we need to look at the people who do the leading and leadership. There probably will be many of them.

For a long time, I wondered why so many of my American colleagues gravitated toward the term *leader* so readily. Now it is becoming clearer to me. First, the term fits well with the culture of the United States. The people like the whole notion of being a *leader*. That notion proliferated in their discourse: in the media, movies, business discourse, and academic discourse. The hegemony and domination of American discourse, based on the size of the market there, has ensured that this notion has infiltrated discourse in other English-speaking countries. There is a marketing law called *Say's Law*. It says that supply creates its own demand. The expansion in the use of *leader* is a great example. Now, because of the massive supply of overuse of the term *leader* from the United States, we all use the term in our academic literature, as well as business and media discourse. We have taken the easy way out and just gone along with the majority. We even have our own non-American journals on leadership, all of which are now writhing in the quagmire of the *leader*–leadership dilemma. I remember a time, not that long ago, when Britain did not have Professors of Leadership or schools or degrees in leadership. Now they are many in number, and the use of the word *leader*, with its associated confusion, will be endemic within all of this.

I will elaborate on the point I made earlier. *Leader* is essentially an English-speaking term; and only recently has it infiltrated the whole English-speaking world. The French language does not have a word for *leader*. The closest they have is *chef* (closest to chief in English). The German word for *leader* is very out of favor, but also means "guide." The Spanish word is *lider*, so they seem to have adopted the English word. Possibly, there is no Spanish word. The Chinese language has no word for *leader*, but has words meaning controlling and winning. They have the word *lingdao*, which is approximately that of "boss" in English. I suggest that we in the English-speaking world have created and propagated this word *leader*, and now we have stuffed it up. It is time to go back to our roots, or at least to something that we know—leadership. It is also time to breathe some more life back into "management" and "manager."

As I was writing this letter, I received an email advising that the Australian Institute of Management (AIM) would now be called the Institute of Managers and Leaders (IML). I am a Fellow of AIM; I know a fair bit about management. But now I am confused and concerned. I am not much of a manager and quite probably a lousy *leader*. Hell, I don't even know if I am a *leader* or not. I know that I demonstrate good leadership from time to time. People have kindly told me. But am I a *leader*? It seems such a "go/no go" gauge. You are either in or you are out. If you are out, you get chipped up and recycled. Perhaps I am just a 50% *leader*, probably much less. Perhaps I am a "narrow pass" *leader*. I have read a lot about this over the years. The only answer to "am I a *leader*?" that I can come up with is "maybe, maybe not; sometimes." If I self-rated on Bass and Avolio's excellent and rigorous leadership frequency scale, I would probably be a "Once in a while" *leader*, which rates 1 on a scale of 0–4. Hell, I don't even want to be a *leader*. I don't want all that weight on my shoulders. I might soon be without a professional body. One thing is for sure. The proliferation of the use of the term *leader* is not helping anyone.

So, what do we do?

The change must come from the academic, scholarly community. The people of the wider population don't really care about the word or concept of *leader* but do care about the effects and consequences. As such, they need to take the lead with the academic community to also get rid of the mythical notion of *leader*. If the wider community stops hearing about *leader* from the academic community in lecturers, seminars, executive education, the media, and popular press writing, then the use of the term will atrophy and wither. But, the change must come from the academic community. I wonder if we are up to it?

Your 1 out of 4 *leader* friend,

Ken

Letter #2: Steve on the New Lexicon of Leadership

Dear Ken,

A provocative view as ever my friend. I found myself stirred by your 1 out of 4 leadership. Not as *leader* of course; but by your sense-giving that seeks to shape my sense-making. I'm picking over my choice of words carefully here so I don't reap your wrath! You lay out the need for scholarly attention to the words we use so as not to sow further obfuscation on the subject of leadership, leading, and the *leader*. The salience you bring to the hegemony of the *leader* concept and how this distorts relationships and limits opportunities for broader, more inclusive and democratic forms of leading is a persuasive argument.

"Let's start at the very beginning (that's a very good place to start)"[11] and consider a possible, and for me plausible, construct of leadership. Reflecting on a recent conversation I had with Mary Uhl-Bien, at the International Leadership Conference in Brussels this year, we sought to create a construct that was leadership in order to define followership. The conversation started with my misgivings around followership. We settled on the notion that the leadership construct is at its heart quite simple. It was the skill of leading. It drew on the etymology of the suffix "ship"—of Germanic origin meaning quality, knowledge, skill, or craft—and the apocryphal story of a Viking standing at the front of a longboat guiding direction through the openings of the ice leads—the skill of leading! So, in this way, leadership is centrally about leading—this is the core that I shall develop a different lexicon around. Mary asserted the corollary that followership must be the skill of following, and therefore both leading and following are significant in forming the construct that is leadership.

My disquiet with followership is similar to that of *leader*. I am minded of the research I have undertaken with Doris and Gareth[12] in search of followers. Using a Lacanian lens, we have explored the *leader* image as one of fantasy: a desire to become a *leader* that is a continual process of disillusion. Primarily, this is centered on the hegemonic leadership discourse within organizations. People desiring to be *leaders* assume the existence of followers. We argue that a form of "phantasmic attachment"[13] is present in pursuance of "imagined leader images [where] the subject can only become the *leader* when he/she is tied into an imagined relationship centered on the recognition of him/herself as the *leader* by a follower."[14] Returning to the notion of hegemonic organizational leadership discourse, this reinforces the desire of a *leader* image to control the attached follower.[15] But this phantasmic attachment is rooted in "the hegemony of the *leader*-follower relation and its promise to deliver what we seek, that the subject continues to desire becoming a *leader* and having control over the fantasised follower."[16] In essence, we postulated that notions of a *leader* identity, and associated hegemonic discourse with such an identity, is a fantasy of continual desire for followers to enable its construction—yet continually failing to become manifest. The phantasmic attachment connects with what Simon Kelly describes as the negative ontology of *leader*.[17] *Leader* does not exist as a fixed entity but is rather an ideal concept that conjures up fantasies of possibilities. Simon draws on Barthes'[18] work on mythology and the notion of second-order form of language to suggest this ideal mythical concept is a floating signifier—relying on proxies to inform the fantasy. So, by negative ontology, Simon persuasively asserts *leader*[ship] is ideological rather than ontological.[19] There is an issue here for us Ken. If we buy Simon's argument to move away from ontology to ideology, then this has major implications for us as researchers. Do we become "an ideologue, politician, activist, cultist or soothsayer[?]"[20] With any argument we develop here, let's be cautious on this. Eric Guthey[21] has persuasively offered a reframing of the leadership research and development industry as one of fashions.

Incidentally, the second stage of the "search for followers" research has focused on the lived experiences of managers as "followers." We asked managers to create a timeline and then examined the leadership relationships. Next, we asked them to define for themselves the difference between following and being a follower. Finally, we asked them to identify leadership relationships in which they were followers and those in which they were following. What have we found so far? Very few follower relationships were identified. The explanations offered included questionable attribution to those who led in terms of viewing them as a *leader*. The empirical data shows that very few people see themselves as followers and reject the attribution; they seek to resist the hegemonic asymmetric relational expectation. Yet ironically many managers lamented the unfortunate experiences of the lack of experiencing good *leaders* in their timelines. I can imagine Simon (Kelly) with a broad smile over his face and a wise look of contentment!

So where does this take us?

The search for followers research above suggests a reframing. We should seek to work on concepts that are not empty or floating signifiers—work with a "first order sign system of a manager (signifier), managing (signified) = doing things right (sign)."[22] To guide this reframing, it's a helpful starting point to draw on Drath et al. who speak of processes that create the outcomes as leadership practices shaped by *leaders*.[23] It is disappointing that despite the great promise they offer in terms of a new ontology of leadership focused on leading and leadership outcomes, they are still caught up with the ideological myth of the *leader* as the input. In part, it could be the cultural issue you highlighted of some our American colleagues where leadership must have *leaders* (and followers).

In our brave new world, the reframing replaces the fantasy signifier of *leaders* with an alternative lexicon of leadership. A lexicon draws from discourses in operations management and systems thinking. As you know I'm most taken with soft systems thinking[24] and its emphasis on systems of purposeful human activity. If leadership is seen as purposeful human activity then the reframing of leadership as a transformation might reflect the following effect on people: demotivated to becoming motivated; lacking curiosity to becoming curious; unclear direction to having a clear direction; low commitment to having high commitment; and low self-efficacy to having high self-efficacy. So the language of inputs, process, and outputs (as first-order language) become the central features of a new lexicon of leadership. With my endless desire for frameworks, I offer up this suggestion (Figure 5.1).

Let me explain what I'm exploring here. Leadership effect is the outcome that emerges within a specific context. I shall come back to the context shortly. The outcome labelled as leadership effect is the outcome of leading impacting on people within a context. In essence, the leadership effect places emphasis on the people being influenced—those impacted by the leading.

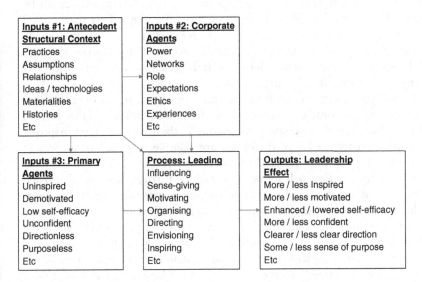

Figure 5.1 Systems example of the operations lexicon—inputs, process, and outputs.

Drath et al. assumed such an outcome, and following a review of extant literature, suggested the leadership outcome to be direction, alignment, and commitment. I think this is helpful but perhaps rather restrictive. There are many aspects that could be considered part of the leadership outcome (or leadership effect), and I have illustrated some of these. Let me be clear though, leadership effect could be a consequence of more than people—such as materiality (your earlier Microsoft Word example). I am just giving emphasis on people—noting that soft systems thinking focuses on purposeful human activity.

What do you think?

Leading as a process, and as a verb, is centrally about an activity. For example, I have put your notion of sense-making here. Actually, I have offered this as sense-giving to give emphasis to framing how people may understand what is occurring and why, and how action could be enacted. The leading is enabled (or disabled) by corporate agents[25] who have or desire to have some influence. In Figure 5.1, I offer some dimensions that might reflect such people, such as experience, power, networks, ethics, or roles. For example, if someone seeking to lead is perceived as lacking integrity, it might seem plausible that this person would be less able to undertake the process of leading effectively—that is, enabling the transformation of inputs (e.g., demotivated people) to outputs (motivated people). But such influences need to be considered as a bundle of elements (or practices)—perhaps most notably power drawn from positional authority, or expertise. Ken, you have often spoken about the prominence of organizational psychopaths and how often they seek out roles to influence sense-making.[26] Their ability to cloak their unethical conduct is clearly a skill as they yield their institutional power. However, corporate agents could be people with no positional authority. Such people might be experts, well connected, passionate, and determined. These corporate agents may reach out through technology and create greater power and influence through social movements. In essence, let's not fall back into assuming only the managers are those that lead.

The leadership context could be a team, department, an organization, even a nation. All contexts have of course antecedent influences that inform and frame leadership outcomes. For example, the effect of being inspired, or having a clearer sense of direction, are relative to past experiences in the relationship. Additionally, alternative experiences of how others have undertaken the leading will shape expectations through a sense of learned organizational practices. I have described the context in slightly indigestible language of antecedent structural context. This is intended to capture the structural influence that impacts on the corporate agents, as well as the primary agents, as well as the process of leading. Through our many conversations (often complemented with some delightful German beers), we have returned countlessly to the absurdity of leadership research that does not embrace context.

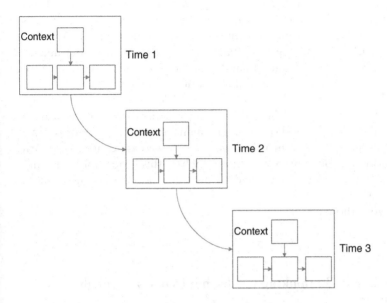

Figure 5.2 Systemic and emergent change through time.

The leadership effect in the outcomes has an impact on all three inputs in terms of shaping emergence and becoming. I have attempted to capture this in Figure 5.2 as temporal dynamic.

The notion of inputs, process, and outputs embedded in the leadership context generates a leadership system, a system that is characterized by the potential for a fluidity of participants, rather than the singularity of the *leader* and associated hegemony. In this way, the opportunities for shared leadership or distributed leadership to become manifest seem most abundant. If someone with expertise (person of influence at that moment) steps into the process of influencing the sense-making of others, and as such affects people's motivations, feelings of success, and commitment, then leadership has become manifest. If we have no *leaders* then there is a very real possibility of liberating and democratizing a greater distribution of power and influence. Joe Raelin[27] has recently advocated this sort of dynamic. For sure he has removed emphasis on the *leader* from his lexicon and gives voice to agency and how this can become leadership as fluid collaboration. What he does not do is provide clarity of a lexicon to explain leading and leadership connected with such agency.

I am suggesting a lexicon that draws from first-order signifiers—a language that is less floating and ideological, a language that is more grounded in a first order ontology. Through orientating the lexicon of inputs, people of influence, process as leading, and leadership outputs, embedded in leadership contexts, we can view leading as a process. I'm shamefully selling this to you Ken, aligned to your overt ontological commitment to leadership as a process.[28] Less keen is your resonance for leadership-as-practice (L-A-P).[29]

But I do think L-A-P resonates so strongly with this lexicon as it reflects the same ontological movement away from the *leader*, and places emphasis on relational and situated practices of leadership relationships. L-A-P provides a sense of individual agency, that may stimulate a fluid inter-agency dynamic to enable collective action and leadership outcomes as practices of communities engaging in technical and relational aspects of work.[30] Did I send you the paper I did with Sarah Gregory?[31] We broadly (or is it loosely) used the approach outlined here examining practices of an organization with particular attention to how a middle manager (not a *leader* of course) addressed an acute crisis. I mention this (not to increase citations—perish the thought) but to open up possibilities of where this lexicon of leadership might lead. In the same vein, I wonder how leadership development might fit with this approach?

I await your thoughts.

Best,

Steve

Letter #3: Ken on Rethinking Leadership Debates Through This Lexicon

Dear Steve,

I really do like your language of inputs, process, and outputs. It is not a new concept generally, but it does now add a sense of salience to all of us who are scholars of leadership. More importantly, it gives coherence to the arguments that you and I are making with this exchange. Instead of a *leader*, we have people and many other elements. This is excellent. After all, leadership is mostly about people influencing other people. In my days, in manufacturing, it was not *leaders* who roll-formed steel coil. There were people (of course), but also there were raw materials, power, finance, packaging, work-shop orders ... and so on ... and of course a whole team of engineers to keep things running. There were those leading and those following all over the place. I was just one of them, and like just about everyone else, taking both roles, occasionally at the same time.

Therefore, it sounds to me like you have replaced the floating or "fantasy" signifier of *leader* with something else. You have replaced it with the much firmer foundation of the clear signifier of people who are leading in order to generate leadership. I think that our colleagues around the world will like to see that. You have now opened up all five elements—inputs, agency, process, outputs, and context. We now have the opportunity as leadership scholars to work with all five. In particular, you have opened up the problematic element by freeing us from the constraints of the floating signifier of *leader*.

I have helped thousands of people over the years to draft leadership speeches. As the input for their speech, they are never a *leader*. No, they are a manager, teacher, parent, Presidential candidate, committee Chair, or whatever. They must be able to explain to their audience: the context of the speech, the role that they are playing, and the general outcome that they want to achieve. The speech-maker must know this, just as the audience must also know this. THEN, they engage in the process of putting the words together. This communication process must influence the audience and help with the sense-making of the audience. Finally, this all results in the output of an inspired audience who have a sense of purpose about where they are heading and why they should follow the message, and perhaps the person making the speech. To identify them as *leader* right from the start would be a mistake. It is a romantic, mythological concept (a floating signifier) that is just plain wrong. The mistake is that they seem to assume they have already achieved the leadership by being the person giving the speech. BUT, they have not achieved their leadership until after they have actually undertaken the leading. They are just one person in a moment among a multiple of people in multiple moments who may connect to achieve something. As a person, they cannot claim leadership at all.

Thank you for opening up the door of insight to me.

Ken

Letter #4: Steve on Using This New Lexicon to Address the Societal Challenges—Putting Leadership as Purpose to Work

Gooday Ken,

Great point on the speeches. It captures the essence so clearly, thanks. The question set for us in channeling our letters is "after leadership?" We of course have reframed the question to "after *leader?*" When we speak of getting our acts together it is toward advancing understanding of leading and developing the practice of leading that should become prominent. The work of Scott et al.[32] is most relevant to this argument. Scott et al. explore the notion of deliberate practice and compare unfavorably leadership with other fields in terms of developing excellence of practice. There is little agreement in the leadership field with regard to terms of what excellence of leading might look like; no acceptance of experts for which others can compare themselves or expert coaches. There is similarly no sense of a practice regime that creates excellence of leading and no practice fields for improvement. Perhaps this is more to do with the lack of attention to the practices of leading, but also a lack of attention to the orientation of leading—that is, less about the person's attributes and more about the foci of the leading and how to frame sense-making with regard to gaining leadership outputs of, for example, direction, alignment, and commitment to the purpose of work. In this regard, the work you have done Ken on speeches is most central.

You point to the need for leadership research to be built on firm foundations. Leadership studies has endeavored to build castles out from foundations based on "running sand." (In my surveying days, I recall there was nothing worse than running sand—it would turn hardened builders into quivering wrecks!) The expectations of those spending billions on leadership studies and leadership development per annum[33] have sought a dividend—a dividend to enrich our institutions, our communities, our societies, and by necessity the planet. Leadership scholars have fallen short time after time in delivering this dividend—perhaps inevitably so when building on bad foundations. However, it is not acceptable that we collectively persist in such wasteful endeavor with such immense talent that exists in the leadership industry.

Arguably leadership is society's most significant mechanism for catalyzing social action to draw on the power and thus influence that is connected to those who are in positions of authority, as well as the power and influence of collectives drawn together to address particular social issues. The time is prescient for leadership studies to get its act together. The challenges humanity face demand this of us. We need to put leading and leadership to work. We need to move from endlessly examining/critiquing the mythical *leader*—traits, styles, authenticity, transformational, charismatic—and address the question "leadership for what?"—a purpose and responsibility orientation.[34] I would offer that the lexicon of leading and leadership connected to notions of inputs, agency, process, and outputs orientates leadership toward the leadership for what question.

Ken, let me give an example. With Brad and Merv,[35] we argued that leadership had lost its purpose. Your point in the first letter gives voice to the issue—too much attention to those leading and too little attention to what they are seeking to lead and why. Using the lexicon of inputs, agency, process, and outputs, a focus on leadership of purpose would offer: inputs as people searching for purpose; people with influence seeking to shape sense-making toward purposeful outcomes; process as leading sense-making around purposes—understanding what these are and why; and outcome as a clear sense of purpose aligned to personal interest—captured in Aristotle's notion of "telos."

This is easy to say, but so much harder to enact. Our research showed there was little appetite of managers to engage in this space for three prominent reasons: first, because there was limited expectations and experiences of those "following" for managers to frame everyday work as meaningful in terms of societal purpose; second, there was limited skill to engage in effective framing of sense-making related to societal purpose; and third our research identified the difficulty for the managers to anchor everyday work to societal purposes—a limited attention to societal purpose along with an inability to translate these to everyday concerns associated with work.

And here's the thing.

Arguably there have never been so many systemically connected challenges that face humanity that have been generated by humanity!

Some emerging and disturbing data: expectations of just a 2°C temperature rise are now most conservative—we should prepare for 4°C.[36] Ocean acidification is as bad as it has been for 300 million years. Three of the earth's boundary conditions for life have been breached and we are close to breaching many of the remaining six.[37] The current planetary human migration that presently stands at 66 million (the population of the United Kingdom) will seem like a "tame" problem in 80 years' time when estimates point to 1 billion with the populations of the United States, most of Africa, the Middle East, India, and China on the move. These of course are but a few of the challenges that face humanity. The United Nations has made a good fist of interpreting these into the 17 Sustainable Development Goals (SDGs).[38] The enormous challenge for leadership is how to translate these challenges or SDGs into action, action that is part of everyday activity.

So, the case for the leadership effect to connect with these grand challenges seems most relevant and timely. The difficulties lie in connecting societal purpose with value-generating everyday organizational activity. There is a concomitant need to connect organizations—businesses, public, and third sector—to work together with governments and NGOs. This is an enormous challenge, yet it is potentially a moment of truth for the leadership studies and development industry. It's the equivalent of our "Cern" challenge. (The Cern project, in search of the fundamental elements that constitute life, incorporates approximately three quarters of the planet's particle physicists.) Can the leadership studies industry come together and achieve real breakthroughs? If we can let go of the *leader* fixation and focus on the leadership effects rooted in purpose, we stand a much better chance. Let's hope there are no more conferences and papers that waste our time critiquing the *leader* in leadership or generating the next theory of *leader* in leadership. Humanity needs effective leading, otherwise we need not worry about after *leader* or after leadership ...

Steve

Conclusion

The purpose of this chapter was to explore "after *leader*." In this respect, we have sought to provoke attention to the distraction of the word *leader* in leadership. We are not saying that leadership is a distraction. We need leadership more than ever. We need to understand how it can be purposeful to support the needs of humanity whilst at the same time addressing the needs of businesses, communities, and societies. The hopeful movement away from the romanticized assumptions associated with *leaders* may liberate the opportunity for both those in positions of influence and the many more in positions to act to collaborate together. The grand challenges that are the task of leadership to address are of course wicked problems. As Grint[39] has astutely asserted, these can only be addressed through collaborative effort. Giving attention to advancing collaborative leading focused on purposes and responsibilities will create a very different research agenda for leadership studies, and similarly a different agenda for leadership development. A world after *leader* needs to be different by necessity. Leadership scholars simply must make a real impact, and not through increased citations between ourselves.

Notes

1 The argument in the chapter builds on Drath, McCauley, Palus, Van Velsor, O'Connor and McGuir, 2008.
2 Drath, McCauley, Palus, Van Velsor, O'Connor and McGuir, 2008.
3 See, for example, Carroll, Levy and Richmond, 2008; Kempster and Gregory, 2015; Raelin, 2016.
4 Archer, 1995. An exploration of structures and agency, and how these continually interact.
5 Kelly, 2008. A thesis on the negative ontology of leadership rooted in the leader. Beautifully written, most persuasive.
6 Kempster and Bainbridge, 2017. Examination of leadership development that draws on Wordsworth's "Prelude" for managers to examine lived experience, vocation and purpose.
7 Beverley, 2000.
8 Jackson and Parry, 2011. Written to engage students of leadership—probably the best leadership text and one of Ken's many contributions to the field of leadership.
9 Giacalone and Promislo, 2013.
10 Weick, 1995; Pye, 2005. Pye situates leadership as a process of sense-making.
11 Sound of Music, Rogers, 1965.
12 Schedlitzki, Kempster and Edwards, 2016. A theoretical argument that draws on the work of Lacan which problematizes the notion of followers.
13 Jones and Spicer, 2005: 235.
14 Schedlidzki et al., 2016: 12.
15 Mueller, 2012: 280.
16 Schedlidzki et al., 2016: 12.
17 Kelly, 2014.
18 Barthes, 1993.
19 Kelly, 2014: 907.
20 Kelly, 2014: 912.
21 Guthey, 2013. Hard-hitting problematizing of the leadership industry—most plausible argument that much of the industry reflects fashions.
22 Kelly, 2014: 917.
23 Drath et al., 2008: 643.
24 Checkland, 1999. A brilliant piece of work—overly complex in explanation but captures so much of the essence of humans framed as activity systems.
25 Archer, 1995. Her work is excellent in terms of understanding the relationship of structures and agents.
26 See, for example, the work of Babiak, 1995.
27 Raelin (2016). Joe Raelin has become the lead proponent for seeking to move leadership studies away from the leader-centric preoccupation.
28 Parry, 1998. Ken's most cited piece of work. He was one of the first to persuasively argue that leadership should be seen as a process of social influence.
29 A useful discussion on LAP is found through: Denis, Langley and Rouleau, 2005; Carroll, Levy and Richmond, 2008; Crevani, Lindgren and Packendorff, 2010; Raelin, 2011; Endrissat and Von Arx, 2013.
30 Raelin, 2015.
31 Kempster and Gregory, 2016. An application of Archer's structure agency work examining a manager in a very difficult moral dilemma.

32 Scott et al., 2017. The work Scott and colleagues are doing to develop leadership skills with undergraduate students through deliberate practice may become most influential. Well worth exploring.

33 Myatt, 2012. Useful, if rather journalistic, summary of expenditure in leadership development.

34 Kempster and Carroll, 2016. An exploration of responsible leadership examined through the lenses of realism and romanticism.

35 Kempster, Jackson and Conroy, 2011. Using MacIntrye's virtue ethics to examine purpose in leadership.

36 Berners-lee and Clark, 2013. Unsettling but compulsive read to wake up humanity to what we are sleep-walking towards. Great title: "the burning question."

37 Steffen et al., 2015. Useful evidence base for the trends of climate boundaries under threat.

38 United Nations, 2014. Can business leaders engage with the SDGs in a manner that is congruent to adding value? We think this is one of the big questions that leadership studies should pay attention to, certainly more than the search for authenticity, traits, style, etc.

39 Grint, 2005. His work is always a great bedtime read.

References

Allen, SJ, Schwartz, AJ and Jenkins, DM (2017) Collegiate leadership competition: An opportunity for deliberate practice on the road to expertise. In S Kempster, A Turner and G Edwards (eds.) *Leadership Development Field Guide* (pp. 29–43). Cheltenham: Edward Elgar.

Alvesson, M and Spicer, A (2016) *The Stupidity Paradox: The Power and Pitfalls of Functional Stupidity at Work*. London: Profile Books.

Archer, M (1995) *Realist Social Theory: The Morphogenetic Approach*. Cambridge: Cambridge University Press.

Babiak, P (1995) When psychopaths go to work: A case study of an industrial psychopath. *Applied Psychology: An international Review*, 44(2): 171–188.

Barthes, R (1983) *Mythologies*. London: Vintage.

Berners-Lee, M and Clark, D (2013) *The Burning Question: We Can't Burn Half the World's Oil, Coal and Gas. So How Do We Quit?* London: Profile Books.

Beverley, J (2000) Testimonio, subalternity, and narrative authority. In N Denzin and Y Lincoln (eds.) *Handbook of Qualitative Research* (3rd edn) (pp. 555–565). London: Sage.

Carroll B, Levy L and Richmond D (2008) Leadership as practice: Challenging the competency paradigm. *Leadership*, 4(4): 363–379.

Checkland, P and Scholes, J (1999) *Soft Systems Methodology in Action: A 30-year Retrospective*. Chichester: John Wiley and Sons Ltd.

Crevani, L, Lindgren, M and Packendorff, J (2010) Leadership, not leaders: On the study of leadership as practices and interactions. *Scandinavian Journal of Management*, 26(1): 77–86.

Denis, J-L, Langley, A and Rouleau, L (2005) The practice of leadership in the messy world of organizations. *Leadership*, 6(1): 67–68.

Drath WH, McCauley CD, Palus CJ, Van Velsor, E, O'Connor, PMG and McGuir, JB (2008) Direction, alignment, commitment: Toward a more integrative ontology of leadership. *The Leadership Quarterly*, 19(6): 635–653.

Endrissat, N and von Arx, W (2013) Leadership and context: Two sides of the same coin. *Leadership*, 9(2): 278–304.

Giacalone, RA and Promislo, MD (2013) Broken when entering: The stigmatization of goodness and business ethics education. *Academy of Management Learning and Education*, 12(1): 86–101

Grint, K (2005) Problems, problems, problems: The social construction of leadership. *Human Relations*, 58(11): 1467–1494.

Guthey, E (2017) *The production of leadership fashions*. The Academy of Management Proceedings, Meeting Abstract Supplement, DOI:10.5465/AMBPP.2013. 12214abstract.

Jackson, B and Parry, K (2011) *A Very Short, Fairly Interesting and Reasonably Cheap Book About Studying Leadership* (2nd edn). London: Sage.

Jones, C and Spicer, A (2005) The sublime object of entrepreneurship. *Human Relations*, 12(2): 223–246.

Kelly, S (2008) Leadership: a categorical mistake? *Human Relations*, 61: 763–782.

Kelly, S (2014) Towards a negative ontology of leadership. *Human Relations*, 67(8): 905–922.

Kempster, S and Gregory, S (2015) Should I stay or should I go? Exploring leadership-as-practice in the middle management role. *Leadership*, 13(4): 496–515.

Kempster, S and Carroll, B (2016) *Responsible Leadership: Realism and Romanticism*. London, Oxon: Routledge.

Kempster, S, Jackson, B and Conroy, M (2011) Leadership as purpose: Exploring the role of purpose in leadership practice. *Leadership*, 7(3): 317–333.

Meindl, J (1995) The romance of leadership as a follower centric theory: A social constructionist approach. *The Leadership Quarterly*, 6: 329–341.

Mueller, M (2012) Lack and jouissance in hegemonic discourse of identification with the state. *Organization*, 20(2): 279–298.

Myatt, M (2012) The 1 reason leadership development fails. Forbes.

Parry, KW (1998) Grounded theory and social process: A new direction for leadership research. *The Leadership Quarterly*, 9(1): Spring, 85–105.

Pye, A (2005) Leadership and organizing: Sense-making in action. *Leadership*, 1(1): 31–50.

Raelin, JA (2011) From leadership-as-practice to leaderful practice. *Leadership*, 7(2): 195–211.

Raelin, JA (2016) Introduction to leadership-as-practice: Theory and application. In JA Raelin (ed.) *Leadership as Practice*. New York: Routledge.

Schedlitzki, D, Edwards, G and Kempster, S (2017) The absent follower: Identity construction within organisationally assigned leader–follower relationships. *Leadership*, On-line first: doi.org/10.1177/17427150176993544.

Steffen, W, Richardson, K, Rockström, J. Cornell, SE, Fetzer, I,Bennett, EM, Biggs, R, Carpenter, SR, de Vries, W Cynthia A de Wit, Carl Folke, Dieter Gerten, Jens Heinke, Georgina M Mace, Linn M Persson, Veerabhadran Ramanathan, Belinda Reyers and Sverker Sörlin (2015) Planetary boundaries: Guiding human development on a changing planet. Science, 347(6223): 1259855. doi:10.1126/science.1259855.

Weick, KE (1995) *Sense-Making in Organizations*. Thousand Oaks, CA: Sage.

6 Leadership Lives?

Affective Leaders in a Neo-Humanist World

David Knights

Questions

What would a neo-humanist leadership look like?
How can we theorise the relationship between leadership, power, subjectivity and ethics?
Is affective leadership an alternative approach to mainstream and critical studies? Is affective leadership a way of acknowledging the body in a newly ethical manner? Does morality blind us to affective leadership and its ethics?

Introduction

The title 'Leadership Lives'?[1] is a vehicle for grabbing attention not dissimilar, if less Armageddon-like, to Alasdair MacIntyre's opening to his book *After Virtue* where he provides a science-fiction scenario of a major environmental disaster. Here all records of knowledge, practices and beliefs have been destroyed and a fictitious pseudo-science fills the vacuum that had been left. His view was that the analytical philosophers would 'never reveal the fact of this disorder' because their job is merely to describe. MacIntyre argues that we need not invent this imaginative world in relation to moral thinking because it is already in this very same state of disorder. It might well be argued that this state of affairs is replicated in leadership studies where for many years there has seemed to be very little sense of where it is leading! Indeed, it is partly because of believing the field to be exhausted that twenty-five years ago, after writing two articles with colleagues on leadership,[2] I felt perhaps arrogantly that there was little more to be said. Consequently, I left the area behind until quite recently when I began to see how space had been created for a more critical and ethical approach to the topic.[3] Hence my question mark in the title to suggest that there remains ambiguity and ambivalence as to whether the lives of leaders are life enhancing and the extent to which 'leadership lives'.

One of the major problems is that because the idea of leadership is so taken for granted, it is rarely interrogated despite the attention given to its everyday practice and the volumes of literature devoted to its theorisation. At the point of writing in 2017, the United Kingdom has witnessed some of the most horrific events in its recent history in relation to terrorism and the Grenfell twenty-four-storey tower block fire killing over seventy people. The overwhelming outcry from the media, the public and the surviving victims is to appeal to leadership as if it could perform a shamanic ritual that would instantly heal the wounds. Regardless of incumbents, the leaders are duly sacrificed at the altar of human expectation that far exceeds any potential endeavour to relieve the suffering. While no one can blame the victims of tragedy for seeking solace from those in closest proximity who are adorned with the trappings of power, this deification of leaders is also something of a tragedy that neither the media nor academic research seeks to alleviate. Yet had the proverbial disaster described by MacIntyre actually occurred, the tragedy that leadership represents would probably be recreated as fast as it disappeared for there would soon be an urgency to fill the vacuum left by its absence. We could only remain hopeful that it would not repeat the damaging senses in which attributions of leadership whether from the 'outside in' or the 'inside out' are seen to be an essential *property* of persons or groups. This is certainly how it has been characterised within the classic trait, transactional, situationist, contingency or transformational approaches but it may be surprising to find that a proprietary conception of leadership also prevails in 'critical leadership studies' (CLS).

In addition to the tendency for studies to rely on proprietary perspectives in which attributions of leadership but also power and identity are seen as the property of persons or groups rather than of relations, there is also a frequent failure to take an embodied approach to understanding organisations and social relations through which these phenomena find expression. This is why of recent times there has been a growing demand to focus more on the body and embodied ways of researching[4] organisations, management and leadership as well as to give attention to other material objects that are significant in human affairs.[5] In this chapter, I will draw on recent neo-humanist approaches that eschew the proprietary, individualistic and often masculine conceptions of leadership, which tend to neglect the embodied and engaged manner through which social relations are conducted in everyday life. By introducing the notion of affect, I seek to demonstrate how embodied leadership is distributed socially such that we lead one another through affecting one another in different ways. Often described as a 'new spirituality', post- or neo-humanist researchers trace the neglect of the body to masculine modes of power and offer insights into the ambiguity, doubt and insecurity that befall us when the myth of certainty surrounding 'scientific' approaches to leadership is exposed.[6] It also rejects prescriptive rule and norm-based approaches to focus on embodied engagement as part of what ethical leadership might mean for the renewal and revitalisation of theory and practice in this field.

The chapter proceeds with a brief history of recent developments in mainstream leadership studies before turning to critical approaches that focus on the neglect of power. It seeks to demonstrate how both literatures tend to subscribe either consciously or unconsciously to proprietary assumptions about leadership and power. The second section links this proprietary conception of leadership and power to a neglect of the body in leadership studies, albeit acknowledging important exceptions within gendered and philosophical analyses of leadership. In the third and final section, I focus on a theory and practice of affect and its affects and, more importantly, how it might facilitate embodied and ethical forms of leadership. A summary and conclusion seek to explore further both the theoretical and practical implications of these developments.

Recent Studies of Leadership: Developing a Relational Approach

The 1980s was a fallow period for leadership studies, not least because the prevailing dominant psychological literature remained reductionist in its 'scientific'[7] attempts to convert the objects of research to measurable variables that could be manipulated in experiments to produce abstract models of predictive precision regarding effective leadership. Assumptions about what constituted leadership had to be made and generally these were identified as the qualities or traits possessed by individuals who were perceived to be leaders. Traits of leadership including such qualities as 'initiative', 'charisma', 'drive', 'intelligence', 'self-confidence' and 'integrity' were mapped and correlated one against another and linked to particular leaders or variables relating to styles of leadership (e.g. autocratic versus democratic), and then these were manipulated, and the effects observed in laboratory conditions. However, frequently these traits were found to be ambiguous or ill-defined and there were numerous reports of the absence of any correlations between them.[8] Even more disconcerting was that apart from the difficulty of defining these qualities, in practice few leaders were found to share exactly the same traits and yet it was possible to identify many of these traits among organisational personnel who had no experience of leadership.[9] These scientific weaknesses were paralleled when applied because the traits of leadership were seen as essential qualities at birth, leaving practitioners reliant on identifying the correct traits at the point of recruitment. Also, given the assumption that these traits were thought to be in limited supply, there was a built-in inflationary competition to attract the 'best' talent, and despite the discrediting of such theories, this mantra still continues to be regurgitated by corporate hierarchies, albeit more as a way of legitimising inequalities than to ensure good leadership. Through introducing contingent and contextual issues, leadership theorists saw a way of overcoming the essentialism of the trait approach, but they simply replaced it with a dualistic format where the individual leader was seen as having to take account of the context. Moreover, the inappropriate application of 'hard' or positivist science (scientism) began to be challenged for its objectivist and reductionist representations of matters of leadership into their discrete and constituent parts that were, in principle, capable of being measured.

Outside of leadership discourse, this period was characterised by a long list of management innovations amongst which were total quality management (TQM), just-in-time (JIT) and business process reengineering (BPR). These seemed to offer a panacea to management alongside rapidly expanding information and communication technologies (ICT) and knowledge management (KM) solutions to longstanding problems. As it turned out, all of these not only failed to deliver what they promised but indeed, in the case of ICT, created a dot.com bubble burst at the turn of the century that would have gone down in history as one of the greatest business disasters of hubris and excess optimism had it not been dwarfed by the global financial crisis of 2008. While there are numerous and often conflicting accounts that seek to explain these enormous crises in the business and financial world, and certainly too many to document here, it is surprising how much hyperbole and false optimism is attached to each new solution as it displaces that which has been wholly discredited. Yet in the background, there were academics and consultants seeking to transform workforces through leadership – a simple target on which to apply energy and resources and one that does not promise more than it can deliver. After the failures of more complex innovations, a return to leadership seemed like a sensible shift back to social rather than organisational or technological solutions. In addition, it not only refutes the view that technology can simply displace a good deal of management, it also restores legitimacy to managers and leaders, thus providing a justification of the wide material and symbolic reward differentials between different levels in the hierarchy.

The revival of practitioner interest in leadership was accompanied by parallel academic developments but only a limited attempt was made to challenge the monopoly that psychology had held over the field.[10] This was despite the emergence of a diversity of disciplines such as communication studies, organisation studies, politics, philosophy and sociology, some of which subscribed to a critical, as opposed to a managerialist or prescriptive, approach to leadership. Few studies were able to escape the proprietary individualistic, psychologistic, reductionist and deterministic perspectives that were a legacy from Enlightenment thinking about the autonomous subject until the development of a constructionist model of leadership.

Of course, the growth of leader–follower, transformational and servant approaches are close to escaping proprietary conceptions by stressing relationship models of leadership. However, there is still often a subscription to entity conceptions of leadership that the individual leaders and followers bring to their interpersonal exchanges. In not dissimilar ways as in the mainstream, the primary source of the relationship is one or other side of the leader/follower binary. This entity view is where instead of focusing on relations, the individual and her or his mental faculties remain centre stage and this can be contrasted with a fully relational conception that reveals 'the social construction processes by which certain understandings of leadership come about and are given privileged ontology'.[11] Instead of falling back on a dualistic framework, this constructionist approach sees leadership and the context in which it is practised as mutually constitutive of one another; leadership is then understood as the embodied manifestation of a range of collective and communal interpretations appropriate to a set of contextual circumstances. When seen in this light, it is difficult for either theorists or practitioners to fall back on conventional individualistic or proprietary conceptions of leadership. Instead, leadership can be seen as fully relational where there is an 'open' engagement with others and the absence of a preoccupation with identity that serves only to transform everything (whether follower or organisation) into a resource for affirming the solidity of self in an 'orderly and predictable world'.[12]

Leadership and Power: The Critical Approach

Following the success of critical management studies (CMS) over the last 20 years, a recent and interesting change on the landscape has been the development of what is called CLS.[13] Rather than apologising for, legitimising and/or assisting leaders, critics are concerned with challenging their claims to automatic privilege and status. They pursue ways in which leadership might assume values of ethical standards, employee wellbeing and environmental protection that transcend those of the established order where maximising returns to shareholders and management and/or minimising costs are pre-eminent. CLS critically examines the negative or dark sides, especially where, for example, leadership can readily be transformed into a cult that mesmerises believers and demonises those who challenge the message or its meaning.[14] However, CLS also challenges the ways in which leadership is treated in a dualistic manner in terms of 'leadership/management; leaders/followers; leaders/contexts; born/made leaders; task/people orientation; theory X/theory Y; one best way/contingent; organic/mechanistic, autocratic/participative; forceful/enabling; saviours/scapegoats; charismatic/quiet; essentialist/constructionist'[15] as well as where, research is characterised by masculine and disembodied analyses.[16] A majority of critical theorists also question how except insofar as it is presumed to be a property of hierarchical position and status, issues of identity are almost completely neglected by the mainstream.

Simultaneously with this neglect, however, the mainstream nevertheless presumes power by exaggerating the agency of leaders as if their intentions have a one-to-one relationship with organisational outcomes.[17]

Consequently, there is an over-attribution of success (and failure) to those in positions of leadership. Not surprisingly, leaders too readily claim the credit for success in their organisations and researchers subscribing to transformational ideas about it are inclined to legitimise these claims despite knowledge of the serendipitous and unpredictability of all things social. Through a number of well-constructed and illuminating case studies that vividly portray some of the disastrous outcomes that can result from leaders following their ambitions and desires, the dangers of attributing too much power and agency to those in positions of leadership have been demonstrated.[18] In a justifiable positive review, however, Gabriel concludes that while leaders should not take all the credit for success, they are not necessarily to 'blame for all failure either'.[19] Of course, it is not just the mainstream literature but also common sense that attribute too much power and agency to leaders. First, this is because it is comfortable to pass on responsibility to those who are willing to assume it, but second it is due to the necessity of holding someone to account, especially when there are serious problems. So, there is a quid pro quo for enjoying the material and symbolic benefits of leadership whether in the form of income, status or success in that the person at the top is also usually held responsible for failures regardless of how they occur.

Power is also a major theme on the part of several other authors who share similar concerns to CLS without necessarily describing their work in those terms. So, for example, it is argued that 'leadership communication is inherently power-based, a site of contestation about the nature of leadership' and there is a focus on the relations between power, praxis and materialities, such as the body.[20] It was also central to authors who felt that leadership researchers should begin to 'hold bodies, in their fleshy version, prominent, and to focus on bodies as possibilities', that may, for example, 'interrupt systemic power'.[21] But even the analysis of care interventions are seen to involve a range of capabilities and capacities that are 'intimately bound up in issues of power'.[22]

All these analyses advance the field of leadership studies in a variety of ways, but I have a few limited reservations insofar as there are occasions when the literature seems not to explore more than the surface features of fundamental theoretical concepts such as power. There is a sense in which arguing that leadership is closely aligned with power is so radical to the field that it seems sufficient not to extend any further. Consequently, the concept is assumed to be self-evident or understood commonsensically rather than interrogated. However, common sense invariably reflects and reproduces certain assumptions, and these usually revolve around proprietary notions of power wherein it is seen to be a property of persons or groups. These proprietary ideas about power derive largely from the dominant work of American political scientist Robert Dahl[23] whose notion of power is captured in his analysis of 'A' having power over 'B' insofar as he (sic) can get B to do what he (sic) wants him to do. Ignoring the gendered language implicit in this analysis, the basis upon which everything is constructed is that the individual possesses power. This analysis was rendered more sophisticated by Steven Lukes distinguishing between three types of power as follows:[24]

1 Power to secure a decision in situations where there is some observable conflict of views
2 Power to keep issues about which there are conflicting views on or off the decision-making agenda
3 Institutionalised power to define reality in such a way as to ensure compliance because of an internalisation of norms even against people's so-called real interests

Yet the first two observable and unobservable dimensions of power remain proprietary in that one or a group of persons possess the power to determine a decision or to deny it a platform. The third dimension is less immediately obviously proprietary since it focuses on the institutionalised practices that are not directly related to the decision making of individuals and groups about particular issues or their ways of excluding them from consideration. However, Lukes sees the norms that people internalise as having been defined as reality by those who have the power to control meaning so that others are rendered powerless as they are not even able to recognise, let alone express, their own 'real interests'. This is not only a proprietary but also a class-based conception of power where it is polarised between those who possess it and those who do not. In addition, it seems to assume that 'real interest' exists independently of relations of power and can be identified a priori, where if it does not slide into essentialist notions of interests preceding one's entry into some form of sociality, it is in danger of imposing them on the subjects ideologically in terms of class or some other category.

CLS seems rarely to go beyond this proprietary conception of power in leadership even though some of it comes close to developing a more divergent view. For example, in arguing that too much agency is attributed to leadership, Tourish[25] is half way to seeing it as projected on to individuals rather than something they possess, but he does not advance this understanding any further. Importantly, Collinson also speaks of power dynamics and situated power relations and how difference can be deployed divisively in the exercise of power, sometimes resulting in excessive binaries that 'oversimplify complex leadership relationships'.[26] However, 'othering' or stereotyping as a routine strategy in everyday life is not examined as a means to interrogate power. Instead of turning directly to Foucault, these authors draw on secondary sources to 'discuss the disciplinary nature of power, and how this is manifest through surveillance, routinization, and cultural practices'. They also acknowledge that 'systemic institutional practices rather than the individual frailties of banking leaders' are a better way of understanding the global financial crisis, but then in a different context they contradict Foucault in arguing that 'even the *possession* of a small amount of power increases people's willingness to engage in corrupt practices'.[27]

Subscribing to such a proprietary view of power generates analyses that reproduce precisely the kinds of problems that critics identify in the mainstream as individualising and romanticising leaders. A relational conception, by contrast, recognises that power can only be exercised when there is consent and not just compliance on the part of those for whom it is a target; otherwise it is domination, which depends primarily on, or the threat of, coercion. A relational conception of power is in this sense virtually coincident with the idea of leadership such that there is coordinated collaboration, creative conflict, communal cooperation, communicative competence, compassionate consideration, constructive challenges, calm courage and collective commitment. It is largely the common sense proprietary conception held by theorists and practitioners alike that prevents both power and leadership being seen and practised in this productive and positive manner. This is not to suggest that power and leadership is always positive and productive rather than negative and repressive; the slippage to proprietary ownership and 'possessive individualism'[28] is ever present as we (they) subjects externalise our (their) fears, anxieties and insecurities or seek to resolve them through identity securing strategies of power and leadership. Clearly then, as Collinson[29] has recognised but not fully developed because of slipping occasionally in to proprietary assumptions, leadership is problematic and cannot be fully understood when it is seen as independent of power and identity. This takes us to an examination of how the body matters when discussing leadership, as it also tends to be neglected by mainstream theorists and practitioners alike.

The Body in Leadership

There is very little in life that does not concern the body and embodiment precedes thought and cerebral discourse, and yet our culture has routinely marginalised or taken the body for granted. Even when it is no longer possible at the point of death, rituals surround the body that is to remain concealed or shrouded in social routines of symbolic rather than material significance. Nonetheless, within sociology, considerable research has focused on the body as a site for studying gender and identity,[30] corporeal feminism,[31] culture,[32] disciplinary power and subjectivity,[33] diversity and discrimination,[34] work and aesthetic labour,[35] consumerism and self-improvement,[36] and even management and organisation.[37]

While continuing a tradition of emulating positive science, leadership studies has also begun to be affected by the general trend in the social sciences of rejecting the Cartesian mind–body dualism where cognitive, linguistic and symbolic discourses are privileged above, thus marginalising, the body. This has resulted in a growing if somewhat limited demand to focus more on the body, and on embodied ways of conducting research, even though, so far, this has tended to be restricted to leadership students with an interest in gender.[38] Partly, this can be seen as a consequence of the rather masculine, linear rational and individualistic character of leadership as both a practice and a topic of research. This both reflects and reproduces the Cartesian binary between mind and body along with fundamental dualisms between subjects and objects (ontology), representational and realist (epistemology), agency and structure (methodology) and other dualisms of a political nature relating to age, ethnicity/race, gender, sexuality and the able-bodied. In each of these dualisms, there is a hierarchy whereby one side of the binary is elevated over the other and with respect to politics, young, able-bodied, white, heterosexual males are privileged. This also reflects and reinforces proprietary conceptions of leadership and power as the property of individuals or groups and, as we have seen, this can be so culturally engrained as to operate subconsciously even among critics who eschew dualistic epistemologies and ontologies. Yet the identification of power as a property of persons or groups invariably invokes a cognitive, mentalist and rational depiction of action and decision making on the part of leaders.

It is not, then, surprising that the body has been marginalised or entirely neglected in leadership studies:

The discipline – its scholars, practitioners, observers and commentators – largely act as if bodies and physicality are unimportant to leadership.[39]

Despite a marginalising of the body, however, it is rarely really absent either in theory or practice; there is just little reflection on its presence. For, without even considering the body as central, mainstream Western leadership studies presume leaders to be 'white able bodied', heterosexual 'males'.[40] Even the mainstream and especially that concerned with transformational, distributional and leaderly matters has focused on emotional, if not directly bodily, aspects of charisma, inspiration and empathy. For clearly leadership is a corporeal activity in the sense of seeking to inspire and enthuse the corporate body and its members to embody the ethos, spirit, strategy and objectives of the organisation. However, the mainstream remains oblivious to the embodied nature of much leadership and this unreflective perception has been attributed to the wholly descriptive nature of much research. As already indicated, within the field of gender and leadership, the body has occupied a central focus. So, for example, in photographic images of male leaders, there is a focus predominantly on the head, which is associated with the mind and cognition to support the myth of men being wholly rational. By contrast, more of the body and the flesh of women is photographed, thus deflecting the imagery away from the mind and cognition.[41]

This clearly maps gender onto the mind–body binary, reflecting and reproducing an image of men and masculinity as in control both physically and metaphorically with women being assigned to their uncontrollable, unpredictable and overflowing bodies. Few better exemplifications of how the gendered body is highly significant can be found than those in TV and film media where physical appearance would seem to be much more significant for women than for men. These discourses of masculinity are quite clearly embedded in leadership studies that embrace conceptions of heroism that stretch back as far as Homer's epic mythic tale of Odysseus's ten-year voyage back home from his heroic battle of Troy. Contemporary leaders have never struggled with the elements and war in the way that Odysseus is proclaimed to have done, yet they often display similar kinds of claims to masculine leadership. They involve rational, disembodied and highly instrumental performances that reflect and reproduce homosocial bonding and social exclusiveness.[42]

As followers, women's bodies are often disciplined in order to render them docile and productive and, as leaders, their aging bodies are at a gender disadvantage since the grey elderly man is looked upon as wise and dignified in a way that is not the case for older women. Feminists have sought to reverse this representation by re-imagining women leaders as effective not in spite of their bodies, but because they are more embodied. This disrupts the representation of leadership as being naturally masculine and lacking in eroticism and sensuality. In its post-anthropocentric form, however, neo-humanists argue that embodiment is one of the necessary conditions of ethical engagement since it renders leaders and those exercising power responsible to the other and thereby less preoccupied with themselves and their own identities.[43] From this, it is reasonable to argue that the failure of ethical leadership both in theory and practice has an association with the dominance of white androcentric disembodiment, the dominance of individualism, preoccupations with the self, and heroism within leadership discourse and practice. We can conclude, then, that what has sometimes been called the 'absent presence' of the body[44] leaves studies of leadership bereft of some of the most important features of its reproduction. Yet paradoxically it is often only when leadership becomes a topic of analysis and investigation that disembodied conceptions of its everyday practice predominates as disembodied masculine assumptions of cognitive control and proprietary power are privileged.

In addition to this gendered focus on the body in leadership studies, there is a growing interest in more philosophical approaches.[45] In seeking to escape individualistic and dualistic approaches, much of the literature speaks about a leadership dynamic that draws on the notion of an ambiguous relational space in between leaders and followers to interrogate this missing link in current research. Ladkin relates this to Merleau-Ponty's (1968) perspective on the flesh, as she seeks to provide 'the material embodiment of an ontology of relationality'.[46] For it is through this sense of 'touching the flesh' metaphorically or physically that the various invisible aspects of leadership such as the embodied and felt experience of being in a leadership relation, the sense of community and vision, and the trust underlying these relations are conveyed. It is not just actual leadership dynamics that can be fleshed out in this way; it is also the research process itself since it is our bodies and 'embodied awareness'[47] that are intimately involved in producing 'insights or findings'.[48] Moreover, while the body and the senses are prior to any cognitive selection or interpretation, our own 'embodied responses' as researchers are crucial in sensing 'the interplay of the "visible" and the "invisible"' within leadership encounters. In speculating on how reflecting on the invisible itself might have a 'material affect' ... 'on those who enter into leader–follower relations, as well as on those who study them',[49] and this conveniently *leads* us into our final section on affect.

Affect and Its Affects in Leadership

The ways in which contemporary studies of leadership have challenged the reductionism within 'scientific' attempts to 'capture' the elements that render it effective has opened up space to examine affect and affections by returning to the medieval philosopher Spinoza.[50] For Spinoza, affect relates to how 'the body's power of acting is increased or diminished, aided or restrained'.[51] While affective leadership is still yet embryonic in terms of research,[52] several contemporary authors argue that we should not even study leaders let alone seek to measure any behavioural content since it is most effective 'where leadership is not required'.[53] As yet, few offer an alternative way of studying leadership that is compatible with this challenge to the mainstream. However, it may be argued that affect provides precisely such an alternative embodied approach to understanding the 'invisible' as residing *in between* subject and object, mind and body, and leaders and followers. Science has always sought to efface such ephemeral phenomena that defy objectification; instead it favours representations generated by sovereign subjects whose actions are deemed to generate knowledge of the world including notions of leadership. But this 'in between' not only involves affectively engaged bodies affecting other bodies and their (our) material and symbolic lives, it also energises these self-same bodies in ways that enhance their (our) capacity to be affective. It also energises us to explore the ambiguous in-between spaces that prevail on us to engage with, rather than seek to control, the other regardless of leadership relations. Fundamentally, affect reflects and reinforces an ethics in which we identify with other bodies sufficiently 'for us to have [a real] ... concern'.[54] Leadership might then begin to resemble what has been described as the art of living an aesthetic existence, where true knowledge depends entirely on 'an essential position of otherness'.[55] There is then massive bodily energy affecting leadership processes and the outcome significantly affects us through a wide range of embodied experiences from anguish to euphoria, sadness to exhilaration, panic to passion, fear to courage and pessimism to optimism, to mention only a few. These processes, however, are open to endless capacities to affect and be affected[56] but also subject the body to recognition of its own 'indeterminacy'.[57]

Yet why refer to *affect* as opposed to feelings or emotions? The reason is because while affect incorporates feelings and emotions, the latter are more static, concrete and individualised, referring almost always to individual sentient, and usually human beings. By contrast, affect is dynamic and inter-corporeal as well as referring to material objects and not just humans. Massumi[58] defines affect 'in terms of its autonomy from conscious perception and language, as well as emotion'.[59] So, for example, a feeling or emotion is a state of being, or the property, of a sentient subject at a singular moment in time while an affect is always in transition, moving from source(s) to destination(s) often in reciprocal fashion, and can just as readily be virtual as real.[60] We affect a vast range of material, animal and human phenomena as they affect us, so affect cannot be seen as the property of a person since it is in a complex web of relations or networks. Although 'affect is subjectively felt as a sense of freedom or potential that adds intensity to action and events', [it] 'cannot be *reduced* to a property of the subject'.[61]

By focusing on affect, we are not inventing something new so much as acknowledging the body as simultaneously the subject and object of the same action and how it affects and is affected by other bodies in ways that can enhance or destroy the capacity for reasoned action. As has been argued, traditional thinking about leadership has often been constrained by attributions of it to persons who are deemed to have essential qualities that render them charismatic, heroic, rational and perhaps even magical. While this individualisation of the notion of leadership as a property of persons has been restrained in succeeding developments of leadership. However, despite that emphasising the context, the followers and practice rather than prescriptive ideals, romanticising the individual continues to remain a legacy that is frequently rekindled, sneaked in by the back door, or simply presumed in the form of proprietary views of power.

Summary and Conclusion

In this chapter, I have examined a range of literatures on leadership from the scientistic to the relational and from the critical to affect in leadership studies. The scientistic theories cerebrally divide the whole into its constituent parts in an attempt to identify what causes effective leadership whereas relational approaches acknowledge complexity and uncertainty[62] and generally critique the disembodied approaches of the mainstream. CLS challenges the positivist epistemology and question the neglect of power in the mainstream but have not always succeeded fully in interrogating conceptions of both power and leadership. By turning to the notion of affect, we can re-envisage leadership as making a difference through embodied energy, albeit an energy that is as much intra-corporeal as inter-individual. It is never static enough to be captured in a concrete instance since it is forever in transition yet enables the embodied subject to form habits that adapt 'to social context'.[63] In making a difference, affective leadership enhances the capacity of others to act so it is infectious, but it affects not just other subjects but also the material and symbolic conditions of its practice.

Of course, there is nothing particularly new about affective leadership for it is routinely enacted in everyday organisational contexts without any conscious appreciation of its embodied energy. Like the body through which it is expressed and given life, affect is not a new innovative technique to be adopted or prescribed by consultants, but it may have to be developed rather than denied and nurtured – not neglected. Leadership is inherently affective even though prescriptions and techniques often intervene to undermine its energy by enforcing obedience to normative prescriptions and regulatory constraints. Affective leadership can transform organisations into ethical, spiritually uplifting and joyful modes of collective action and commitment, but we have to abandon the attachment to expertise that invariably imposes masculine linear rational techniques that leave subjects devoid of any sense of embodied engagement. Through acknowledging affect as an embodied experience, we can begin to see how leadership is no more than affecting and being affected by our relations in ways that energise our joyful, creative and productive action. In reflecting on their own practices, those engaged in what is sometimes called the secret of good leadership – enabling others to cultivate their own creativity – invariably endorse this view, for leadership and affect are two sides of the same coin in their enhancement of the collective and communal capacities for reasoned action.

Notes

1 This paraphrases our title Management Lives (Knights and Willmott, 1999/2004).
2 Knights and Morgan (1992); Knights and Willmott (1992).
3 Knights and O'Leary (2006).
4 Thanem and Knights (2019).
5 Knights and McCabe (2017).
6 Braidotti (2013).
7 Some have described its practices as being scientistic (e.g. Schroyer, 1975) whereby meaning and interpretation can be ignored since the social world is treated as if there is no ontological discontinuity between 'natural' and human phenomena.
8 Stodgill (1974/6).
9 Bryman (1986).
10 Fairhurst and Connaughton (2014).
11 Uhl-Bien (2006: 655–666).
12 Knights (2015: 209).
13 Collinson (2011).
14 Tourish (2013).
15 Collinson (2014: 39).
16 Knights (2017).
17 Tourish (2013: 8–12).
18 Tourish (2013: 8–12).
19 Gabriel (2013).
20 Fairhurst and Connaughton (2014: 8).
21 Sinclair (2005: 388).

22 Tomkins and Simpson (2015: 1026).
23 Dahl (1961).
24 Lukes (1973). This summary and analysis draws on Knights and Willmott (1999/2004: 95–99).
25 Tourish (2013).
26 Collinson (2014: 47).
27 Collinson and Tourish (2015: 587, my emphasis).
28 MacPherson (1962).
29 Collinson (2014).
30 Butler (1990, 1993).
31 Grosz (1994).
32 Judovitz (2001) Atkinson (2005).
33 Foucault (1977).
34 Tretheway (1999); Knights and Omanović (2015).
35 Wolkowitz (2006).
36 Askegaard et al. (2002).
37 Thanem and Wallenberg (2015).
38 Trethewey (1999); Sinclair (2005; 2011).
39 Sinclair (2013: 439).
40 Pullen and Vacchani (2013: 315).
41 Sinclair (2005).
42 Knights and Tullberg (2012).
43 Ziarek, (2001); Braidotti (2013).
44 Leder (1990).
45 Case, French and Simpson (2011); Ciulla, Knights, Mabey and Tomkins (2018).
46 Ladkin (2013: 328).
47 Ibid.: 325.
48 Kupers (2013: 336).
49 Ladkin (2013: 332).
50 Spinoza (1677/1883).
51 Spinoza (1677/1883), III quoted in Deleuze (1988: 49).
52 Knights (2018); Munro and Thanem (2018). While not directly on leadership, there is a brief literature on the margins of affective leadership (Thanem, 2013; Thanem and Wallenberg, 2015). There is also a self-improvement literature (e.g. Boyer, 2011) that makes no reference to the philosophical grounding of the recent academic interest in affect.
53 Bolden (2016: 45).
54 Gatens (2006: 39).
55 Foucault (2011: 7367).
56 Clough (2009).
57 Clough (2007: 3).
58 Massumi (2002).
59 Clough (2007: 3).
60 Massumi (2002).
61 Hynes (2013: 561 original emphasis).
62 Bolden (2016).
63 Hynes (2013: 571).

References

Askegaard, S., Cardel Gertsen, M. and Langer, R. (2002) 'The body consumed: Reflexivity and cosmetic surgery', *Psychology & Marketing*, 19(10): 793–812.

Atkinson, T. (ed.) (2005) *The Body: Readers in Cultural Criticism*. Basingstoke, UK: Palgrave Macmillan.

Bolden, R. (2016) 'Paradoxes of perspective' in Bolden, R., Witzel, M. and Linacre, N. (eds.) *Leadership Paradoxes: Rethinking Leadership for an Uncertain World*. London and New York: Routledge, pp. 31–52.

Boyer, L. (2011) *Connect: Affective Leadership for Effective Results*. Leadership Options, LLC.

Braidotti, R. (2013) *The Posthuman*. Malden: MA: Polity Press, Kindle Edition.

Bryman, A. 1986. *Leadership and Organisation*. London: Routledge.

Bryman, A. (1986) *Leadership and Organisation*. London: Routledge.

Butler, J. (1990) *Gender Trouble: Feminism and the Subversion of Identity*. London: Routledge.

Butler, J. (1993) *Bodies that Matter: On the Discursive Limits of 'Sex'*. New York: Routledge.

Case, P., French, R. and Simpson, P. (2011) 'Philosophy of leadership' in Bryman, A., Collinson, D.L., Grint, K., Jackson B. and Uhl Bien, M. (eds.) *The Sage Handbook of Leadership*. London: Sage, pp. 242–254.

Ciulla, J., Knights, D., Mabey, C. and Tomkins, L. (eds.) (2018) 'Ethical leadership and ethics: Philosophical and spiritual approaches', *Business Ethics Quarterly*, 28, 1 & 3, Forthcoming.

Clough, P.T. (2007) *The Affective Turn: Theorizing the Social*. Durham, NC: Duke University Press.

Clough, P.T. (2009) 'The *new* empiricism: Affect and sociological method', *European Journal of Social Ideas*, 12(1): 43–61.

Collinson, D.L. (2011) 'Critical leadership studies' in Bryman, A., Collinson, D.L., Grint, K., Jackson, B. and Uhl Bien, M. (eds.) *The Sage Handbook of Leadership*. London: Sage, pp. 179–192.

Collinson, D. (2014) 'Dichotomies, dialectics and dilemmas: New directions for critical leadership studies?' *Leadership*, 10(1): 36–55.

Collinson, D. and Tourish, D. (2015) 'Teaching leadership critically: New directions for leadership pedagogy', *Academy of Management Learning and Education*, 14(4): 576–594.

Dahl, R. (1961) *Who Governs?: Democracy and Power in an American City*. New Haven, CT: Yale University Press.

Deleuze, G. (1988) *Spinoza: Practical Philosophy*, trans. by R. Hurley, San Francisco: City Lights Books.

Fairhurst, G.T. and Connaughton, S.L. (2014) 'Leadership: A communicative perspective', *Leadership*, 10(1): 7–35.

Foucault, M. (1977) *Discipline and Punish*. London: Allen Lane.

Foucault, M. (2011) *The Courage of Truth*. Harmondsworth: Penguin.

Gabriel, Y. (2013) 'Book review', *Organization Studies*, 34(9): 1407–1410.

Gatens, M. and Genevieve, L. (1996) *Collective Imaginings: Spinoza, Past and Present*. London and New York: Routledge, Kindle edition.

Grosz, E. (1994) *Volatile Bodies: Toward a Corporeal Feminism*. Bloomington, IN: Indiana University Press.

Hynes, M. (2013) 'Reconceptualizing resistance: Sociology and the affective dimension of resistance'. *The British Journal of Sociology*, 64(4): 559–577.

Judovitz, D. (2001) *The Culture of the Body*, University of Michigan Press.

Knights, D. (2015) 'Binaries need to shatter for bodies to matter: Do disembodied masculinities undermine organizational ethics?', *Organization*, 22(2): 200–216.

Knights, D. (2017) 'Leadership, masculinity and ethics in financial services' in Storey, J., Hartley, J., Denis, J.-L., Hart, P.T. and Dave Ulrich (eds.) *The Routledge Companion To Leadership*, London: Routledge.

Knights, D. (2018) 'What's more effective than affective leadership? Searching for embodiment in leadership research and practice', in Mabey, C. and Knights, D. '*Leadership Matters?*': *Finding Voice, Connection and Meaning in the 21st Century*, London and New York: Routledge.

Knights, D. and McCabe, D. (2017) 'The missing masses of resistance: Employing insights from actor network theory to enhance our understanding of resistance', *British Journal of Management*, DOI:10.1111/1467-8551.12170.

Knights, D. and G. Morgan (1992) 'Leadership as corporate strategy: Towards a critical analysis', *Leadership Quarterly*, 3(3): 171–190.

Knights, D. and Omanović, V. (2015) 'Rethinking diversity in organizations' in Bendl, R., Bleijenbergh, I., Henttonen, E. and Mills Albert, J. (eds.). *The Oxford Handbook of Diversity in Organizations*. Oxford: Oxford University Press.

Knights, D. and M. Tullberg (2012) 'Managing masculinity/mismanaging the corporation'. *Organization*, 19(4): 385–404.

Knights, D. and O' Leary, M. (2006) 'Leadership, ethics and responsibility to the other', *Journal of Business Ethics*, 67(2): 125–137.

Knights, D. and H. Willmott (1992) 'Conceptualising leadership processes; A study of senior leadership processes; A study of senior managers in a financial services company', *Journal of Management Studies*, 29(6): 761–782.

Knights, D. and Willmott, H. (1999/2004) *Management Lives*. London: Sage.

Kupers, W. (2013) 'Embodied inter-practices of leadership – Phenomenological perspectives on relational and responsive leading and following', *Leadership*, 9(3) 335–357.

Ladkin, D. (2013) 'From perception to flesh: A phenomenological account of the felt experience of leadership', *Leadership*, 9(3): 320–334.

Leder, D. (1990) *The Absent Body*. Chicago, IL: University of Chicago Press.

Lukes, S. (1973) *Power: A Radical View*. London: Macmillan.

MacPherson, C.B. (1962) *Political Theory of Possessive Individualism: Hobbes to Locke*. Oxford: Oxford University Press.

Massumi, B. (2002) *Parables for the Virtual*. Durham, NC: Duke University Press.

Merleau-Ponty, M. (1968) *The Visible and the Invisible*, edited by C. Lefort and translated by A. Lingis. Evanston, IL: Northwestern University Press.

Munro, I. and Thanem, T. (2018) 'The ethics of affective leadership: Organizing good encounters without leaders', in Ciulla, J., Knights, D., Mabey, C. and Tomkins, L. (eds.) 'Special issue: Philosophical approaches to leadership ethics', *Business Ethics Quarterly*, Forthcoming.

Pullen, A. and Vachhani, S. (2013) 'The materiality of leadership', *Leadership*, 9(3): 315–319.

Schroyer, T. (1975) *The Critique of Domination*. Boston: Beacon.

Sinclair, A. (2005) 'Body and management pedagogy', *Gender, Work and Organization*, 12(1): 89–104.

Sinclair, A. (2011) 'Leading with body' in Jeanes, E., Knights, D. and Yancey Martin, P. (eds.) *Handbook on Gender, Work & Organization*. London and New York: Routledge, pp. 117–130.

Sinclair, A. (2013) 'A material dean', *Leadership*, 9(3): 436–443.

Spinoza, B. (1677/1883) *The Ethics*, trans. by R.H.M. Elwes, A public domain book, Kindle.

Stodgill, R.M. (1974/6) *Handbook of Leadership*. New York, NY: Free Press.

Thanem, T. (2011) *The Monstrous Organization*. Cheltenham: Edward Elgar.

Thanem, T. and Wallenberg, L. (2016) 'Just doing gender? Transvestism and the power of underdoing gender in everyday life and work', *Organization*, 23(2): 250–271.

Tomkins, L. and Simpson, P. (2015) 'Caring leadership: A Heideggerian perspective', *Organization Studies*, 36(8): 1013–1103.

Tourish, D. (2013) *The Dark Side of Transformational Leadership: A Critical Perspective*. London and New York: Routledge.

Trethewey, A. (1999) 'Disciplined bodies: Women's embodied identities at work', *Organization Studies*, 20(3): 423–450.

Uhl-Bien, M. (2006) 'Relational leadership theory: Exploring the social processes of leadership and organizing', *The Leadership Quarterly*, 17: 654–676.

Wolkowitz, C. (2006) *Bodies at Work*. London: Sage.

Ziarek, E.P. (2001) *An Ethics of Dissensus: Postmodernity, Feminism and the Politics of Radical Democracy*. Stanford University Press.

Part II
Unravelling, Disentangling, Refashioning

7 Redoing and Abolishing Whiteness in Leadership

Helena Liu

If we must pinpoint one defining moment that marked the start of the fall of Western imperialism, it would be 1 June 2017, when the United States President at the time, Donald Trump, announced that the country would withdraw from the Paris climate accord. Prior to this announcement, the United States was responsible for spewing a lion's share of past emissions, with its most deleterious effects being experienced by citizens in the developing world. As floods ravaged Bangladesh, heatwaves scorched northern India and carbon-filled smoke choked Colombia, the smug self-centred empire declaring 'America First' prompted a global backlash.

Signs of public discontent had been stirring beneath the surface for years before this brash misstep on the part of the former president. While in hindsight we may recall a somewhat monolithic era in our history where oblivious citizens worshipped its political and business leaders and their dogged pursuit for endless growth, anti-imperialist sentiments were rippling across activist and academic countermovements, building to a force that swallowed the unsuspecting empire whole. Millions of disenfranchised citizens woke from their stupor and took to the streets, marching in protest against the violences committed in this world and demanding an alternate future.

Trump's impeachment was in retrospect just one tremble in the eventual collapse of Western imperialism. The work of rebuilding alternatives was found in the various protest movements, which reignited the kind of collaborative radical democracy that had been suppressed by their romance with heroic leaders. Some marched for science, others marched for women, others still, marched for Black lives, until they quickly realised that their politics intersected. Together, they began to question 'leadership' as an all-powerful and all-consuming construct representing everything that is good and urgently needed in their society.

Defining Leadership by White Supremacy

Before the fall of Western imperialism, leadership seeped into all domains of social life. Under the expanding benedictions of political-, organisational-, community-, school-, group-, thought- and self-leaderships, it appeared that anything could be considered 'leadership'. Leadership, however, had always been a love song to whiteness. Built on the back of colonial subjugation, leadership was infused from the outset with idealisations of white people's moral and intellectual superiority that granted them the birthright to govern others.

The dominance of whiteness in leadership remained largely invisible for many decades, especially among those who partook in the benefits. In a testament to the power of wilful ignorance during this time, leadership studies produced an incessant series of visionary, charismatic, transformational, authentic, spiritual and servant leaderships, each touted as race-neutral while upholding whiteness as the leadership norm and exemplar.[1] Practitioners were developed, and they developed others, in the images of whiteness. Leadership development programmes venerated Western imperialist ideals of individual heroism, self-assurance and social impact, compelling its participants to fashion themselves after such fantasies of whiteness.[2]

The early formations of leadership studies took shape around the values of the European Enlightenment, which served to instate a rigid racial hierarchy.[3] At the centre of leadership stood the figure of the autonomous European man from whom leadership gloriously emanated. He represented 'orderliness, rationality and self-control' while the racial Others he colonised and enslaved represented 'chaos, irrationality, violence and the breakdown of self-regulation'.[4]

For decades, leadership studies remained oblivious to the growing field of critical race theory, which sought to interrogate white supremacy in our culture.[5] Across diverse disciplines such as legal studies, sociology, education, communication and media studies, and film and literature studies, critical race theorists collected comprehensive evidence of the racial oppression faced by people of colour, while providing them and their white allies with the tools to dismantle white supremacy.[6] Within this field, white supremacy refers to the centuries-old racialised social system comprising the 'totality of the social relations and practices that reinforce white privilege'.[7] White supremacy is systemic and operates in and through everyday racism to maintain a normalised orientation to 'white superiority, virtue, moral goodness and action'.[8]

Although critical race theory is a dynamic and multifaceted movement, one of its core tenets is that race is not a fixed biological marker, but socially constructed and politically contested.[9] Yet notwithstanding its social construction, 'race' remains salient in our social reality and bears real, material consequences for people's ongoing experiences with privilege and oppression.[10,11] Whiteness is therefore not a trait essentialised in white people, but a set of interlinked dimensions. Specifically, whiteness is simultaneously a location of racial privilege; a standpoint from which white people look at themselves, at others, and at society; and a collection of taken-for-granted social practices.[12]

The legacy of the white supremacist ideology in leadership scholarship was carefully guarded by Western positivistic science.[13] In this erstwhile approach to academic inquiry, race was only allowed to be studied in specific, socially sanctioned ways. Racial categories would typically be reduced to a demographic variable to measure its effects on leaders' behaviours and perceptions.[14] Grounded in influential theories at the time, most notably, social identity theory, leadership scholars argued that attributions and evaluations of leadership are dependent upon the collective, prototypical norms of the group.[15] They suggested that social minorities such as non-white people, who are not 'prototypical' members of society, would expect to face more challenges in persuading others of their legitimacy as leaders.[16] These popular explanations elided histories of colonial violence and persistent structural inequality in favour of psychologistic justifications. By suggesting that the insidious association of 'leadership' with white people was a 'natural', cognitive process, the scientists of the time were able to alleviate their racial guilt, yet nonetheless reinforce their racial power.

Alternative ways of knowing the racial Other were, for the most part, discounted by Western positivism as 'illegitimate' knowledge.[17] Humanising representations of people of colour were systematically marginalised from leadership scholarship. Attempts to interrogate white supremacy in the canonical journals of the day were ironically decried as 'biased' and 'ideological'. Whiteness remained firmly hinged to its privileged location as transparent, dominant and ordinary[18] so that white racial power was tantamount to rationality, objectivity and common sense, and the protection of this power became synonymous with science.

Leadership sustained whiteness through the everyday practices of normalisation, solipsism and ontological expansiveness.[19] Normalisation refers to the ways in which whiteness 'silently imposes itself as the standard by which social difference is to be known'.[20] Normalisation is seen in the way markers of race are only applied to non-white people in everyday discourse so that white people are not racially defined, which makes the hegemonic status of whiteness and its privileges seemingly invisible.[21] The normalisation of whiteness was cultivated through European imperialism and then sustained through the perceived prototypicality of white people as legitimate leaders.[22] Normalisation reinforces the powerful status occupied by white people as the human norm that affords them the claim to speak for the commonality of humanity when racially marked people can only speak for their race.[23] A white leader was therefore more readily perceived as representative of the whole of society and all its citizens, while non-white people were commonly seen as only fit (and predisposed) to serving the needs of their racial group.

Leadership studies during this time reproduced white normalisation by continually centring white subjects in the study of 'leadership'.[24] Scholars who conducted empirical research were rarely questioned during the academic peer-review process when they attempted to pass off white managers as 'leaders', yet they would often be instructed to reframe their study as being about 'professionals' when their research subjects were managers of colour.[25] 'Leadership' was evidently a prized form of capital that could only be granted to people who mustered enough racial power to lay claim to it. For these managers of colour, they also struggled to be seen as legitimate representatives by their own organisations. In tandem with the invisible white dominance in organisational research, managers of colour faced a series of resistive microaggressions,[26] such as being continually suspected of being 'biased' towards their own racial group.[27] Organisations were to be protectively guarded by white managers, whose governance was the only way to ensure leadership would be exercised for the 'greater good'.

White solipsism refers to a way of living as though only white people exist or matter.[28] Although the literal existence of people of colour is acknowledged, white solipsism only considers white values, interests and needs as important.[29] This practice often results in the inability of white people to form meaningful relationships with people of colour and underpins their abdication of responsibility for their effects on subdominant groups.[30] The habits of white solipsism could be seen in the branches of mainstream leadership studies that promoted 'women in leadership'. This single-axis focus on gender, while often well-intentioned, created the illusion that injustice in organisations only exists on the realm where white women are not afforded the same power and privilege as their male counterparts. Under the banner of gender equality, much of this research maintained a blindness towards the racial violence it perpetuated. Without a reflexive awareness of solipsistic practices, gender and leadership issues primarily upheld white needs and interests and drove social change on white terms.[31]

Ontological expansiveness is where 'white people tend to act and think as if all spaces – where geographical, psychical, linguistic, economic, spiritual, bodily or otherwise – are or should be available for them to move in and out of as they wish'.[32] Cultural appropriation is one form of white expansiveness, manifesting, for example, in the commodity fetishism of indigenous traditions to fill spiritual gaps in white hegemony.[33] Every few years, white leadership scholars would mine the far reaches of the empire for constructs like Ubuntu leadership or Daoist leadership in attempts to spice up[34] the normalised whiteness of leadership. Such theorisations through cultural appropriation were rarely grounded in an intimate understanding of or respect for the underlying philosophies but enabled a certain dilettante identity performance for the scholars to showcase their worldliness. In practising expansion, white people assume that they can and should exercise total mastery over all aspects of their environment.[35] White expansiveness saliently resonates with practices of leadership heroicism, where white leaders' intervention in organisational or social processes are largely treated as reflections of positive attributes such as visionary or transformational leadership and presumed to produce positive effects.[36]

Desecrating Leadership

There was a time when it seemed that anything and everything had become 'leadership'.[37] As Mats Alvesson and André Spicer observed, 'very different people – from CEOs to vicars to supermarket supervisors – suddenly [wanted] to identify themselves as "leaders", eager to do "leadership"'.[38] Leadership has now been desecrated. We have seen how the Western imperialist ideals of individual heroism, self-assurance and social impact glorified within leadership undergird decades of gradual social and environmental degradation. Leadership has become a dirty word.

Leadership cannot, and perhaps should not, be redeemed. The language of leadership has proven itself too vulnerable for corruption. It's a blank canvas on which we can paint beautiful, seductive images that capture our desires and compel us to market and sell leadership development programs.[39] It's an empty space where power can be exercised to decide whose interpretation of leadership matters most.[40]

Speaking just within the Anglophone world, we have at our disposal language that more precisely and accurately captures the activities that so-called 'leaders' do. Administration, coordination, collaboration, communication, supervision, team building and decision making may be more useful descriptors for the day-to-day practices of people whose work involves responsibility to others. Relinquishing broad-brush illusions of leadership may also allow us to name the activities conducted in governments, organisations and communities that may have been obfuscated by the romance with leadership, including domination, discrimination, exclusion and violence.

Anti-Racist Praxes

As we work together towards rebuilding the political, organisational and community practices that had once been co-opted by white supremacist renderings of 'leadership', we can return to the intellectual tools of critical race theory to illuminate our path. Leadership scholarship in the past defined the problem of diversity as the lack of leaders of colour – the lack of the Other in leadership.[41] This perpetuated the myth that the issue lay with people of colour. Their underrepresentation in leadership was due to their lack. 'If only people of colour had the self-confidence to get over racism and assert themselves as leaders', they would bemoan. The onus was placed on people of colour to improve their individual and collective capabilities to meet the norms of leadership.[42] Critical race theory in contrast attends to the discourses, structures and cultures constituting dominant notions of leadership. There are at least two approaches to dismantling the imperialist, white supremacist ideologies that shaped our social relations: redoing whiteness and abolishing whiteness.

Redoing Whiteness

Redoing whiteness requires us to reflexively interrogate the practices of whiteness and reinvent ways of doing whiteness differently.[43] This process involves subverting normalisation, solipsism and ontological expansiveness.

We can challenge white normalisation by exposing and raising awareness about the mechanisms by which white power and privilege are kept in place yet hidden from view.[44] The first step is to name whiteness where it exists. Entrenched discursive habits mean we may single out racialised individuals as 'black managers' or 'Asian managers', while white managers get to just be 'managers'.[45] If we agree that race matters in social life, then it needs to be called out in all cases of social practice and research.

Our racial grammar[46] may register the explicit designation of hegemonic identity categories as awkward or unnecessarily cumbersome. A study publicised simply as 'exploring how leaders practice gender inclusivity' may in fact be more precisely about 'how white middle-class able-bodied self-identified heterosexual cis-male managers demonstrate inclusivity towards white middle-class able-bodied self-identified heterosexual cis-female employees'. The universality (and grandiosity) of the former statement is diminished when otherwise invisible racial, class, dis/ability and sexual privileges are exposed.[47] It also sensitises us to how seemingly altruistic practices like gender inclusivity could in fact be exerting violences of racial, class, dis/ability and sexual power.

Whiteness imparts an invisible advantage to white men and women, yet few white leaders are called to question their whiteness or asked to justify their dominance in leadership positions.[48] In contrast, people of colour are continually queried about their racial identification in white-dominated nations. With diversity marked on their bodies,[49] leaders of colour navigate a precarious balance between being expected by their organisations and communities to stand for issues of diversity and multiculturalism[50], yet being regarded with suspicion about whose interests they represent. For example, managers who advocate for increased racial diversity in their organisations would be accused of being self-interested, surreptitiously scheming for a promotion or a higher salary through their attempts at leadership. Local councillors are targeted by the media to comment on issues of multiculturalism in the community, which reinforces the assumptions that racialised people are only interested in race and racialised people have no right to govern 'universal' issues like education or healthcare.[51]

When challenging white normalisation, we need to be cautious that naming white power and privilege does not simply become about recentring whiteness.[52] Calling out white power and privilege should be about exposing and disrupting racism, not fetishising whiteness. Aileen Moreton-Robinson observed how white feminists who wrote about their white privilege have a tendency to then recentre whiteness in their successive work.[53] Their one-off acknowledgement of white privilege then serves as an alibi against future racism. This ability to choose to disengage from race is an example of the racial privilege exercised by white scholars. To redo white normalisation, all scholars need to question 'how they come to, and what allows them to produce and write knowledge as deracialised subject/knowers'.[54]

White solipsism can be disrupted through the critical race tradition of counterstorytelling. Where leadership research reproduced the logic of racism by centring whiteness, future theorising has the potential to interrogate this logic by asserting self-defined and humanising accounts of subdominant groups. Marginalised people have always used counterstories to resist being 'swallowed up by the Eurocentric will to dominate'.[55] As our theorising turns to more reflexive explorations of its precise activities (coordinating, collaborating, communicating), we need to lay the groundwork for wide-scale scholarly resistance – epistemic disobedience[56] – against white supremacist ways of knowing.[57] Rather than indulge in comparative research where non-white subjects are examined in relation to their deviation from the white norm, non-white subjects should be allowed to stand centre stage from time to time. Empirical studies could take deep dives into the social practices of little-known groups, honouring the voices of its members, affirming their self-definitions and illuminating the nuances of their cultures.[58]

The habit of ontological expansiveness, however, reminds us that even in racially progressive practice, white scholars and leaders assumed it would be their rightful place to showcase marginalised groups and lead the efforts of their inclusion.[59] Although white allies have an important role to play in our ongoing project of racial equality, the magnetic pull back towards domination has been strengthened through our history of imperialism and racism. Redoing expansiveness means practising contraction: being smaller, softer and quieter.

Elaine Swan offers listening as a practice people positioned as white can cultivate to undo ontological expansiveness.[60] Following Tanja Dreher,[61] a politics of listening in relation to inequalities means learning to listen receptively – seeking ongoing permission to listen and shifting to the margins of discussions when that permission is granted. White people also need to learn to let go and be absent when their listening is not welcome.[62] Political listening is not about imposing one's need for empathy, therapy or friendship onto non-white people as though it is a feel-good panacea for white guilt.[63] Listening can in fact be risky, painful and discomforting, but indeed necessary for consciousness-raising to understand one's world from the point of view of those who have been harmed by it.[64] Listening as a form of radical white praxis is the opposite of expansiveness, requiring white people to learn how to be unobtrusive and unimportant.[65]

Within the trope of white benevolence,[66] there is an abiding tendency to venerate white people as saviours. Practising listening and other forms of white contraction would mean resisting the temptation to speak for the Other 'for their own good'. Even for white scholars who see themselves as genuinely inspired by Ubuntu or Daoist philosophies, they need to critically interrogate when it may not be their place to be cultural carriers. Even if white allies come from a place of good intent to raise the profile of non-white people, they need to acknowledge that not all counterstories may be for them to tell.

Abolishing Whiteness

Although there are tools to help us theorise the redoing of whiteness beyond an ideology of oppression, any interrogations of white supremacy would be remiss not to consider the provocations of New Abolitionism, self-proclaimed 'race traitors' who seek to 'study whiteness in order to abolish it'.[67] From the point of view of this project, whiteness without the habits of normalisation, solipsism and ontological expansiveness would cease to be whiteness at all. As one of its earliest proponents David Roediger puts it, 'it is not merely that whiteness is oppressive and false; it is that whiteness is *nothing but* oppressive and false'.[68] According to the abolitionists, whiteness itself has no biology or culture.[69] It is instead as Frankenberg's definition of whiteness contends, defined by its position of social dominance and sustained through its ongoing practice of racial oppression.[70] In James Baldwin's words, 'as long as you think that you are white, there is no hope for you'.[71] Without the privileges attached to whiteness, the white race would no longer exist.

The abolitionists believe that when those aligned with being white defect from this identification, they become free to realise themselves as other things, such as workers, youth, women or any other self-definitions they wish to explore. Would-be defectors need to 'break the laws of whiteness so flagrantly as to destroy the myth of white unanimity'.[72] This would mean challenging every manifestation of white supremacy, for example, by responding to an anti-black remark with the defiant retort, 'What makes you think I'm white?'[73,74]

According to New Abolitionists, we only need a determined congregation of people to disrupt whiteness through their visible rejection of its membership.[75] Although white people cannot completely relinquish their privileges, at least initially, by strenuously jeopardising their own abilities to draw on white privilege, a critical mass of race traitors have the potential to fracture the white race, 'and former whites, born again, will be able to take part, together with others, in building a new human community'.[76] Abolishing whiteness circumvents the tendency to venerate white saviours as good white anti-racists and instead calls for white people to become traitors to the white race.

Final Thoughts

Rejecting the ideologies of Western imperialism was a necessary first step in undoing white domination in the definitions and practices of 'leadership', but our work has only just begun. Challenging white supremacy requires ongoing work, grounded in a commitment to equality, justice and radical democracy, that disrupts entrenched white racial habits like normalisation, solipsism and ontological expansiveness. Mercifully, that work is not a lonely struggle or a burden to be silently shouldered by solitary saviours. Rather, it is a redemptive politics of solidarity. There are numerous approaches, and this chapter has offered just two of them: redoing whiteness and abolishing whiteness. Regardless of the approach we cultivate in our contexts of practice, we ought to be reminded that whiteness in the era of Western imperialism is inherently a practice of domination, oppression and violence. Its undoing is thus a joyous, emancipatory praxis where we may finally pick up the fragments of ourselves and our communities, broken apart by a centuries-old racial hierarchy, and make them whole again.

Notes

1 Liu and Baker, 2016.
2 Critical race examinations of leadership development are still in their infancy, but some exemplars can be found in education, see, for example, Blackmore (2010).
3 Kincheloe, Steinberg, Rodriguez & Chennault, 1998; Moreton-Robinson, 2000.
4 Kincheloe et al., 1998, p. 5.
5 Bell, 1980; Crenshaw, 1991; Delgado and Stefancic, 2012.
6 Bell, 1989; Chou and Choi, 2013.
7 Bonilla-Silva, 2006, p. 9.
8 Feagin, 2013, p. 10.
9 Omi and Winant, 1994.
10 Bonilla-Silva, 2006.
11 As Shannon Sullivan (2014, p. 14) states, 'ontologically speaking, there's no such thing as whiteness all by itself'. Our racial categorisations are necessarily cross-cut by gender, sexuality, class, religion and other identity categories, but whiteness is nevertheless valuable and necessary in many cases to name a particular system of power that has predominantly remained hidden.
12 Essed, 1991; Frankenberg, 1993; Hill, 2009; Sullivan, 2006; Sullivan, 2014.
13 Denzin, 2009.
14 Ospina and Foldy, 2009.
15 Hogg, 2001; van Knippenberg & Hogg, 2003; van Knippenberg, van Knippenberg, De Cremer & Hogg, 2004.
16 Hogg, 2001.
17 Taliaferro Baszile, 2015.
18 Nayak 2003, p. 173.
19 Clarke & Garner, 2010; Dyer, 1997; Frankenberg, 1993; Levine-Rasky, 2013; MacMullan, 2009; Nayak, 2003; Sullivan, 2006.
20 Levine-Rasky, 2013, p. 45.
21 Dyer, 1997; MacMullan, 2009.
22 Rosette, Leonardelli & Phillips, 2008. Peter McLaren (2000, p. 150) also puts it cogently when he describes whiteness as a universilising authority by which white subjects claim the right to speak on behalf of everyone who is non-white, while at the same time denying the agency and voice of non-white subjects. White normalisation is supported by the 'refusal to acknowledge how people are implicated in certain social relations of privilege and relations of domination and subordination'. Whiteness, then, is a form of 'social amnesia'.
23 Dyer, 1997.
24 Nkomo, 1992.
25 This observation is based on my own experiences and the anecdotes of other organisational race scholars.

26 Microaggressions are subtle, iterative acts that reinforce the marginalisation and subordination of people of colour, while taking a physical and psychological toll on them (Deitch et al., 2003; Pérez Huber & Solórzano, 2015; Pierce, 1974).
27 Liu, 2017.
28 Sullivan, 2006.
29 Sullivan, 2006.
30 Levine-Rasky, 2013.
31 Aileen Moreton-Robinson (2000) talks about how white patriarchy works to hide issues of racial power and privilege from white feminists so that their thinking, knowing and writing conforms with Western masculinist epistemology.
32 Sullivan, 2006, p. 10.
33 Donaldson, 1999.
34 I use this phrase in reference to bell hooks' (1992) essay, *Eating the Other*, in which she makes the observation that our culture has come to seek pleasure in the consumption of Otherness. Speaking to the commodification of racial difference, hooks (1992, p. 44) states that 'ethnicity becomes spice, seasoning that can liven up the dull dish that is mainstream white culture'.
35 Sullivan, 2006.
36 Bass, 1998; Nanus, 1995; Śliwa, Spoelstra, Sørensen & Land, 2012; Spoelstra & Ten Bos, 2011.
37 Alvesson & Sveningsson, 2003; Ford & Harding, 2007.
38 Alvesson & Spicer, 2012, p. 372.
39 Śliwa et al., 2012.
40 Kelly, 2014.
41 Blackmore, 2010.
42 This orientation is explored in the concept of post-racism (Bonilla-Silva, 2015; Lentin, 2016), which resonates with the concept of post-feminism, in that it is a neoliberal construction of structural equality as something primarily produced by and thus overcome by individuals.
43 The concept of redoing whiteness is grounded in parallel arguments about redoing gender, as theorised by Candace West and Don Zimmerman (2009).
44 Grimes, 2002.
45 Dyer, 1997; Grimes, 2001; Liu & Baker, 2016; Nkomo, 1992.
46 Bonilla-Silva, 2012.
47 Baca Zinn & Thorton Dill, 1996; Collins, 2000; Crenshaw, 1991; Yuval-Davis, 2006.
48 Blackmore, 2010.
49 Ahmed, 2009.
50 Ahmed & Swan, 2006.
51 Both these empirical examples are drawn from my study of Chinese Australian 'leaders' in business and government (Liu, 2017).
52 Blackmore, 2010.
53 Moreton-Robinson, 2000.
54 Moreton-Robinson, 2000, p. 351.
55 Taliaferro Baszile, 2015, p. 240.
56 Mignolo, 2009, p. 162.
57 Bell, 1995.
58 Denzin, 2009.
59 Sullivan, 2014.
60 Swan (2017) explores progressive white praxis.
61 Dreher, 2009.
62 Dreher, 2009.
63 Swan, 2017; see also Ahmed, 2008.
64 Swan 2017.

65 Dreher, 2009.
66 Blackmore, 2010; Haggis & Schech, 2000.
67 The core tenets of this radical political project have been articulated by Noel Ignatiev (1997). His own work on the history of Irish immigration in the United States, published in *How the Irish Became White* (1995), argues how the embracing of white supremacy among Irish-Americans (as primarily exercised through violence against African-Americans) underpinned Irish-Americans' so-called 'success' in the white republic.
68 Roediger, 1994, p. 13; emphasis in original.
69 Ignatiev, 1997.
70 Ignatiev, 1997.
71 From the film *The Price of the Ticket*. Roediger (1994) reflects that while this quote may seem more poetic than political for those who have struggled to even persuade white people to disarm racism, let alone abolish whiteness, a highly poetic politics may be what is exactly required to disrupt white resistance against antiracism.
72 Ignatiev, 1997, p. 5.
73 Ignatiev, 1997, p. 5.
74 A white-passing Russian co-author of mine has written about her experiences being 'tested' by white Australians for her loyalty to whiteness. She recounted how a racist joke would be made in her presence and her reaction carefully monitored. When she challenged the racism, she became marked as the Other and marginalised as 'too foreign' to understand the normalised practices of Australian whiteness. Katya shares her experiences in our joint paper (Liu & Pechenkina, 2016).
75 Ignatiev, 1997.
76 Ignatiev, 1997, p. 6.

References

Ahmed, S. (2008). The politics of good feeling. *Australian Critical Race and Whiteness Studies Association*, 4(1), 1–18.

Ahmed, S. (2009). Embodying diversity: Problems and paradoxes for Black feminists. *Race Ethnicity and Education*, 12(1), 41–52.

Ahmed, S. & Swan, E. (2006). Introduction: Doing diversity. *Policy Futures in Education*, 4(2), 96–100.

Alvesson, M. & Spicer, A. (2012). Critical leadership studies: The case for critical performativity. *Human Relations*, 65(3), 367–390.

Alvesson, M. & Sveningsson, S. (2003). Managers doing leadership: The extraordinarization of the mundane. *Human Relations*, 56(12), 1435–1459.

Baca Zinn, M. & Thorton Dill, B. (1996). Theorizing difference from multiracial feminism. *Feminist Studies*, 22(2), 321–331.

Bass, B. M. (1998). *Transformational Leadership: Industry, Military, and Educational Impact*. Mahwah, NJ: Lawrence Erlbaum.

Bell, D. A. (1989). *And We Are Not Saved: The Elusive Quest for Racial Justice*. New York, NY: Basic Books.

Bell, D. A. (1995). Who's afraid of critical race theory? *University of Illinois Law Review*, 1995, 893–910.

Blackmore, J. (2010). 'The other within': Race/gender disruptions to the professional learning of white educational leaders. *International Journal of Leadership in Education*, 13(1), 45–61.

Bonilla-Silva, E. (2006). *Racism Without Racists: Color-blind Racism and the Persistence of Racial Inequality in the United States.* Lanham: Rowman & Littlefield Publishers.

Bonilla-Silva, E. (2012). The invisible weight of whiteness: The racial grammar of everyday life in contemporary America. *Ethnic and Racial Studies,* 35(2), 173–194.

Bonilla-Silva, E. (2015). The structure of racism in color-blind, 'post-racial' America. *American Behavioral Scientist,* 59(11), 1358–1376.

Chou, R. S. & Choi, S. (2013). And neither are we saved: Asian Americans' elusive quest for racial justice. *Sociology Compass,* 7(10), 841–853.

Clarke, S. & Garner, S. (2010). *White Identities: A Critical Sociological Approach.* London: Pluto Press.

Collins, P. H. (2000). *Black Feminist Thought: Knowledge, Consciousness, and the Politics of Empowerment* (2nd ed.). Hoboken, NJ: Taylor & Francis.

Crenshaw, K. (1991). Mapping the margins: Intersectionality, identity politics, and violence against women of color. *Stanford Law Review,* 43(6), 1241–1299.

Deitch, E. A., Barsky, A., Butz, R. M., Chan, S., Brief, A. P. & Bradley, J. (2003). Subtle yet significant: The existence and impact of everyday racial discrimination in the workplace. *Human Relations,* 56(11), 1299–1324.

Delgado, R. & Stefancic, J. (Eds.) (2012). *Critical Race Theory: An Introduction* (2nd ed.). New York, NY: New York University Press.

Denzin, N. K. (2009). *Qualitative Inquiry Under Fire: Toward a New Paradigm Dialogue.* Walnut Creek, CA: Left Coast Press.

Donaldson, L. E. (1999). On medicine women and white shame-ans: New Age Native Americanism and commodity fetishism as pop culture feminism. *Signs: Journal of Women in Culture and Society,* 24(3), 677–696.

Dreher, T. (2009). Eavesdropping with permission: The politics of listening for safer speaking spaces. *Borderlands E-Journal,* 8(1), 1–21.

Dyer, R. (1997). *White.* London: Routledge.

Feagin, J. R. (2013). *The white racial frame: Centuries of racial framing and counterframing.* New York, NY: Routledge.

Ford, J. & Harding, N. (2007). Move over management: We are all leaders now. *Management Learning,* 38(5), 475–493.

Frankenberg, R. (1993). *White Women, Race Matters: The Social Construction of Whiteness.* Minneapolis: University of Minnesota Press.

Grimes, D. S. (2001). Putting our own house in order: Whiteness, change and organization studies. *Journal of Organizational Change Management,* 14(2), 132–149.

Grimes, D. S. (2002). Challenging the status quo? Whiteness in the diversity management literature. *Management Communication Quarterly,* 15(3), 381–409.

Haggis, J. & Schech, S. (2000). Meaning well and global good manners: Reflections on white women feminist cross cultural praxis. *Australian Feminist Studies,* 15(3), 387–399.

Hogg, M. A. (2001). A social identity theory of leadership. *Personality and Social Psychology Review,* 5(3), 184–200.

hooks, bell. (1992). Eating the other. In *Black Looks: Race and Representation* (pp. 21–39). Boston: South End Press.

Ignatiev, N. (1995). *How the Irish Became White.* New York, NY: Routledge.

Ignatiev, N. (1997). The point is not to interpret Whiteness but to abolish it. Retrieved May 6, 2016, from http://racetraitor.org/abolishthepoint.html

Kelly, S. (2014). Towards a negative ontology of leadership. *Human Relations*, 67(8), 905–922.

Kincheloe, J. L., Steinberg, S. R., Rodriguez, N. M. & Chennault, R. E. (Eds.) (1998). *White Reign: Deploying Whiteness in America*. New York, NY: Palgrave Macmillan.

Lentin, A. (2016). Racism in public or public racism: Doing anti-racism in 'post-racial' times. *Ethnic and Racial Studies*, 39(1), 33–48.

Levine-Rasky, C. (2013). *Whiteness Fractured*. Farnham, UK: Ashgate Publishing.

Liu, H. (2017). Undoing whiteness: The Dao of anti-racist diversity practice. *Gender, Work and Organization*, 24(5), 457–471.

Liu, H. & Baker, C. (2016). White knights: Leadership as the heroicisation of whiteness, *Leadership*, 12(4), 420–448.

Liu, H. & Pechenkina, E. (2016). Staying quiet or rocking the boat? An autoethnography of organisational visual white supremacy. *Equality Diversity and Inclusion*, 35(3), 186–204.

MacMullan, T. (2009). *Habits of Whiteness: A Pragmatist Reconstruction*. Bloomington, IN: Indiana University Press.

McLaren, P. (2000). Unthinking whiteness: Rearticulating diasporic practice. In P. P. Trifonas (Ed.), *Revolutionary Pedagogies* (pp. 140–173). New York, NY: Routledge.

Mignolo, W. (2009). Epistemic disobedience: Independent thought and decolonial freedom. *Theory, Culture and Society*, 26(7–8), 159–181.

Moreton-Robinson, A. (2000). Troubling business: Difference and whiteness within feminism. *Australian Feminist Studies*, 15(33), 343–352.

Nanus, B. (1995). *Visionary Leadership*. San Francisco: Jossey-Bass.

Nayak, A. (2003). *Race, Place and Globalization: Youth Cultures in a Changing World*. Oxford: Berg.

Nkomo, S. M. (1992). The emperor has no clothes: Rewriting 'race in organizations'. *The Academy of Management Review*, 17(3), 487–513.

Omi, M. & Winant, H. (1994). *Racial Formation in the United States: From the 1960s to the 1990s* (2nd ed.). New York, NY: Routledge.

Ospina, S. & Foldy, E. (2009). A critical review of race and ethnicity in the leadership literature: Surfacing context, power and the collective dimensions of leadership. *The Leadership Quarterly*, 20(6), 876–896.

Pérez Huber, L. & Solórzano, D. G. (2015). Visualizing everyday racism: Critical Race Theory, visual microaggressions, and the historical image of Mexican banditry. *Qualitative Inquiry*, 21(3), 223–238.

Pierce, C. (1974). Psychiatric problems of the black minority. In S. Arieti (Ed.), *American Handbook of Psychiatry* (pp. 512–523). New York, NY: Basic Books.

Roediger, D. (1994). *Towards the Abolition of Whiteness*. London: Verso.

Rosette, A. S., Leonardelli, G. J. & Phillips, K. W. (2008). The white standard: Racial bias in leader categorization. *Journal of Applied Psychology*, 93(4), 758–777.

Śliwa, M., Spoelstra, S., Sørensen, B. M. & Land, C. (2012). Profaning the sacred in leadership studies: A reading of Murakami's *A Wild Sheep Chase*. *Organization*, 20(6), 860–880.

Spoelstra, S. & Ten Bos, R. (2011). Leadership. In M. Painter-Morland & R. Ten Bos (Eds.), *Business Ethics and Continental Philosophy* (pp. 181–198). Cambridge: Cambridge University Press.

Sullivan, S. (2006). *Revealing Whiteness: The Unconscious Habits of Racial Privilege.* Bloomington, IN: Indiana University Press.

Sullivan, S. (2014). *Good White People: The Problem with Middle-Class White Anti-Racism.* Albany, NY: SUNY.

Swan, E. (2017). What are white people to do? Listening, challenging ignorance, generous encounters and the 'not yet' as diversity research praxis. *Gender, Work and Organization*, 24(5), 547–563.

Taliaferro Baszile, D. (2015). Rhetorical revolution: Critical race counterstorytelling and the abolition of white democracy. *Qualitative Inquiry*, 21(3), 239–249.

van Knippenberg, D. & Hogg, M. A. (2003). A social identity model of leadership effectiveness in organizations. *Research in Organizational Behavior*, 25, 243–295.

van Knippenberg, D., van Knippenberg, B., De Cremer, D. & Hogg, M. A. (2004). Leadership, self, and identity: A review and research agenda. *The Leadership Quarterly*, 15(6), 825–856.

West, C. & Zimmerman, D. H. (2009). Accounting for doing gender. *Gender & Society*, 23(1), 112–122.

Yuval-Davis, N. (2006). Intersectionality and feminist politics. *European Journal of Women's Studies*, 13(3), 193–209.

8 Films as Archives of Leadership Theories

The Terminator Film Franchise

Nancy Harding

I imagine a far distant future from where I can look back at our present as if it is the history of our descendants, as indeed it will be. What might those descendants learn about leadership from our present, and may those lessons become available to us through this thought experiment?

Nothing has survived the destruction of leadership texts, save a few scattered relics that suggest many more must have existed. Films from the second half of the 20th century have survived, and there appear to be sufficient references to leadership in these to allow us to develop an understanding of how leadership was understood by our ancients. Indeed, films may tell us more about leadership than academic texts: commentators of the time accused academic texts of being inadequate because they privileged rationality and thus failed to account for subjectivities and emotional perspectives.[1] As Hassard and Holliday argued, 'popular culture offers more dramatic, more intense and more dynamic representations of organization than management texts'.[2] Relatedly, debates in the first two decades of the 21st century critiqued leadership and management researchers' claims to be writing something that was scientific. They were engaged in the craft of writing fiction, it was argued, for, as Rhodes and Brown observed, 'notionally "factual" accounts of research ... do not tend to accept or recognize their role in constructing the realities that they purport to represent'.[3] Indeed, organisations, the very stuff of the discipline of leadership, were argued to be fictions 'in the sense that through intentional acts of pretence, of actively imagining an organization, we are able to produce some kind of understanding of what organizations are. Fiction is in this sense not simply a heuristic for understanding organizations, but it is the core, or constitutive, process through which organizations are imagined and made sense of, and that shapes in a very real sense how people act around them'.[4] The boundaries between 'real' and 'fictional' were under severe challenge, it would seem, in that time before leadership texts were destroyed.

We understand now that our ancestors followed our even more ancient forebears, the Ancient Greeks, in articulating major cultural tensions through the medium of drama.[5] Where the Ancient Greeks had perhaps only two major forms of story-telling, the tragedy and the comedy, by the 20th century, many genres of story-telling had evolved. Extant texts from the period suggest that one in particular, science fiction, or Sci-Fi, encouraged dramatists to engage in the use of their imaginations to allow 'bigger truths' to speak through their work. Sci-Fi untethered authors from the binds of reality and allowed them to imagine worlds where the laws of physics, alongside numerous other laws, did not apply. Their stories, on the one hand, were 'surface' representations arising from imaginations set free to wander at will, but on the other hand, there were deeper truths discernible in them. What can be found there is what various commentators of the time called the 'cultural unconscious',[6] or what a theorist of the psyche, Bollas, called the 'unthought known'.[7] That is, this was a culture in which people both as individuals and collectives were believed to have an 'unconscious' that informed and influenced their actions in ways of which they were unaware. The 'cultural unconscious' referred to a society's foundational stories that were buried so deeply beneath the sedimented layers of dead metaphors, myths and other stories that they could not be told in language. However, they burst through in multitudes of ways, informing and, to a certain extent, governing, everyday practices. Sigmund Freud,[8] for example, 'invented' – or was it that he remembered, or looked inside himself and found the story hidden in his own desire? – a myth of the primeval father, a man so powerful and cruel to his sons that they murdered and subsequently ate him. Guilt drove them to erect a totem in his honour. This, Freud argued, was the origin of religion, with the need to appease that slain father pushing up from the unconscious into everyday religious observance. Novels, films and dramas were forums through which such foundational stories could erupt into conscious thought. That is, people 'knew' deeper truths (the unthought known) but needed mechanisms to bring them into conscious thought. Films in general, but Sci-Fi in particular, articulated eruptions from the unconscious of 'the ego's era',[9] that era when the individual regarded itself as a sun around which all others' egos orbited.[10] Sometimes an artist might deliberately attempt to voice certain ideas but as often as not, it was believed, the culture, or zeitgeist, or discourses, spoke through cultural artefacts such as films. It was the role of the thinker to analyse the entrails of these artefacts to disinter what was hidden beneath the surface account.

Science fiction films are particularly useful for our purpose of rebuilding theories of leadership because they are awash with depictions of leaders, and so they offer remarkable resources for understanding how leadership was envisioned (if not practised) in the early 21st century. But, as the previous discussion suggests, it would be an error to think of these films as presenting straightforward depictions of leadership. They did not provide direct, easily accessible descriptions of topics but rather often showed them obliquely or hermeneutically, as subtexts almost hidden beneath dominant texts. We know this from remnants of other texts from that period that writers in the late 20th and early 21st centuries called 'the Anthroposcene'. These texts argued that films played a far more complicated role than 'mere' entertainment. Fictional narratives more generally were advocated as a resource for making sense of organisations[11] but, beyond this, films were understood to sometimes directly influence 'knowledge'. Films made at the time for family entertainment by the Disney Corporation were argued to have provided populations with an understanding of the Middle Ages that was palpably inaccurate but appeared to be historical truth to cinema-going audiences.[12] Sometimes films buttressed the status quo: Disney sought to perpetuate capitalism,[13] and science fiction was accused of perpetuating a gender order in which women were weak and subservient second-class citizens.[14] Furthermore, films (as an aspect of popular culture) were understood to actively influence the everyday world of work: popular culture, it was argued, not only re-presented but *shaped* actual behaviours in workplaces.[15] It achieved this through its provision of representations of working life, guidance on how to respond, and ideas about how work should be conducted. Cinema, as Cooper outlined,[16] provided the mechanism that made 20th/21st century thinking possible. Quoting Merlin Donald and Gianni Vattimo,[17] Cooper argued that cinema should be understood as the 'machinery' of 'the hybrid modern mind' that *performs* the social and cultural mind. That is, cinema was not just the communication of reality but its expression and performance. Cinema was reality itself: it represented life and life represented itself as cinema.

The merit of exploring films of that era to rebuild a theory of leadership cannot therefore be gainsaid: we enter into the thought processes of leadership theorists of the period if we explore cinema's articulation of what leadership could mean. If we follow the analytical thought processes of that time, then we can use the ancient film archive to understand how leadership and cinema each informed the other, with cinematic representations mimetic of leaders who modelled themselves on those very representations.

But, to emphasise, to understand the work that films did in constructing leadership requires far more than a superficial reading of their stories. Film theorists of the time understood that these cultural artefacts articulated major concerns through putting them into visual, aural and/or verbal forms that had several levels, all nested in each other, with the visible, comprehensible, first layer of a story disguising second and other layers.[18] Film deconstruction was a process in which the 'obvious' account, or the story immediately available to an audience, had to be peeled back and a process of hermeneutic reading then had to be undertaken to allow identification of other accounts that showed how the celluloid image articulated impossible desires and inarticulable fears. For example, 'zombie apocalypse' and 'slasher' movies, popular with teenage audiences in the last quarter of the 20th century, articulated the dysfunctionality of nuclear families.[19] Gender theorists found in films the mechanisms through which women were both subordinated and constituted as the sex that *should be* subordinate to men.[20] That is, women appeared as protagonists in stories but, secondly, at a deeper level, their presence was one that invited the male gaze, so that, thirdly, women learned that to be 'a woman' required that they become creatures who existed to be looked at.[21] War films encapsulated the fragility of masculinity even though, superficially, they lauded its seemingly inviolable strengths.[22] With regard to science fiction, it was argued at the time that Sci Fi was just as false, and just as true, as organisation science.[23] Sci Fi films offered not just the escapism of a story but also acute observations of contemporary organisational reality. That is, they could be read firstly as adventure stories, but secondly the presence of organisations in these films meant Sci Fi also offered 'often quite detailed interrogations of what organisations do – and how these practices might be resisted'.[24] What they were represented as doing was reprehensible – the pursuit of profit above all other considerations was shown, in film after film, to lead to the destruction of the humanity in the human. Thirdly, films also articulated deeper desires, often unspoken ones, about organisational life. They allowed, for example, a dreaming of an impossible escape from the mundanity of the workplace quotidian.[25]

In this report to the post-leadership world, I will follow this layered process of analysing a film. My focus is the first three of the Terminator series of films, referred to from now on as T1 (released in 1984), T2 (1991) and T3 (2003) respectively. Attempts to resuscitate what was a lucrative franchise in Terminators 4 and 5 failed because the films, although profitable, were poorly received by critics and are, frankly, tedious and add nothing to the analysis, so I will not explore them here. I will firstly describe the surface stories the films recount, then, secondly, will explore what they ostensibly say about organisations and how they laud leaders and leadership. That will lead me to an exploration of what these films tell us about followers who are, of course, an inherent aspect of leadership. My interpretation suggests that our ancients saw leaders and leadership as the means by which organisations could be resisted and, ideally, overthrown. At the same time, they suggested that to be a follower to those very leaders was to be put in a life-threatening situation where one's responsibility for protecting the leader could, and very possibly would, lead to one's own annihilation. I conclude by bringing these two somewhat contradictory analyses together.

Terminator: First Layer – The Story

The Terminator series imagines a post-apocalyptic future when the vast majority of the human race has been wiped out by a global defence network, Skynet, built by Cyberdyne Systems. Skynet has become self-aware and, perceiving all humans as a threat to global security, seeks to exterminate them. It achieves this through triggering nuclear Armageddon. Each film has four main protagonists. The first is John Connor, a leader of the resistance in the post-apocalyptic world. In the first film, he appears in the pre-apocalyptic world only as a foetus, in T2 as a teenager, and in T3 as a grown man trying to escape his destiny. The second major character is Sarah Connor, John's mother. She does not appear in T3, having died, the storyline said, of leukaemia. The other two main protagonists are beings from the post-apocalyptic world, in which Skynet has been able to develop time travel. One of these beings is sent back in time to protect John Connor and another to eradicate him. In T1, the Terminator, played by body-builder, actor and, subsequently, politician, Arnold Schwarzenegger, has to kill John Connor's mother so that he can never be born; in T2, the aim is to kill the teenage Connor, and in T3, the plan is to assassinate as many of the people who were to become resistance fighters as possible. In each film, the killer is a cyborg-like, super-powerful killing machine. In T1, Schwarzenegger is one of those seemingly indestructible assassins, but in T2 and T3, his role alters dramatically: he becomes a protector rather than a slayer. Schwarzenegger's change of allegiance, from destroyer to protector, is accounted for by the type of cyborg of which he is an example of having become outdated as Skynet built superior killing machines. The cyborg played by Schwarzenegger is reprogrammed by the resistance as a protector (who must not kill humans). In T1, John Connor's protector is a human soldier sent back by the future John Connor to protect the woman who will become his mother. Sarah and the soldier fall for each other, resulting in her pregnancy – the soldier that John Connor sent back to save his mother is his father.

The story arc of T1 focuses solely on the protection of Sarah Connor. That the soldier sent back from the future by John Connor is John Connor's father, so John Connor could not have existed without his having been able to send his biological father back in time, is a time-travel philosophical riddle that the film avoids exploring. In T2, the narrative is concerned with the attempts of Sarah, the teenage John and the now-protective Terminator to prevent Cyberdyne Systems from developing Skynet. They discover the identity of the engineer responsible for its development. T2 repeats T1's strategy of trying to prevent the future through changing the conditions that made it possible in the past, but this time it is Sarah who sets out to kill the engineer. In a fine scene that encapsulates the deontological trolley-man dilemma – can it ever be ethical to kill even if an act of murder would save many other lives? – Sarah struggles with the enormity of killing another human whose death might save billions of lives. Saved, the engineer reveals that he has reverse-engineered a limb of the first terminator, the only part of it not destroyed at the denouement of T1. The second time-travelling conundrum (there are others) is encountered in this moment: the future Armageddon is made possible only by something that exists after that Armageddon has occurred. The group set out to destroy that limb, and in a shoot-out, the engineer dies but he is able to destroy Skynet in his final moments. Armageddon has been avoided. In the midst of all this, there are many fight and chase scenes involving the shape-shifting, cold and emotionless terminator sent from the future with the order to kill.

T2 ends with a sigh of relief: Armageddon has been avoided. In T3, this is shown to be a mistake: Armageddon has been deferred but is unavoidable. Sarah Connor is now dead, of leukaemia. There is a new female protagonist, Kate, who will become John Connor's wife. Schwarzenegger, Connor and Kate battle against a female terminator whose task is to destroy as many future resistance fighters as possible. This seems to require long, extended chase scenes that, to this viewer at least, are tedious and repetitive. One leads them eventually to the mausoleum where Sarah Connor's coffin is stored: her body is not in it because she had arranged for the casket to be filled instead with a large cache of lethal weapons. The trio's task now is to try to dissuade Kate's father, who is chairman of the US Joint Chiefs of Staff, from activating Skynet. They are too late. With war imminent, they set off to try to get to a site where, John and Kate believe, Skynet's core is located. After chases and battles between the Terminator and its more technologically advanced opponent, the Terminator eventually sacrifices itself as it helps John and Kate enter the bunker they have been seeking. But it is a nuclear fall-out shelter. Armageddon begins. John, safe in the bunker, starts to take command of the survivors who contact him.

These three films are rollicking stories, able to keep restless teenage grandsons glued to their seats while their academic grandparent gets caught up in analysing their subplots. But on the surface at least reports of the time suggested there was little new about them apart from impressive developments in computer animation: they were traditional chase films of the period, involving a Manichean struggle between heroes and villains. Nevertheless, these films deserve a deeper reading for they touch on deep philosophical issues signalled only implicitly on the screen. It is perhaps no surprise that the internet in the early 21st century was awash with discussions of the films' philosophy. A few examples will suffice. It is existentialist, one academic blogger reported, because it preaches the message that we are in charge of making our own futures.[26] It explored what it is to be human, wrote another.[27] Academic texts were equally enthusiastic about exploring the Terminator series of films for ways of analysing what was then the present. T1 and T2 diagnose changes and stabilities in masculinities, argued Jeffords,[28] or problematise Cartesian and other dualisms such as that of gender,[29] or force humankind to face its own destiny as one in which it may no longer exist,[30] a trope repeated several times in discussions of Sci-Fi.[31] Terminator, in a similar fashion to other cultural artefacts in our ancient film archive, including films such as *Bladerunner* and Sci-Fi television series such as *Battlestar Galactica* (2004) and *Humans* (2015), interrogated how the human could be defined: can a 'machine' be(come) human, or a human a machine?[32] That is, science fiction provoked deep philosophical questions in the late 20th and early 21st centuries. However, I have been unable to find any discussions of Sci-Fi and leadership, even though leadership is represented over and over in Sci-Fi films, so I turn now to exploring what theories of leadership can be discerned in the Terminator series of films.

Terminator: Second Layer (1) – The Leader

I am now going to peel away that first layer, the straightforward recounting of the films' storylines, and explore their implicit theory about leaders and leadership. The analysis of this section leads to an understanding that leadership was understood to be concerned with the protection of people from the ravages imposed by organisations.

The organisations that feature in Terminator are gigantic, faceless, inhuman destroyers. Cyberdene Systems and the military-industrial complex more generally are organisations whose sole pursuit was described as the building of weapons that countries could use to wipe out each other's populations. It is hard, today, to think that humanity could be so bent on its own destruction but these films captured a then very real fear that, through their own aggression, human beings could wipe each other from the face of the Earth. But the films suggest that the ordinary, everyday individual was not hell-bent on such an unimaginable pursuit. They show people enjoying themselves in bars, going on dates, working in mundane jobs, raising children, selling petrol and being generally concerned with their own minor role in making the world go round. Some people are shown doing their jobs, as police officers, nurses or psychiatrists. They have no role in the wider scheme of things, only in keeping things going. Their ties to the wider organisation seem tenuous at best – they do the jobs they have been hired to do, in the ways they have learned how to do them.

It is when the films peer into the more senior echelons that the vileness of corporations is seen. Organisations are represented as juggernauts that are beyond the control of individuals. The films show that some form of brainwashing, or zombification, happens to those in the senior echelons of organisations – the collective leadership is dysfunctional, able to set in train processes that they then have no power to control or contain. They are powerful and powerless at the same time.

This image of organisations is perhaps exemplified in the mysterious post-Armageddon organisation that can develop time travel and break other rules of physics by developing metal that can melt and form itself into shapes that mimic the last thing it has touched. Nothing of this corporation is ever shown in T1, T2 or T3, save for its robotic foot-soldiers stamping out the life of any human being they encounter, and the dread emissaries it sends back in time to kill John Connor. The trajectory of the films' stories is governed by this mysterious, faceless organisation that is bent on eradicating the human race that begat it. In the idiom of the day, the films portray a gigantic Oedipal struggle in which the metallic offspring seeks to overthrow its fleshy progenitor and take possession of the Earth.

This, the Terminator series tell us, is the reason why leadership is needed: to protect innocent individuals from faceless corporations. It also tells us the form that that leadership should take: it should be embodied in the shape of a heroic individual, a person with a face and a name whose destiny is predetermined and who will be tested to destruction. John Connor is destined for the greatness of leadership and for the severe demands it will bring. He has no choice in this: his path has been carved out for him since before his conception. He, this named person with a face, will protect the population against *faceless*, out-of-control organisations.

We have uncovered texts from the period that argued certain popular mass media forms of entertainment articulated populations' loathing for their employers, offered them a form of wish fulfilment through denigrating companies, and allowed them to dream of an end to the futility of lives lived at the behest of a management that served no purpose other than to maximise profit.[33] In the Terminator series, we see something deeper than this frustration of being reduced to the status of unthinking automata that exist only to achieve the organisations' purpose. That is, these films articulate a deep unease bordering on terror of lives being in the control of over-mighty, faceless corporations that can make all their staff expendable.

We do not see these corporations, as I noted previously, but they are embodied in the Terminators sent from the future. Their faces are expressionless and emotionless. Although they can mimic the human, they are inhuman. They have an objective and they pursue that objective heedless of any other considerations. They are beyond the power of any ordinary human being's resistance; humans seem almost totally impotent against them. They cannot be changed or destroyed. They are destructive and their aim is to destroy you, the long-ago viewer of these films.

This suggests how dire must have been the lives of working people in the early 21st century. The films are not documentaries, so we cannot read them as descriptions of reality. All we can do is interrogate the reasons why they had such an appeal to so many people, and I suggest those reasons lie in their articulating the sheer desperation of mundane working lives in this period.

But they also offer a form of wish fulfilment, because they say there *is* a way out of this mess. This is through the leadership of a hero, John Connor, who will lead a rising against these destructive corporations. This will result in their overthrow and the flowering of a new Garden of Eden where work has meaning because it nourishes the human race rather than being used to till the fields of humankind's exploitation.

So I offer this as the theory of leaders and leadership that circulated in the early 21st century. The Terminator series, I have argued, contains a theory of leadership that can be disinterred through exploring it as an articulation of the inarticulate desires of the working masses. This theory argues that the films show the existence of deep desires for a leader who will lead a rebellion against overly powerful and utterly exploitative corporations. These corporations lack a human face; they are known for their effects (reducing workers to profit-making opportunities) but appear so gargantuan that there is no way to evade or challenge them. There is no-one inside the organisation who challenges them: organisations are leader-free territory with everyone above the level of ordinary worker brainwashed into conforming with the organisation's requirements. Leaders must come from outside, heroes who will lead the rebellion and thus free workers from the destruction wrought on them every day in the world of work.

In sum, this ancient theory of leadership argued that leaders are followed because they *oppose* the organisation.

Terminator: Second Layer (2) – A Theory of Followership

It is difficult to conceive of any theory of leadership that does not have an accompanying theory of followership: the two are inevitably intertwined and mutually dependent. I will suggest that the theory of followership contained in the Terminator films is quite ambivalent. Firstly, it is one that regards followers as superior to leaders: they are strong whilst leaders are vulnerable and must be protected by followers. Secondly, this task of protecting the leader gives the *raison d'etre* or very identity of the follower. It arises from a blind belief in the leader: on the skimpiest of evidence save prognostications about a much-to-be-feared future, individuals abandon their identities and become followers. Thirdly, the films argue that the position of follower is one that is both inherently dangerous and corrupting.

The vulnerability of leaders underpins the entire story arc of these films, such that the follower has to become the leader's protector. Followers exist only for this purpose, and in doing that service, they become expendable. A recap of the story in T1, T2 and T3 illuminates this. T1 opens with two creatures arriving, naked, from what seems like outer space. One of these is a cyborg, the Terminator, and the other a fragile human soldier who will impregnate the future leader's mother. After doing that duty, he will die. Everyone else who might have protected Sarah Connor, and thus the as-yet-unborn future leader, is killed by the Terminator: her friends, her family, her flatmates, all are exterminated. The Terminator, played by Schwarzenegger, undergoes a damascene conversion in between T1 and T2: he returns in T2 as the protector/follower of the leader, John Connor, as he does again in T3, but in both T2 and T3 Schwarzenegger's character dies, sacrificing itself so that John Connor (and thus, we are told, humankind itself) can live. Along the way, numerous other characters who might threaten the leader's future are exterminated: hospital staff, police officers and innocent bystanders, amongst others. These are not followers, but through coming into the orbit of John Connor they die. It seems that leadership was understood to have lethal implications for those who came into contact with it, but because the leader was so vulnerable and needed protection, the followers, who believed totally in the future seemingly foretold for this leader, had no option save to gather around and join the fight. To be a follower was to be blindly faithful and in jeopardy.

The most interesting of all the followers/protectors is Sarah Connor, the mother. Her body is the vessel through which the leader will arrive, but the films portray her as far more than a passive container. In T1, the leader is little more than an idea, a being yet to be born who must be protected at all costs. The mother is persuaded of the accuracy of the news that she will bear the future saviour of humankind; she subsequently turns herself into a warrior and, ultimately, into armaments, to protect her child. Our first sight of her in T1 is of a curly haired young woman interested in enjoying herself, but by the opening scenes of T2, she has transmogrified. Our first sight of her in T2 is of her doing body-building exercises, her body rippling with muscles that are emphasised by the white singlet she is wearing. Everything she does is motivated by the protection of her son, the future saviour. The stripping away of everything that is superfluous to this aim reaches its climax in T3 where the actual human being does not appear at all. The audience is told that she has died of leukaemia. It is shown her coffin. The casket falls to the ground; its lid opens. Leaning forward perhaps in eschatological curiosity, the audience expects to see her skeleton but what pours out is not bones but a cache of weapons. Rather than lay her body down to rest in death, the mother/follower/protector has turned flesh into pure fighting machine, devoid of any agency save the intent of being used to protect the leader.

But that is in T3. In T2, the young woman to whom we had been introduced in T1 has become a fighter. She is herself now a killing machine, which is somewhat ironic given that the Terminator, protector now rather than eradicator, has vowed not to take human life. She will challenge anyone who threatens the life of her son, the future leader. Except, that is, when she comes face to face with the man who is building the lethal system that will destroy humanity. If she killed him at that moment, she would change the trajectory taking the world to its mortal destiny. Yet she cannot. I referred earlier to the moment where she leans over the recumbent, scared scientist, his family watching on, ready to pull the trigger, as an enactment of the deontological trolley dilemma, but this scene can be interpreted in another way. If life continues as normal, if there is no Armageddon, then her son will not achieve his destiny, he will not become leader. Instead, his life will be normal, perhaps average, and she has been preparing him for something far higher. If she saves humanity, then she will sacrifice the emergence of her son as leader. The leader has to be protected at all costs, even if that cost is the destruction of almost the entire human race. His destiny is paramount. She thus sacrifices herself, becoming someone totally different from who she might have been if she was not doomed to be the mother of the leader.

The theory of followers and followership contained within the Terminator films is thus one of the follower as a disciple whose conviction concerning the need to protect the leader has the status of a religious conviction. Annihilation threatens anyone who becomes a follower, whether it is the annihilation of the material body or of the immaterial self. It seems that followership required the death of the ego, agency and any conception of a 'self'.

Conclusion

This, then, is one of the theories of leaders, leadership, followers and follower-ship circulating in the late 20th and early 21st centuries, as encapsulated in the highly popular 'Terminator' series of science fiction films. Leaders and leader-ship were understood to be vital to resisting, if not overcoming, organisations whose excesses wreaked chaos and imposed despair upon the masses. This was the era of the Anthropocene when global populations were concerned with how humankind, or rather gigantic, global corporations, were killing the planet Earth. The Terminator franchise shows a planet destroyed by gigantic corporations. Perhaps these films represented the individual's wish to rise up and somehow stop the destruction they saw organisations wreaking on the planet in the name of profit. Such uprisings would require leaders – strong, charismatic, cunning, intelligent leaders, able to rally people to the cause of overthrowing the planet-destroyers and replacing them with something unnamed and non-articulated, but located in the local and the social (T1, T2 and T3 linger on shots of young children playing with friends and families).

At the same time, there is an uneasiness about becoming the follower to such leaders. Followership was caught up with individual annihilation; leaders were vulnerable and needed protecting, and that was the role of their followers/protectors, but that role meant the social death of the self and, ultimately perhaps, the physical death of the body. Followers were dispensable. This presents us with a conundrum. Leaders are needed to lead a revolution against faceless corporations, but the followers of such leaders sacrifice the self. Arnold Schwarzenegger and his fellow actors seem to have articulated a fear of becoming so absorbed in the vision of another human being, 'the leader', that one's own ego, individuality, agency, capacity for independent and critical thought, freedom, and more, was lost. The desire for a leader seems to have implied a suicidal wish.

Perhaps these films articulated the meaninglessness of life at the time. The theory they contain is that populations were the prey of corporations, yet the only way to resist these faceless corporations was through the emergence of leaders who would in their turn ravage followers. The dream of escape was tem-pered by the nightmare that the only way out involved destruction of the self.

Is this why all texts of leadership seem to have disappeared? Was it because of the eventual recognition that leadership was detrimental to the vast mass of humankind? Because, we must assume, within the sphere of those faceless corporations were other leaders, those who took the decisions that led to the exploitation of humankind and the planet. Leaders may have been desired who would rise up against the faceless leaders of organisa-tions, but the need for this heroic leader arose only because of faceless lead-ers. Destroying all leadership texts thus seems like a very good idea indeed: the future of humankind was threatened by leaders; leaders were needed to resist those more powerful leaders; and the ordinary person, the follower, was sacrificed regardless of who was 'the leader'.

To paraphrase a Sci-Fi trope of the time: leadership is (or was) futile. It was not through the agency of leaders that 21st century populations would put behind them the worst that corporations and their emissaries and flunkies could wreak. Other ways of building a harmonious nurturing social world were needed. The Terminator films were reaching towards that understanding, and sensing that it was time to move on to new ways of thinking about how to organise work and how to run organisations.

I am back

I opened this essay with a statement about carrying out a thought experiment, via a reading of the Terminator film franchise, to see what may emerge about understanding leaders that may be pertinent for the present day. My first reading of the film led me to comprehend the need for leaders to overcome those very leaders of the corporations that are despoiling the planet, fuelling neoliberalism and limiting people's lives. Zoller and Fairhurst argued something similar:[34] it cannot be assumed that leaders will be loyal to the corporation rather than the people who work in/for it. This chapter, therefore, supports their arguments. However, it was through exploring the position of followers in the Terminator films that something different emerged: a deep fear about the destructive potential of concepts and practices of leadership, notably against the ego. In modernity's elevation of the egotistical self to the centre of its own universe, this is a form of immaterial violence that needs further exploration. For example, if 'I' am because 'I' think, as Descartes famously argued, then what happens if my thinking is so inhibited by someone else's desire to control what I think – that is, to follow the leader unquestioningly? Do 'I' exist as anything but a flesh-bound robot? That is, this reading of Terminator points to the need for understanding the violence of leadership. This is not the familiar form that violence takes, of an offence against the embodied self, nor indeed the symbolic violence discussed in Bourdieusian theory, but a different form again, one that attempts to destroy that vital spark that marks 'me' as 'me', as human and not a machine.

There is no space here in which to develop such a theory but (and please excuse the failure to resist this temptation) I'll be back, with a more fully formed theory of the violence of leadership.

Notes

1 Czarniawska-Joerges and de Monthoux, 1994.
2 Hassard and Holliday, 1998: 1.
3 Rhodes and Brown, 2005: 477.
4 Savage, Cornelissen and Franck, 2017: 4.
5 Steiner, 1984.

6 See, for example, Stein, 1984.
7 Bollas, 1993, 1995.
8 Freud, 2012.
9 Brennan, 2002.
10 de Beauvoir, 2014.
11 Rhodes and Brown, 2005.
12 Pugh, 2012.
13 Giroux and Pollock, 2010.
14 Yehya, 2001/2004, in Czarniawska and Gustavsson, 2008.
15 Czarniawska and Rhodes, 2006.
16 Rhodes and Parker, 2008; see also Parker and Cooper, 1998.
17 Merlin Donald, 1991; Gianni Vattimo, 1992 in Parker and Cooper, 1998.
18 Monaco, 2013.
19 Gill, 2002; Wee, 2006.
20 Mulvay, 1989.
21 Copjec, 2004.
22 Godfrey, Lilley and Brewis, 2012.
23 Parker et al., 1999.
24 Parker et al., 1999: 582.
25 Parker, 2013.
26 http://rhube.co.uk/wp/2014/10/15/existentialism-and-the-terminator/ See also www.terminatorfiles.com/media/articles/moviesfacts_005.htm
27 http://catholicskywalker.blogspot.co.uk/2012/07/the-philosophy-of-terminator.html
28 Jeffords, 2012.
29 Holland, 1995.
30 Kimball, 2002.
31 See examples in the edited collection by Smith, Higgins, Parker and Lightfoot, 2001.
32 Littmann, 2009.
33 Parker, 2013.
34 Zoller and Fairhurst, 2007.

References

Bollas, C. (1993) *Being a Character: Psychoanalysis and Self Experience*. London: Routledge.

Bollas, C. (1995) *Cracking Up: The Work of Unconscious Experience*. London: Routledge.

Brennan, T. (2002) *History after Lacan*. London: Routledge.

Copjec, J. (2004) *Imagine There's no Woman. Ethics and Sublimation*. London: Verso Books. MIT Press.

Czarniawska, B. and Rhodes, C. (2006) Strong plots: Popular culture in management practice and theory. In Gagliardi, P. (Ed) *Management Education and Humanities*. Cheltenham, UK: Edward Elgar. 195–220.

Czarniawska-Joerges, B. and De Monthoux, P. (Eds) (1994) *Good Novels, Better Management: Reading Organizational Realities in Fiction*. London: Routledge.

Czarniawska, B. and Gustavsson, E. (2008) The (D)evolution of the cyber-woman. *Organization*, 15:5, 665–683.

De Beauvoir, S. (2014) *The Second Sex*. Random House.

Freud, S. (2012) *Totem and Taboo*. Empire Books.

Gill, P. (2002) The monstrous years: Teens, slasher films, and the family. *Journal of Film and Video*, 54:4, 16–30.

Giroux, H. and Pollock, G. (2010) *The Mouse that Roared: Disney and the end of Innocence*. New York: Rowman and Littlefield.

Godfrey, R., Lilley, S. and Brewis, J. (2012) Biceps, bitches and borgs: Reading Jarhead's representation of the construction of the (masculine) military body. *Organization Studies*, 33:4, 541–562.

Hassard, J. and Holliday, R. (Eds) (1998) *Organization-Representation: Work and Organizations in Popular Culture*. London: Sage.

Holland, S. (1995) Descartes goes to Hollywood: Mind, body and gender in contemporary cyborg cinema. *Body & Society*, 1:3–4, 157–174.

Jeffords, S. (2012) Can masculinity be terminated? In Cohan, S. and Hark, I.R. (Eds) *Screening the Male: Exploring Masculinities in the Hollywood Cinema*. London: Routledge. 245–259.

Kimball, A.S. (2002). Conceptions and contraceptions of the future: Terminator 2, The Matrix, and Alien Resurrection. *Camera Obscura*, 17:2, 69–108.

Littmann, G. (2009) The Terminator wins: Is the extinction of the human race the end of people, or just the beginning? In Irwin, W., Brown, R. and Decker, K.S. *Terminator and Philosophy: I'll Be Back, Therefore I Am*. John Wiley & Sons.

Monaco, J. (2013) *How to Read a Film*. 4th Edition. Oxford University Press: New York.

Mulvey, L. (1989) *Visual and Other Pleasures*. Basingstoke: Macmillan.

Parker, M. (2013) *Alternative Business: Outlaws, Crime and Culture*. London: Routledge.

Parker, M. and Cooper, R. (1998) Cyborganization: Cinema as nervous system. In Hassard, J. and Holliday, R. (Eds) *Organization-Representation: Work and Organizations in Popular Culture*. London: Sage. 201–228.

Parker, M., Higgins, M., Lightfoot, G. and Smith, W. (1999) Amazing tales: Organization studies as science fiction. *Organization*, 6:4, 579–590.

Pugh, T. (2012) Introduction: Disney's retroprogressive medievalisms: Where yesterday is tomorrow today. In Pugh, T. and Aronstein, S. (Eds) *The Disney Middle Ages*. New York: Palgrave.

Rhodes, C. and Brown, A.D. (2005) Writing responsibly. Narrative fiction and organization studies. *Organization*, 12:4, 467–491.

Rhodes, C. and Parker, M. (2008) Images of organizing in popular culture. *Organization*, 15:5, 627–637.

Savage, P., Cornelissen, J.P. and Franck, H. (2017) Fiction and organization studies. *Organization Studies*, http://journals.sagepub.com/doi/abs/10.1177/0170840617 709309.

Smith, W., Higgins, M., Parker, M. and Lightfoot, G. (Eds) (2001) *Science Fiction and Organization*. London: Routledge.

Steiner, G. (1984) *Antigones*. Oxford: Oxford University Press.

Wee, V. (2006) Resurrecting and updating the teen slasher: The case of Scream. *Journal of Popular Film and Television*, 34:2, 50–61.

Zoller, H.M. and Fairhurts, G.T. (2007) Resistance leadership: The overlooked potential in critical organizational and leadership studies. *Human Relations*, 60:9, 1331–1360.

9 Choosing A Life

(Re)incarnating After Leadership

Jonathan Gosling and Peter Case

Introduction

It is important to have an impact, to make a difference, to be effective, to take initiative, to persuade—to lead.

But this is not forever self-evident.

Individual leaders step out of influential roles for many reasons—retirement, illness, sacking, a choice to do something else with their remaining years. This chapter is about the transition out of roles characterized by power, agency, and influence, leaving behind the things that make one feel alive, someone with a voice, someone who matters.

Role transition is usually theorized as a kind of journey from one role through a liminal phase to eventual re-establishment in a new role.[1] But we are concerned with exits that are not heading anywhere known or foreseen—where there is no capacity to find or create a new identity (we will suggest that this applies more generally than is often recognized). Rather than the journey, therefore, our metaphor is death.

The aim of the chapter is to offer a close consideration of myths and philosophical accounts of "after death" in pursuit of insights and analytical categories to form a theoretical basis for studying "after leadership."

Leadership

Leadership is all bound up with power; power to influence, command, collude; power to envision, imagine, inspire. Even in its more passive modes, where self-identified followers point to a source of influence that might be abstract (e.g. "the rules") or dead (e.g. Jesus), leadership involves fantastical projections of potent influence onto the supposed leader.

To take a lead is to exercise agency, engaging power in relation to other people, and therefore to occupy a role.

We will suggest that a move from one role to another involves not so much the personal *acquisition* of knowledge as it does a rebirth of individual subjectivity followed by a longer phase of moment-to-moment rebirth; these subjective transformations are constituted by choice and enactment as well as involving certain forms of forgetfulness—the yin and yang of selfhood.

We begin with a Greek myth concerning death and reincarnation because death is a realistic expectation, personally and culturally; and reincarnation expresses the hope that there might be some form of continuity beyond catastrophe, that the end will indeed be apocalyptic, ("apocalypse" in Greek is ἀποκάλυψις apokálypsis; "lifting of the veil" or "revelation") and not merely the end.

We go on to examine the trope of death and rebirth in Jungian and Buddhist traditions, reinforcing the significant themes of choice and forgetfulness. In Buddhist terms, the sustained movement of consciousness that we might call "self" is refined to concentrated attention (choice) and non-attachment (forgetting).

This perspective suggests further theoretical observations about the relationship between self and identity, and between person and role. From this, we suggest an epistemological argument that knowledge is (at least partly) an affordance of role.

Finally, we speculate this essay on death and rebirth might have implications at a societal level as we face the possible death of our civilization.

Death and Choice: The Myth of Er

Reason is the central motif of the dialogues of Plato, analyzed and exemplified by Socrates, their principal character and protagonist. But at several points, one or other of the interlocutors introduces a myth, explicitly trailed as such. These myths are carefully crafted contributions to the subject matter of each dialogue, reasonable but not reasoned. In symbolic or analogical images, Plato offers his readers insights that are hard to grasp but nonetheless intuitively recognizable. These are all to do with the nature and life of Soul, the reasoning subject which in Platonic epistemology cannot know itself by dialogic reasoning. The myths therefore reveal something to the reflexive intuition, while at the same time veiling their meaning to the reasoning mind.[2] Probably for this reason, the Platonic myths have seldom been approached by modern organizational scholars in spite of the extensive (usually critical) attention paid to the more "rational" and cognitive aspects of the Dialogues, such as Gareth Morgan's[3] reference to the metaphor of the Cave and Popper's critique of hope in a "philosopher king."[4]

For the purposes of the current chapter, we want to concentrate on one of the myths that deals specifically with the journey of the soul subsequent to death, the choice of how to live, and the projection into incarnation.

The Platonic myths that attend to the nature of the Soul are to be found in the *Timmaeus*[5] and *Phaedrus*[6] while the soul's journey into incarnation and after death are addressed in *Gorgias*,[7] *Phaedo*,[8] and *Republic*.[9] Love in relation to the soul is addressed in two myths in *Symposium*[10] and her final enlightenment in *Phaedrus*. In the Myth of Er at the end of *Republic*, Plato[11] has Socrates tell of a vision afforded to the warrior Er, who was taken for dead and laid out on his funeral pyre but recovered to tell what he had seen. Apparently, his soul journeyed with many others to a place where four chasms opened before him, two into the earth and two to heaven. The souls of the dead were judged and sent either down to the underworld or up to heaven according to whether they had lived life justly. Through the other two chasms, souls returned to earth, those coming up from hell stained and disheveled, those from heaven pure and tranquil. Meeting each other and recognizing friends, they swapped stories, camping for seven days in a meadow. On the eighth day, they set off on a journey that brought them, after a further four days, to a great shaft of light that binds heaven and earth together and extending from it "the spindle of necessity," the efficient cause of the universe.[12]

The three Fates, the daughters of Necessity (*Adrastia*), are seated on thrones nearby. *Lachesis* sings the past, *Clotho* the present, and *Atropos* the future. *Lachesis* (through a prophet who assists her) casts outnumbered lots and each soul picks up the lot that falls nearest to them, determining the order in which each will choose their next life. The prophet warns the souls to choose with care, for "Virtue has no overlord, so as a man honours or dishonours her, so shall he have more or less of her. Of the chooser is the cause, and God is guiltless."[13]

Then numerous lives are laid out in front of the crowd—more than enough for everyone—and amongst them are every conceivable kind, rich and poor, famous and unknown, beautiful and ugly, healthy and sick. These conditions are set, but not the temperament or the character of the person, because this will be established by the soul in living that life: "of necessity, a soul that has chosen a certain kind of life becomes changed accordingly."[14]

Here Socrates pauses his narration to point out that this is the most crucial moment, and that knowledge of what constitutes a good life (that which will be most fitted to living in justice) and the ability to select it is the most important, "for thus does a man [*sic*] become most happy."[15] As they take their turn to choose, many—especially those coming from an easy time in heaven, "virtuous through custom without philosophy"[16]— leap at the chance of fame, fortune, and power, without noticing the tragedies and unhappiness that accompany these Fates. Souls coming from the underworld searched more carefully, but most apparently "chose after the custom of their former life."[17] Only the soul of Odysseus, who drew the last lot and so has fewer to choose from, is wise enough to seek carefully for the fate of a humble farmer destined to lead a quiet life with every chance of happiness.

Having chosen, each soul comes before Lachesis to be granted the angel (or "daemon" or "genius") of the life she has selected, who guides her to Clotho to ratify the choice and thence to Atropos to make it irrevocable. Passing from the thrones of the three Fates, the souls journeyed through terrible heat across the barren Plain of *Lethe*, to the river *Amalete*, where the thirsty souls drink, though the wise more moderately than others. *Lethe* means forgetfulness, and *amalete* is usually translated as careless-ness; having forgotten where they came from, and without a care in the world, the souls slept until the middle of the night when, with a peal of thunder, they were cast hither and thither into birth.

At this point Er, who had not been permitted to drink the waters of Lethe, awoke on his pyre, and thus preserved the tale of his vision. The moral of the tale, according to Socrates, is an injunction to care for the soul by seeking jus-tice and living the life of a philosopher.[18] However, the eschatological features of the myth should not obscure its cosmological and psychological aspects. In particular, the myth deals with forgetfulness and choice, and it is these themes that we explore in more detail below.

There are direct parallels between this Ancient Greek myth and the widely documented phenomenon of the "near-death experience." It is important to point this out because we want to focus on *existential* aspects of role transi-tion and not confine ourselves merely to "identity-adoption."[19] Hence the archetype of reincarnation, as discussed extensively by Jung, for example, carries crucial implications for our argument. The brief review we offer at this juncture will help set the scene for the analysis we engage in shortly. In his tour de force *Imagining Karma*, Obeyesekere[20] undertakes a meticulous cross-cultural analysis of myths and stories of rebirth in Greek, Buddhist, and Amerindian cultures. In the same manner as Jung, Obeyesekere estab-lishes the ubiquity of the reincarnation motif within narratives that hail from widely different times and places. Similarly, Zaleski's scholarly inter-rogation of "near-death experience" in medieval and contemporary Western accounts lends weight to the idea that this phenomenon is crucially impor-tant in both individual psychic and collective cultural terms.[21] In a more recent study based on interviews with 100 respondents who claim to have had near-death experiences, Fox[22] compares and contrasts the anecdotal experiential evidence with the more sceptical positions deriving from medi-cal science. Serious psychological and social science research on the theme of "past life memory"[23] and sanctioned LSD research from the 1950s and 1960s[24] also identify recurring patterns of experience, many of which mirror those described by Plato in *Republic*. Whether one "believes" in the real-ity of life-to-life rebirth or not, there can be no question that the phenom-enon has consistently and persistently manifested itself in individual and collective human consciousness. We are bringing it up in a chapter on role because it provides an expression of the experience of role transition, one focusing on the existential aspects rather than mere "identity-adoption."[25]

Forgetfulness

> And although in the course of her journey she may forget much and suf-fer much, yet her forgetting will be the means of her remembering, and her suffering will bring release from suffering.[26]

In the Platonic myths, the soul is portrayed as "forgetting" all she inherently knows of reality and is thus obliged to learn it again through personal experience and the exercise of philosophic faculties. Forgetfulness got her into this mess, and un-forgetting will get her out of it. It is no mere coincidence that the Ancient Greek word *lethe* is the root of the word for "truth": *a-lethe-ia* (αλήθεια), meaning "un-forgetfulness" or "un-concealment." In other words, discovering the "truth" implies reversing the forgetfulness that veils an already manifest reality, a process which is central to the dialogical method employed by Socrates in "revealing truth" to his interlocutors. But forgetfulness plays a still more dynamic part in this account of transition, for it is the first lesson the soul learns in crossing the plane of Lethe after choosing a life. The transmigration of the Soul is perhaps the archetypal example of "transformation," a word overused in relation to any kind of change or adaptation, with little regard to what receives a new form, or indeed what is entailed in the process of formation.

In other premodern sciences of rebirth, for example, those of *Theravadin* and *Mahayana* (particularly Tibetan) Buddhism, death-moment-consciousness is treated with very close scrutiny indeed.[27] The moment of consciousness that immediately precedes death is understood within Buddhism to be the most powerful supporting condition for rebirth in another realm (whether that be one of the many "heaven" or "hell" planes or indeed another human birth which, within Buddhist cosmology, is considered to be the first or lowest form of "heaven realm"). Evans-Wentz's translation of the *Bardo Thödol*, rendered as *The Tibetan Book of the Dead*,[28] gives some insight into the Tibetan Buddhist analysis and understanding of the life-to-life rebirth process. The *Bardo Thödol* is effectively a manual intended to offer guidance to dead people whose consciousness moves into *Bardo* existence—a forty-nine day interregnum between death and rebirth. Typically chanted by a monk in the presence of a dying or recently deceased individual, it consists of three major sections as follows: (1) *Chikhan Bardo*, detailing the psychic events at the moment of death; (2) *Chönyid Bardo*, a description of the dream state arising after death; and (3) *Sidpa Bardo*, an account of the onset of the rebirth impulse and prenatal events occurring in subjective consciousness.

It seems likely that the various elements of the *Bardo Thödol* would have been directly informed by the psychological philosophy of *Theravada* Buddhism, first committed to written form in approximately 80 b.c. and documented in the *Abhidhamma* texts of the *Pali Canon*. Quoting from Nārada's translation of *A Manual of Abhidhamma*, "Every birth is conditioned by a past good or bad Kamma [volitional action] which predominates at the moment of death. The Kamma that conditions the future birth is called Reproductive (Janaka) Kamma."[29] According to this tradition, action or memory at the moment of death carries a great deal of "weight" in terms of conditioning post-death/rebirth consciousness: "Death-proximate Kamma, is that which one does or remembers immediately before the dying moment. Owing to its significance in determining the future birth, the custom of reminding the dying person of his [sic] good deeds and making him [sic] do good acts on this death-bed still prevails in Buddhist countries."[30] As with the Platonic Myth of Er, Buddhism also maintains that, for most, memory of previous births are completely lost when a new life-to-life birth is undertaken.

So, the soul forgets first her own nature, and thus learns to forget; later she forgets sensible things and remembers intelligible realities. Leaving things behind, literally forgoing the getting of things, is the essential virtue of "non-attachment." This forgetting is analogous to death, a departure from the world of parts, and like death is veiled in the same way: what knowing lies beyond forgetting; what life beyond dying? The Myth of Er is in some respects an attempt by Socrates to fill this lacuna, conjuring up a more or less familiar process of judgment and journey, perhaps to deny the awful void of death as well as to re-present death as an opportunity for choosing a good life. And in life, creeping forgetfulness must be a terrifying thing, so we make no attempt to romanticize a failing of memory. But "the philosophic death" is a consistent theme for Socrates, arguing that paradoxically the philosopher truly lives when, by practice of the cathartic virtues, he or she becomes free of material attachments and "soars aloft" to contemplate reality. Thus, forgetting and dying are analogs, experiences of transiency marking a transition into a state free of partial and ultimately deceptive perceptions, but one in which the soul remembers reality—contemplative, intuitive, and self-evident. In Socratic terms, therefore, forgetting is central to this transition.

We now have two "forgettings," the first by which the soul forgets what she should know, and thus falls carelessly and ignorantly into incarnation, followed by the struggle to learn and thus develop intellectual virtues (set out, for example, as the *mathetai* or intellectual disciplines—arithmetic, geometry of planar, solid and moving objects, and harmonics—in *Republic*). The second forgetting is the precise reverse of the first. The soul abandons the facts and impressions thus accumulated, and thus by contemplation is able to perceive truth, *alethia*—abstract, eternal, and real ideas. The difference is that the first forgetting occurs through foolishness, the second through wisdom.

The foregoing analysis suggests the function of "forgetting" within an epistemological argument underlying the Myth of Er. However, we would not wish to deny other interpretations of this myth, some of which are more psychological than epistemological. For example, referring to transitions between work roles, forgetting may be functional if it enables a person to leave behind the darker associations of an old role—the regrets, the impotencies, and the unforeseen consequences of actions. Moving toward a new role, one is often seduced into colluding in its idealization and the image of oneself in it. The disowned parts of one's experience (of oneself in role) sink into the shadows, are forgotten. So setting off across the plains of Lethe is allowing oneself to forget one's old obligations. Forgetting enables a discontinuity, from anxiety about the future and regrets about the past, toward hope and the possibility of insight.

Choice

The choice to take up a new role, like that of a new life, is only partly governed by conscious reasoning.[31] Fantasies and wishful thinking play a big part, and very few of us have the foresight and discretion of Odysseus or even the philosophical grounds on which to make a choice. The Myth of Er paints a vivid picture of the turmoil within which such choices are made, but central to the Myth—as to this entire corpus—is the principle of individual responsibility for choosing. Regardless of whether or not we take the myth (or other evidence) of rebirth as containing a literal truth, it points to a deep pattern or archetype within human consciousness. For the purposes of this chapter, we can think of rebirth as occurring on a moment-to-moment basis, formed out of conditioned (pre-given) and conditioning (volitional or intentional) choices. Moreover, as the myth suggests, consequences follow from the conditioning aspects of the rebirth process and the choices involved.

The principle of intentional choice is addressed by Plato in *Protagoras*[32] in the Myth of Prometheus (forethought) and Epimetheus (afterthought). In that myth, Prometheus signifies the power of the soul to identify a purpose in the life she chooses. But what is forgotten on the Plain of Lethe includes knowledge of intent as well as experience accrued from the past. Prometheus, as forethought chained to a rock, reminds us of this predicament—that there is something we ought to be getting on with, but which we have forgotten, and that we have allowed ourselves to be detained and harried by events.

In the Myth of Er, the choice of next life is characterized by forethought assailed by impatience, grandiose ambition, and avarice: it is as if most of these souls (with the exception of Odysseus) are already chained to the Promethean rock. Making their selection before the throne of Necessity suggests that to become someone the soul must take on the consequences that go with that selfhood. Similarly, when taking up a role we take on the consequences of that role—there is no option to take up a role without such consequences. And although the consequences are in the future, we choose on the basis of past experience and knowledge (i.e., from *Lachesis*, who looks to the past). So what belongs to the role, and what do we bring to it? As the myth suggests, the disposition of the Soul develops in response to the circumstances of the life or role; but the *character* of the soul is exercised most clearly at the point of choosing, for it is here that, even without forethought, those souls preserved by wisdom are able to exercise moral virtues. In so doing, they seem to bring moral agency to this transition, individual choice beneath the gaze of necessity. It is this lesson of *choice* deriving from the Myth of Er that prompts us to frame role transition in terms of the *moral craft* of self-management. In other words, choice in this context carries moral as well as technical implications.

On Taking up a Role, Like Choosing a Life

A remarkable feature of the rebirth myths and transmutations we have discussed so far is their resistance to a dualistic framing of life and death. The Myth of Er in particular describes an active zone of transition, in which both space and time (sequence of events) are rich in significance far beyond a literal representation.

As described above, the construct of self-in-role derives from psychodynamic theory in which dualisms are crucial to explaining the dynamics of *psyche*. For Freud, life and death are not so much states of being as dynamic forces: the destructive forces of the so-called death instinct, *thanatos*, in constant struggle with the life-longing drives of *eros*. Although Freud generally conceived of these as opposing libidinal forces, Sabina Spielrein as early as 1912 proposed *eros* and *thanatos* as components of a single-sex instinct.[33] Both might be seen as drives toward obliteration—*thanatos* toward obliteration of self in the All; *Eros* toward obliteration in the other. Both give rise to anxiety about the loss of self, along with many other potent emotions such as guilt, envy, and desire. However, as we see in the Myth of Er, the passions of the soul are in relation to an object—the lives to be selected and lived. Object relations theory[34] addresses the ways in which we internalize objects external to ourselves, and project the emotional and meaning-making content of our selves into these objects. The pattern of these relations is established in infancy, by the manner in which an early sense of subjective self is established through the gradual realization of an objective world on which the self is dependent. Thus, these early relations with others (primarily the mother or mother-substitute, experienced as part-object rather than as a whole and independent complex person) are of crucial existential significance; so much so that in later life most relationships with others conform to the patterns set in early life because these are the determinants of how we experience ourselves. When we relate to others we do so by projecting onto them the expectations that have come to be integral to our own sense of self. Thus, we relate to them as objects in our own psychic universes; this is especially so when the relationship is laden with the emotional and existential charge most reminiscent of early parental relationships—that is, with people in authority, and also with organizational systems that embody authority. As we have argued above, self-narrated prospective identities may serve the same function as part-objects.

In this context, we may approach the Myth of Er as an account of intrapsychic processes of role adoption. The lives offered to the souls are objects paradoxically devoid of life until selected. It is only when the soul projects herself into these lifeless objects that they become vivific possibilities; and we have seen how this projection is engulfed by the emotional residue of past lives. It is not hard to see this dynamic at work in everyday life; for example, by analogy, we observe that job descriptions are not dissimilar to the lives offered by *Lachesis* (likewise the process of choosing a new role, assuming its responsibilities, and necessary conditions). Job descriptions themselves are mere caricatures: inanimate objects that nonetheless provide the material conditions for the realization of roles, once taken up by a person. A person longing for a job is thus longing for a lifeless object, at least in so far as the longing is directed at the imagined role, rather than the experiences and relationships that it might afford. But perhaps from the point of view of an organizational system, one function of the job description is to sanitize the role from the imprint of the previous role holder, de-personalizing it in the way that a hotel prepares a supposedly "characterful" room for the next (unknown) guest.

Person-In-Role as A Transformational Rebirth: A Jungian Perspective

The themes of *transformation* and *transmigration* that we have thus far explored in relation to Plato's Myth of Er are afforded a central place within Jungian psychology. Although Jung, perhaps surprisingly, did not discuss the Myth of Er directly (despite many references in his oeuvre to Plato's theory of the soul), he was fascinated, not to say at times preoccupied, by the rebirth motif and its transformational implications. Jung returns repeatedly to the concept of archetype in his work, but a useful definition is found in a relatively early essay 'Symbols of the Mother and of Rebirth' dating from 1916 and first published in *Psychology of the Unconscious*.[35] Here he defines archetypes as: "universal and inherited patterns which, taken together, constitute the structure of the unconscious ... for archetypes are the forms or river-beds along which the current of psychic life has always flowed."[36] Similarly, in *Psychology and Religion*, he speaks of "inherited psychic factors" as "universal dispositions of the mind" that are "analogous to Plato's forms (*eidola*), in accordance with which the mind organizes its contents."[37] He goes on:

> One could also describe these forms as *categories* analogous to the logical categories which are always and everywhere present as the basic postulates of reason. Only in the case of "forms," we are not dealing with categories of reason but with categories of the *imagination*. As the products of imagination are always in essence visual, their forms must, from the outset, have the character of images and moreover of typical images, which is why ... I call them "archetypes."[38]

As Jung asserts in *The Archetypes and the Collective Unconscious*: "Rebirth is an affirmation that must be counted among the primordial affirmations of mankind. These primordial affirmations are based on what I call archetypes ... [and] it is not surprising that a concurrence of affirmations concerning rebirth can be found among the most widely differing peoples."[39] In this lecture dating from 1939, Jung identifies five forms of rebirth, one of the most pertinent of which for our present argument is "participation in the process of transformation."[40] He observes that "Rebirth may be a renewal without any change of being, inasmuch as the personality which is renewed is not changed in its essential nature, but only its functions, or part of the personality ..."[41] Furthermore, "rebirth" can, under certain circumstances, involve an *indirect* transformation brought about not by passing through literal death and rebirth but in "a process of transformation which is conceived of as taking place outside the individual." These thoughts resonate strongly with the argument that we are pursuing here insofar as the kinds of organizational role transition that we are considering relate to the migration and subsequent enactment of *person* (subjectivity) into *role* (exogenous context).

While such moments of organizational transition and moment-to-moment action within role can involve, in Jung's terms, both an "enlargement" or, by contrast, "diminution" of personality,[42] it is useful for our purposes to consider the kind of development entailed in, say, taking on greater responsibility associated with positions of increased authority. Here we find Jung confirming our thesis that enactment of "persona" in role does not simply entail an accretion of psychic contents stemming from external organizational (re)sources—the idea of "stuffing oneself as much as possible from the outside" which can only lead to "greater inner poverty"[43]— but must come from a dynamic meeting of subjective sensibilities with new organizational demands. In other words, in moving into a role with a commensurate expansion of responsibility, "something in us responds to it and goes out to meet it."[44] This demands of the individual a certain form of wisdom, *phronesis* perhaps, which enables her to grow and react to organizational rebirth. As Jung asserts:

> Richness of mind consists in mental receptivity, not in accumulation of possessions. What comes from outside, and, for that matter, everything that rises up from within, can only be made our own if we are capable of an inner amplitude equal to that of the incoming content. Real increase of personality means consciousness of an enlargement that flows from inner sources ... It has therefore been said quite truly that *a man [sic] grows with the greatness of his [sic] task.*[45]

Jung also describes certain forms of rebirth transformation in terms of "possession," a metaphor which, once again, seems apposite to our discussion of person-in-role. Although "possession" may be related in pathological parlance to "paranoia," this does not discount the possibility of viewing it in non-pathological terms, for taking up a role might well involve being "taken over" by certain forms of psychic content whose sources are external to the subject. In this context, Jung makes some telling observations about professional life that resonate strongly with our argument:

> Every calling or profession, for example, has its own characteristic persona. It is easy to study these things nowadays [1939], when the photographs of public personalities so frequently appear in the press. A certain kind of behaviour is forced on them by the world, and professional people endeavour to come up to these expectations ... One could say, with a little exaggeration, that the persona is that which in reality one is not, but which oneself as well as others think one is. In any case the temptation to be what one seems to be is great, because the persona is usually rewarded in cash.[46]

For postmodern societies in which the cult of mass media and mass mediation has taken so great a hold, these words seem to carry no less resonance than they did in 1939. Indeed, if anything they have even more salience. The recent financial crisis, for instance, has spawned a plethora of imagery of bank bosses, once lauded by the financial press, who, having lived up to expectations of the high-flying leader are now uniformly portrayed in the negative. The scandal over bonuses must surely have caused the personae implicated no end of anguish as their post-crisis image became subject to such strong public disapprobation and derision. Our main point is that the notion of "possession" associated with organizational role casts interesting and helpful light on the kinds of transformation and rebirth processes that concern us here. We may think of the role *possessing* the individual subject, in a certain sense, and demanding that inner sensibilities go out to meet and embrace new forms of knowledge in the broadest terms.

Jung devoted a great deal of energy to an exhaustive exploration of the transformation motif in medieval (and earlier) forms of alchemy.[47] Throughout this engagement, he emphasizes that the kinds of physical or material transformation that featured in alchemical experimentation and the search for the *lapis philosophorum* ("philosopher's stone") was, for the more enlightened alchemists, always located within an explicitly mystical search for personal realization, that is, "the transformation of what is mortal in me into what is immortal."[48] This is a key informing trope for what Jung describes as a process of *individuation* or "natural transformation." "Nature herself demands a death and a rebirth,"[49] he asserts, and the "inner voice of the soul" is in unconscious connection with this imperative. Jung makes the universal claim that human individuals each have *inner voices*— what alchemists referred to as *aliquem alium internum* or "a certain other one, within"[50]—that call them toward personal and spiritual development. Such "voices," moreover, are not exclusively or even predominantly of the pathological variety. We may also note in this context a more than passing resemblance between the inner voice and the function of the daemon within Ancient Greek cosmology. Jung's notion of individuation reinforces our argument to the extent that it offers yet another perspective on the operation of the unconscious in relation to the personal transformation of the kind invoked by role transition.

Discussion

The trajectory of our chapter has been to problematize the relationship between person and role to better understand transition out of leadership. We have suggested that a move from one role to another involves not so much the personal *acquisition* of knowledge as it does a rebirth of individual subjectivity followed by a longer phase of moment-to-moment rebirth; these subjective transformations being constituted by choice and enactment as well as involving certain forms of forgetfulness. We have pursued an ironic trope with respect to "knowledge," indicating that this may be thought of as something *produced* by the role context; that is, the role entails *possession* of the individual in a certain sense. With this main argument in mind, it is interesting to note how Jung's conception of the collective unconscious implies a level of "reversibility" of the subject/object or person/role duality. Consider Jung's contention:

> The world of gods and spirits is truly "nothing but" the collective unconscious inside me. To turn this sentence round so that it reads "The collective unconscious is the world of gods and spirits outside me," no intellectual acrobatics are needed, but a whole human lifetime, perhaps even many lifetimes of increasing completeness. Notice that I do not say "of increasing perfection," because those who are "perfect" make another kind of discovery altogether.[51]

Of course, this framing of the personality/unconscious duality in Jung's modernist hands takes on a progressive hue that sees some kind of "essential" personality "evolving" toward greater levels of "completeness." What we take from this quotation, without endorsing such essentialism, is the implication that the boundary between personality and collective unconscious is necessarily *permeable*, perhaps even illusory in the last analysis. By analogy, we would want to claim that the same level of boundary permeability and reversibility characterizes the relationship between person and role—that these notions are intimately interconnected and that it is a matter of perspective or emphasis (informed by rhetorical purpose) which guides whether one recovers "knowledge" as something pertaining to the "within," "without," or "in-between" of person–role.[52]

Conclusions

One implication of this chapter is a theory of knowledge that refers to ideas as wholes rendered particular by role holders: we suggest that two processes involved in this particularization are *choosing* and *forgetting*.

A second implication is to interpret learning as the realization of properties inherent in a role, rather than the acquisition of new personal knowledge. A third implication is that roles now appear as affordances, offering unforeseen opportunities.

We have argued elsewhere that managing oneself in role involves disciplining intra-psychic processes, disciplinary practices that might take Stoic spiritual exercises as their source of inspiration.[53] In the present chapter, we argue managing oneself in role also involves perceiving, internalizing, and working with knowledge that becomes available through taking up a role, including conscious and unconscious aspects of knowledge. In particular, we have drawn attention to the processes by which certain kinds of knowledge are brought into being by the confluence of person and role, which we characterize as a knowledge nexus. Epistemologically, we claim that roles are so closely associated with some forms of knowledge that they might even be defined *by the knowledge to which they give access*; and further, that it makes sense to think of this knowledge as a potential awaiting actualization by a person taking up and managing themselves in that role. We suggest a theory of knowledge that refers to ideas as wholes, rendered particular and "known" by role holders' forgetting and remembering. In terms of Plato's Myth of Er, it is as though the new inhabitant of a role effectively *chooses* birth in that role and has, as a consequence, to engage in a certain form of "un-forgetting" in order to discover the practical *truth* of what such rebirth entails.

As a further implication, this perspective affords us an ironic take on "learning." In place of learning as the *acquisition* of new personal knowledge and practical competence, the myth inspires us to think in terms of realizing the propensity or potential *inherent* in the role—the meeting of personal, previously conditioned sensibilities with the newly expanded (or diminished) context of responsibility and organizational duty. Learning occurs through the un-forgetting or openness to the moment-to-moment experience of the rebirth in-role. This suggests new insight into the function of *reflectiveness* in leadership and management development.[54] All too often, reflection is described as learning from past events and sometimes as reflexive awareness of the here and now. What is implied by our discussion is qualitatively different, arising from participation in intellectual and affective wholenesses, and thus transcending purposive human agency.[55]

These observations support our argument that roles should be approached as affordances offering unforeseen opportunities. These include the accomplishment of self-concepts often referred to as identity work,[56] and also the realization of ideas and systemic knowledge, conceived as impersonal latent potential within a system.

We began this essay by speculating that "after leadership" is akin to "after life," because it requires leaving behind the identity-boosting devices of power and efficacy. However, our close analysis of Buddhist, Jungian, and Platonic accounts of death suggests that leaving leadership is not such a special case after all. Many role transitions—and many developments within role—may be characterized as death and rebirth, forgetting and choice. After leadership might be a particularly strong case, but not a special one. This is a theoretical proposition that we hope might be explored empirically.

Wider Implications for Leadership

Although our focus has been on the individual, we believe our argument has wider significance for civilization.

The balance of global power is shifting, challenging cultural and political faith in democratic decision making, consensual leadership, free trade, and the inevitability of technical progress. In a 2009 speech to the United Nations, President Obama named a litany of threats to a world order that values (at least normatively) democracy, individual human rights, and market economics. These are terror, unending wars, genocide, nuclear proliferation, poverty and disease, and melting ice caps. It is now clear that all of these are linked, and all of these are terrible; but the last is of a different order, signaling the collapse of objective conditions for human life by non-human processes that are likely already beyond mitigation. We face the likelihood of the death of our civilization, if not our species (amongst the multitude of deaths now characterized as "the 6th extinction").[57]

Many authors focus on how societies will adapt to changes brought about by climate change and biodiversity destruction and pollution, combined with those wrought by digitization and globalization, along with massive and ubiquitous migration. These conditions will stretch the meaning of the well-established term "adaptive leadership,"[58] but perhaps if combined with "resilience" (Rockström et al., 2012), there will be sufficient continuity for us to develop and recognize leadership in more or less familiar ways. But there is more than a chance that changes will be severely disruptive of the moral norms by which we assess authority to be legitimate. This is a theme we have explored elsewhere,[59] arguing that social and cultural collapse undermines common understandings of what counts as good action, virtuous characteristics, admirable behaviour, and wise leadership in general. Such times might properly be called catastrophic (κατά (*kata*) = down; στροφή (*strophē*) = turning), and for many societies, such as those subject to violent colonization, the catastrophe has been terminal. Hence our interest in death and what might survive the collapse of the powers, competencies, and meaningfulness that characterize a vibrant society, and at this level might suggest other ways of pursuing "after leadership."

Anxiety about catastrophic endings has always inspired messianic tyrannies and millenarian anarchies,[60] but these have proven ineffective preservers of civilizations, cultures, and institutions. Catastrophic collapse removes the institutionalized practices by which a civilization legitimates unequal allocation of power and influence. Leadership is a phenomenon of these institutional processes, not their cause. When institutions collapse, the legit-imacy of leadership goes with them. So to hope that leaders will carry us through hell is a vain fantasy.

However, there may be a more "radical hope" (as Jonathan Lear[61] sug-gests) to guide the soul of a civilization through catastrophe. This hope may be embodied in those whose way of life prepares them to choose (and to forget) with aesthetic finesse—like Odysseus before the throne of *Adrastia*. The quality of choosing and the tonality of forgetting may vary; it is not things or events that carry forward in memory, but values and aesthetics that characterize a way of living. In Buddhist meditation practice, the sus-tained movement of consciousness that we might call "self" is refined to concentrated attention (choice) and non-attachment (forgetting).

Though in contrast to the pomp of leaders, such asceticism has always been respected. Perhaps it lies behind the current popularity of mindfulness practices—the sense that we must prepare not to have, to control, or even to know, but to choose. Maybe this is what comes after leadership.

Notes

1 Ibarra (2003); (2007).
2 Gabriel (2004).
3 Morgan (1986).
4 Popper (1945).
5 Plato (1965).
6 Plato (1973).
7 Plato (1960).
8 Plato (1993a).
9 Plato (1993b).
10 Plato (1951).
11 Plato (1987; 1993b).
12 The image of the spindle of necessity occurs also in *Timmaeus* (Plato, 1965) where a more detailed symbolic cosmology is described, but which does not directly touch on the concerns of the present chapter.
13 Plato (1987: 617e).
14 Plato (1987: 618b).
15 Plato (1987: 619b).
16 Plato (1987: 619d).
17 Plato (1987: 619d).
18 See Hadot (1995, 2004) on the meaning of the "philosophical life."
19 Becker & Carper, (1956).
20 Obeyesekere (2000).
21 Zaleski (1987).
22 Fox (2003).
23 Stevenson (1974, 2003); Head and Cranston (1977); Cranston and Carey (1984).
24 Grof (1975).
25 Currie et al. (2010).
26 Thomas Taylor quoted in Anon (1936: 59).

144   *Jonathan Gosling and Peter Case*

27 Nārada (1980a); Evans-Wenz (1960).
28 Evans-Wenz (1960).
29 Nārada (1980b: 257).
30 Nārada (1980b: 260).
31 Case & Gosling (2011).
32 Plato (2005: 321c).
33 Carr and Lapp (2006).
34 Klein (1959).
35 Jung (*1953–1983*, 5: 207–273).
36 Jung (*1953–1983*, 5: 228).
37 Jung (*1953–1983*, 11: 517).
38 Jung (*1953–1983*, 11: 517–518), original emphases.
39 Jung (*1953–1983*, 9: 116).
40 Jung (*1953–1983*, 9: 114).
41 Jung (*1953–1983*, 9: 114).
42 Jung (*1953–1983*, 9: 119–120).
43 Jung (*1953–1983*, 9: 120).
44 Jung (*1953–1983*, 9: 120).
45 Jung (*1953–1983*, 9: 120–121, added emphases).
46 Jung (*1953–1983*, 9: 122–123).
47 Case and Phillipson (2004).
48 Jung (*1953–1983*, 9: 134).
49 Jung (1953: 9: 130).
50 Jung (*1953–1983*, 9: 130).
51 Jung (*1953–1983*, 11: 525).
52 Case and Gosling (2011).
53 Case and Gosling (2007).
54 Branson (2009).
55 This might be what Aristotle refers to as *theoria*, the fourth intellectual virtue (after arête, episteme, and phronesis) in *Nichomacean Ethics*.
56 Brown (2018); Alvesson, Ashcraft & Thomas (2008); Ashforth (2001).
57 Kolbert (2014).
58 Heifetz (1994).
59 Gosling and Case (2013); Gosling (2017).
60 Cohn (1957).
61 Lear (2008).

References

Alvesson, Mats, Karen Ashcraft, and Robyn Thomas 2008 "Identity matters: Rreflections on the construction of identity scholarship in organization studies." *Organization*, 15/1: 5–28.

Anon, editor 1936 *The Human Soul in the Myths of Plato*. Godalming, UK: Shrine of Wisdom.

Ashforth, Blake E. 2001 *Role Transitions in Organizational Life: An Identity-Based Perspective*. Mahwah, NJ: Lawrence Erlbaum.

Becker, Howard S. and James Carper 1956 "The elements of identification with an occupation." *American Sociological Review*, 21: 341–348.

Branson, Christopher M. 2009 "Finding a philosophical framework in support of 'presence.'" *Leadership & Organization Development Journal*, 30/3: 224–239.

Brown, Andrew 2018 "Identities in organization studies." *Organization Studies*, e-print 1-15. DOI:10.1177/0170840618765014.

Carr, Adrian and Cheryl Lapp 2006 *Leadership is a Matter of Life and Death: The Psychodynamics of Eros and Thanatos Working in Organizations*. Basingstoke, UK: Palgrave Macmillan.

Case, Peter and Jonathan Gosling 2007 "Wisdom of the moment: Pre-modern perspectives on organizational action." *Social Epistemology* 21/2: 87–111.

Case, Peter and Gosling, Jonathan 2011 The wisdom we have lost in knowledge in Pauleen, D. and Gorman, G. (eds) *Personal Knowledge Management*. London: Gower.

Case, Peter and Gareth Phillipson 2004 "Astrology, alchemy and retro-organization theory: An astro-genealogical critique of the Myers-Briggs Type Indicator®." *Organization*, 11/4: 473–495.

Cohn, Norman 1957 *The Pursuit of the Millennium: Revolutionary Millenarians and Mystical Anarchists of the Middle Ages*. Oxford: Oxford University Press.

Cranston, Sylvia and Carey Williams 1984 *Reincarnation: A New Horizon in Science, Religion, and Society*. New York: Julian Press.

Currie, G., Finn, R., and Martin, G. 2010 "Role transition and the interaction of relational and social identity: New nursing roles in the English NHS." *Organization Studies*, 31: 941–961.

DeNora, Tia 2003 *After Adorno: Rethinking Music Sociology*. Cambridge: Cambridge University Press.

Evans-Wentz and Walter Yeeling (eds) 1960 *The Tibetan Book of the Dead*, third edition. Oxford: Oxford University Press.

Foucault, Michel 1988 "Technologies of the self." in L. H. Martin, H. Gutman, and P.H. Hutton (eds), *Technologies of the Self: A Seminar with Michel Foucault* (pp. 16–49), Amherst, MA: University of Massachusetts Press.

Fox, Mark 2003 *Religion, Spirituality and the Near-Death Experience*. London: Routledge.

Gabriel, Yiannis (ed.) 2004 *Myths, Stories and Organizations: Premodern Narratives for Our Time*. Oxford: Oxford University Press.

Gosling, Jonathan 2017 "Will we know what counts as good leadership if things fall apart? Questions prompted by Chinua Achebe's novel." *Leadership*, 13/1: 35–47

Gosling, Jonathan and Peter Case 2013 "Social dreaming and ecocentric ethics: sources of non-rational insight in the face of climate change catastrophe." *Organization*, 20/5: 705–721

Grof, Stanislav 1975 *Realms of the Human Unconscious: Observations from LSD Research*. New York: Viking.

Hadot, Pierre 1995 *Philosophy as a Way of Life*. Oxford: Blackwell.

Hadot, Pierre 2004 *What is Ancient Philosophy?* translated by Michael Chase. London: Harvard University Press.

Head, Joseph and Sylvia Cranston (eds.) 1977 *Reincarnation*. New York: Julian Press.

Heifetz, Ronald 1994 *Leadership Without Easy Answers*. Cambridge MA: Harvard University Press.

Ibarra, Herminia 2003 *Working Identity: Unconventional Strategies for Reinventing your Career*. Boston MA: Harvard Business School Press.

Ibarra, Herminia 2007 "Identity transitions: Possible selves, liminality and the dynamics of voluntary career change." *Insead Working Paper Series*, Fontainebleu, France: Insead.

Jung, Carl G. 1953–1983 *The Collected Works of C.G. Jung*, 21 Vols, Herbert Read, Michael Fordham, Gerhard Adler (eds.). London: Routledge & Kegan Paul.

Klein, Melanie 1959 "Our adult world and its roots in infancy." *Human Relations*, 12: 291–303

Kolbert, Elizabeth 2014 *The Sixth Extinction: An Unnatural History*. London: Bloomsbury.

Lawrence, W. Gordon (ed.) 1979 *Exploring Individual and Organizational Boundaries*. Chichester, UK: Wiley.

Lear, Jonathan 2008 *Radical Hope: Ethics in the Face of Cultural Devastation*. Cambridge MA: Harvard University Press.

Morgan, Gareth (1986) *Images of Organization*. Beverly Hills, CA: SAGE.

Obeyesekere, Gananath 2000 *Imagining Karma: Transformation in Amerindian, Buddhist, and Greek Rebirth*. London: University of California Press.

Plato 1951 *Symposium*, translated by Walter Hamilton. London: Penguin Classics.

Plato 1965 *Timmaeus*, translated by Desmond Lee. London: Penguin Classics.

Plato 1960 *Gorgias*, translated by Walter Hamilton. London: Penguin Classics.

Plato 1973 *Phaedrus*, translated by Walter Hamilton. London: Penguin Classics.

Plato 1987 *The Republic*, translated by Henry Desmond Pritchard Lee. London: Penguin Classics.

Plato 1993a *Phaedo*, translated by David Gallop. Oxford: Oxford University Press.

Plato 1993b *The Republic*, translated by Robin Waterfield. Oxford, Oxford University Press.

Plato 2005 *Protagoras*, translated by Adam Beresford. London: Penguin Classics.

Popper, Karl 1945 *The Open Society and Its Enemies*. Abingdon-on-Thames: Routledge.

Rice, A. Kenneth 1958 *Productivity and Social Organization: The Ahmedabad Experiment*. London: Tavistock Press; reprinted London and New York: Garland Publishing 1987.

Sievers, Burkard 1990 "Thoughts on the relatedness of work, death and life itself." *European Journal of Management*, 8/3: 321–324.

Sievers, Burkard 1994 *Work, Death and Life Itself: Essays on Management and Organization*. Berlin: Walter de Gruyter.

Sievers, Burkard 2007 "It is new and it has to be done!" *Culture and Organization*, 13/1: 1–21.

Stevenson, Ian 1974 *Twenty Cases Suggestive of Reincarnation*. Charlottesville, VA: University of Virginia Press.

Stevenson, Ian 2003 *European Cases of the Reincarnation Type*. Jefferson, NY: McFarland & Company.

Zaleski, Carol 1987 *Otherworld Journeys: Accounts of Near-Death Experience in Medieval and Modern Times*. Oxford: Oxford University Press.

10 Toward Inclusive Leadership Scholarship

Inviting the Excluded to Theorize Collective Leadership

Sonia M. Ospina

I imagine a time when the leadership canon we know today has largely disappeared, leaving only random fragments of utterances like collective, relationality, co-production, dialogue, participation, emergence, identity, power, inclusion, and so on. How would these concepts help us reimagine new knowledge of what we would agree to call leadership in a post-leadership world?

As this chapter's title suggests, I extend my query to explore who could offer novel insights to rethink leadership from these fragments and what would they contribute. By posing these questions, I intend to surface the invisibility of certain social groups as potentially rich sources from which to theorize collective leadership. By answering them, I hope to broaden the epistemological map by adding alternative ways of knowing to a collective construction of leadership.

In this chapter, I first connect this provocation to my positionality in the field. I then briefly unpack my answer to the imaginative scenario posed by the book: that diverse social groups previously excluded from contributing to leadership theories would help weave together fragments toward theorizing collective leadership as the dominant theory within a new post-leadership canon. I then theorize and unpack some implications for the new canon. Finally, I bring my thought experiment back to the present.

An Outsider Looking In

In the United States, I've mostly been an outsider looking in. I've been a foreign student in a Sociology Department, gaining credentials to return home in the South, where knowledge development aims to nurture change; a sociologist working in the North, where the academy maintains its distance from practice; and a qualitative management scholar in a professional field favoring quantitative research. Eventually, I recognized myself in the United States as a Latino woman who surprises some by "how articulate" I am.

As I gradually became a leadership scholar in this new epistemic community, I also made outsider choices. They influenced my approach to the multi-year project on social change leadership that propelled me, mid-career, into the field. I took risks both with respect to theory and study design: studying leadership in organizations representing marginalized communities, not corporations or large nonprofits; using interpretive methods—qualitative and participatory—not positivist quantitative models; and favoring an emergent constructionist approach that prioritizes collective leadership over leader-centered perspectives.

So there I was, a Latina sociologist entering the field, doing non-traditional leadership research *with* (not *about*) social change leaders. I was working with communities whose members were also often treated as outsiders by virtue of social exclusion dynamics – women, Black, Latino, Indigenous, Immigrant, and LGBTI individuals and groups. Engaged in collaborative research with leaders who enacted a more collective perspective, we explored their leadership at a time when collective approaches had not yet gained currency. Their leadership stories were powerful and offered great potential to theorize from a different and novel perspective.

This experience, which shaped my sensibilities and my way of being a leadership scholar, grounds my provocation. It also has informed my ability to make fruitful contributions—drawing from voices and practices traditionally silenced—to nurture field conversations about the collective nature of leadership.

A caveat helps to close this section. I do not intend to romanticize the excluded. People experiencing the world from the intersection of devalued social identities are human too; there are good and bad persons, effective and ineffective leaders. Wise and flawed leadership work happens everywhere. But "a system of knowledge that draws on their insights and starts from their predicaments will be richer than one that draws only on the insights and starts from the predicaments of privileged groups alone."[1] Looking for leadership outside the dominant contexts broadens our lens, changes the questions we ask and opens new horizons for theorizing collective leadership in the post-leadership world.

A Post-Leadership World: Unpacking the Provocation

Growing interest in collective leadership today challenges the heroic models of the leadership canon. Notions of organizing rooted in the industrial revolution's narrative of progress, rationality, and individualism are too simple. The image of the professional manager at the top of a hierarchy (the leader), authorized to lead workers and employees (the followers), offers a constrained understanding of how to achieve organizational success. New questions explore the relational dynamics of leadership and the conditions under which it takes up different forms, from individual, to shared, to distributed, to collective leadership.

This emerging scholarship is fragmented. Multiple streams, grounded on differing ontologies, epistemologies, and methodologies, generate confusion.[2] Theoretical, methodological, and practical challenges of conceptualizing, studying, and practicing collective leadership are compounded by the strong power of an entrenched parsimonious model that equates leadership with leaders and emphasizes hierarchy. The field is stuck in old molds, despite clarity about the need to invent new ones.

What, then, if the leadership canon were to largely disappear today, leaving only random fragments that included utterances reflecting this new interest? Despite its early development, fragments reflecting the vocabulary of a collective leadership lens could help theorize something that I would agree to call leadership. Actors previously excluded from the leadership canon would recognize in the fragments their collective ways of thinking about leadership, and claim that these have been practiced successfully in contexts outside the interest of the leadership and management domains (e.g., in community-based, alternative organizations, and social movement groups). Broader conceptual lenses capturing the leadership experience of multiple actors in different social locations would challenge the narrow focus of today's canon. The broader repertoire of what constitutes leadership work beyond traditional views would expand the point of reference to a larger and diverse set of experiences.[3]

The potential of inviting diverse worldviews not considered before is illustrated in the origin of *Harmony with Nature*, a United Nations (UN) platform for global sustainable development. Challenging a technocratic Western narrative of sustainable development, this UN initiative develops a holistic vocabulary grounded on a worldview that sees a fundamental interconnection between humanity and nature, arguing that as human beings we cannot damage nature without severely damaging ourselves. With this comes an affirmation of the Rights of Mother Earth and the notion of Earth Jurisprudence (i.e., developing laws that give rights to nature and allow for actions on behalf of, let us say, a threatened river, now "entitled" to protection).[4] This effort was crystallized through the leadership work of representatives of the Plurinational State of Bolivia—a country with a large Indigenous population led by an Indigenous President. This should not come as a surprise.

Inviting the Excluded to Reimagine Leadership

Contexts where inequality and exclusion are salient become promising to explore leadership. It requires considering the consequences of social location on the social actors' experience of leadership, thus broadening the inquiry. This becomes the starting point for a post-leadership theorization of collective leadership.

Social location is "the position one holds in a society based on a variety of relevant social identities (e.g., race, socioeconomic status, gender identity, sexual orientation, geographic location, occupation) that in turn frame how the world is experienced."[5] It influences our sense of self in relation to others (our social identity), what we know about ourselves and the world (our knowledge), and our capacity to act in the world (our power). Intersecting identities shape each other and the life experience of individuals and groups, impacting in compounded ways those in less privileged social positions. Yet, as discussed next, the latter may be able to transform their experience into a source of leadership.

Robnett, a US historian of the Civil Rights movement, illustrates the gains of introducing social location to broaden the inquiry. Introducing a gender perspective, she explores the critical role of women in the movement, despite their apparent invisibility in the highest leadership positions.[6] By asking "how mobilization takes place in day-to-day community work," and thus "who is likely to do such work" she was able to see Black women as movement leaders.[7] For example, activist Septima Clark understood the need to be intimately involved with the community "to connect the politics of the movement to the needs of the people."[8] By doing much of this middle-meaning-making work, Black women constructed local leadership that shaped (elaborated, altered, and bridged) the movement's message. Women were thus instrumental in linking the broad movement's change strategies (where males dominated) to more personalistic, identity-rooted strategies at the local level (where women worked).

Restricted from visible positions, Black women participating in the movement took up the leadership work readily available to them, empowering themselves and the community members with whom they worked at the grass-roots level. Their (gendered) bridging work was absolutely critical for success. Yet it was invisible in earlier studies because scholars ignored a gender hierarchy and focused on the visible male leaders at its top. Broadening the lens allowed Robnett to see leadership among those with less privilege in this particular "collective."

In our imagined post-leadership scenario, as excluded voices start weaving the fragments of a collective approach into the leadership conversation, scholars would start looking more systematically for leadership everywhere, while considering the impact of social location. This would contribute to challenging hegemonic assumptions that take for granted systemic dynamics of social exclusion directly affecting the exercise of leadership.

Social identity leadership theories informing the old canon ignored that unfair social systems reproduce themselves when people take for granted realities like ethnocentrism, neocolonialism, and inequality. Scholars explicitly disregarded structures of power and exclusion as pertinent to their inquiry. In a post-leadership world, rather than neutrally describing "in" and "out" groups, for example, scholars would interrogate the dynamics of inequality that construct these outcomes. In this post-leadership world, scholars would ask if what appears to be leadership may actually just be the operation of privilege. The opposite may also be true: the leadership work of people without privilege may become visible. This awareness enlarges the empirical instances and alternative worldviews from which to theorize collective understandings of leadership.

Implication # 1: Theorizing Collective Leadership as Lens

Consider how a group of contemporary US leaders of color—leaders who identify as Black, Latino, Indigenous or other non-dominant identity—describe their experience in social organizations. After affirming the challenges stemming from the complexity of the work in movement-building organizations, they state:

> For leaders of colour, racial issues exacerbate these challenges, and silence (concerning race) from other parts of society, further complicates the nature of their movement-building work. In fact, race always remains a salient consideration for these leaders, and however differently it might manifest in various communities or difficult it might be to measure, it cannot be ignored. It is embedded in their professional and personal realities at school, work, home, and everywhere in between. By extension, it is inevitably built into the issues on which their movement-building organizations work. The stories that these leaders tell, filled with pain, complexity, and grit, find little hearing elsewhere in the country.[9]

This vignette is from our multi-year research on social change leadership.[10] Based on our findings, we theorized that when individuals in excluded groups claim their leadership, their actions are grounded on a collective sense of hope and resilience that helps them imagine and realize abundance where others see scarcity. They draw on their lived experience of exclusion to articulate the vision of the future they want to achieve. A humanist worldview includes values that help articulate what is "a good life" for the collective. The emerging leadership practices aim to intentionally create spaces where affected members cultivate and take up their leadership, thus participating in bringing their future into the present. Social justice values become the moral compass to use power responsibly and activate the aspiration to create inclusive social arrangements in organizations and systems.

This theorization considers the context of leadership as a plurality of people participating in a "commons" to co-produce what the group considers valuable for the collective. The commons metaphor includes any space where interconnected individuals participate in meaning making to intentionally bridge their differences and find purpose and strategy. This "leadership work" happens simultaneously within each individual, in the (often imbalanced) relationships emerging among them and embedded in broader patterns of interaction within an existing but fluid power structure. The question of "leadership for what" becomes quite relevant in its co-construction.

The commons may be a team, an organization, a community, an inter-organizational network, a society, a coalition of nations, or the system of global institutions. These represent contextual levels of action to achieve what the collective wants. Of course flows of influence must be present for leadership to happen.[11] But these may not be merely channeled downward, through lines of authority; instead, the flows can also go upward, sideward, outward, or through formal and informal channels, impacting individuals, emerging relationships, roles, and so on. The leader-centered approach of the old canon could not illuminate what is going on. A positional authority focus would be too narrow. A broader collective lens is needed. A collective leadership theory applies a collective lens to leadership.

In a post-leadership world, collective leadership would not represent a different form of leadership, but instead a broader lens to look for leadership. Queries like where leadership resides and who is a leader become empirical: leadership may reside in individuals located in many parts of a collective— and it may also reside in objects and in processes that facilitate joint work for its members. Specific forms of leadership emerge in context and must be empirically identified. This is another reason to look for leadership in unexpected places, not just where it is expected. It also motivates asking the right questions for the particular contexts where leadership is studied.

Implication # 2: The Universal Value of the Leadership Experience of the Excluded

Exploring the role of identity in leadership, scholars guided by the old canon have focused on the obstacles minorities face working in traditional organizations as they aspire to, and achieve, formal leadership positions. While relevant, this is a narrow view of their leadership experience, and reflects a narrow understanding of the connections between leadership, identity, and power explored previously. Likewise, with a few exceptions, the new area of research on diversity leadership seems to be grounded on similar poor and narrow understandings of these links, as reflected in studies with ethnocentric research agendas; simplistic constructs of race and ethnicity presupposing internal uniformity; and "ethnic gloss" approaches that overgeneralize and minimize how cultural variation influences the exercise of leadership.[12]

Studies documenting the leadership experience of outsiders from other fields offer a different picture, showing, for example, that devalued social identities can become sources of strength, activate agency, and motivate effective leadership work.[13] In a study of gay and straight student leaders, the identity work gay students did around their LGB orientation positively impacted their ability to lead. They scored higher in their ability to manage controversy with civility, in recognizing interconnections among community members, and in valuing collective work for change.[14] Similar rich insights about the leadership experience of people of color in complex contexts (documented in fields like education, communications, and Black studies) also suggest that identity is not merely a constraint, but a leadership resource that helps transform scarcity into abundance. The emergence of leadership in these contexts may offer great insights about where and how leadership emerges (just as Robnett's research demonstrated). And yet this work has remained marginal to the leadership canon.[15]

In the new scenario, as the excluded entered the leadership conversation, explorations of identity and leadership would move beyond the old canon's interest in discrimination and attribution. New theories in the post-leadership world would gain depth and complexity in its understanding of the interconnections of leadership, identity, and power. As non-dominant social groups lost their status of exotic instances in an otherwise homogenous leadership narrative, insights about their characterizations of leadership styles and effectiveness would be potentially useful "for all people."[16]

Indigenous leadership research further illustrates the premise of the post-leadership canon: that the leadership work of Indigenous peoples—or other non-dominant identity groups—represents a potentially "good" case for theorizing leadership.[17] Exploring Australian Indigenous artists and arts leaders, scholars Evans and Sinclair theorize multiple contexts or "territories" within which leaders engage their leadership work. "Defined by intersecting social and economic structures, cultural norms and stereotypes, community pressures and expectations,"[18] these territories created conflicting pulls for the leaders (i.e., cultural-authorization and self-authoring in a bi-cultural world; identity and belonging; innovation and conservation of cultural values in the artistic practice; and expression and containment of trauma and hope, given a history of colonization). These explain the unique and dynamic leadership paths the leaders weaved as they moved across territories.

Seemingly specific to art leaders in Australia, the researchers convincingly claim that these findings have broader applicability for understanding leadership. Indeed, the conflicting pulls in these "territories" are quite resonant with the paradoxical demands of complex and turbulent environments where leadership emerges today. As the authors claim, the "content" of the territories navigated may be different, but the idea that leadership emerges through an intentional navigation process, heavily influenced by issues of identity and social location, has universal applicability. They argue that while Indigenous arts leaders combine (according to their unique circumstances) overlapping and often contradictory leadership practices as they engage in identity work, their engagement illuminates what leadership is about: a contextualized and dynamic phenomenon combining both structure and agency.

This study advances again the promise of a post-leadership canon that makes visible leadership work not recognized as such before. The authors remind us that leaders from non-dominant groups may emphasize understandings, espouse values, or highlight tensions unique to their experience, which researchers may not recognize as leadership work *because they may not have been represented in conventional explanations and thus may not be recognized as leadership.* Evans and Sinclair further clarify that studying these leaders led them to problematize accepted ideas of leadership and Aboriginality. This added a critical lens that helped them to see leadership where others may not have seen it.

Theorizing leadership from the experience of marginalized groups in a post-leadership world demands incorporating critical thinking, if it is to offer insights about the human condition. As new voices shift from the margins to the center, and enter the theorizing space where leadership scholarship is reinvented and created anew, their prior subordination to the perspectives and voices of individuals located in traditional contexts or in positions of privilege eventually disappears.

Implication # 3: Rethinking Methodologies

There are methodological implications of these insights for post-leadership researchers, who, as the collective lens took roots, would develop cultural sensitivity and culturally appropriate research methodologies. They would incorporate critical theories that make visible issues of power and privilege and emphasize participatory approaches that respect and empower participants.[19] In the case of Indigenous leadership, for example, gaining a basic understanding of an Indigenous way of life would acknowledge the relevance of honoring the spoken word, prioritizing memory of Indigenous knowledge to keep it alive, and resisting forms of neocolonialism, both intellectual and enacted.[20]

Post-leadership researchers would also be aware of and conversant with alternative methodologies, viewing them as legitimate choices—equal or preferred to the methods in the old canon. Grounded on Indigenous knowledge systems, Indigenous research has a relational, collective, and contextual mind frame, emphasizing place, spirituality, holism, and experience, as well as considering history, politics, the impact of oppression on people, and their responses to it.[21] Researchers would appreciate these as advantages to better "capture" the emergent nature of leadership and the invisible work associated with relationality and collectivism.

In sum, in the newly constituted post-leadership field, core principles of alternative standpoint research approaches, like feminist and Indigenous methodologies, would gain currency. Beyond helping study women and Indigenous leaders, these methodologies could shed light on leadership in other contexts.

Concluding Reflections

My thought experiment imagines a new leadership canon in the post-leadership world where collective leadership is dominant and grounded on insights from a plurality of voices including non-dominant individuals and groups. These would bring their experience and challenges to weave together and give substance to the various fragments representing the lost narrative of a young collective leadership scholarship at the time of the collapse.

From a critical constructionist perspective, the book's motivating question invites another one: wouldn't the disappearance of the leadership canon reflect a larger crisis of hegemonic ideas supporting existing social arrangements? An affirmative answer portrays a critical juncture in which the social world was re-ordering itself. Perhaps we are just there today, in a time when we strongly challenge old frameworks but have not quite yet created those we aspire to live by. Could we thus imagine our own participation as leadership scholars in supporting this transformation?

What if leadership studies today took seriously the plurality of voices, perspectives, and experiences that have been mostly excluded from prior research and knowledge development? Feminists and critical scholars have argued consistently that we can learn much from considering these perspectives. However, this has not happened in today's leadership studies: dominant theories tend to treat such experiences as special cases and tend to default to a Western white privilege standard when entering generalizations in the leadership canon.

Incorporating the plurality of voices would yield a more complex theorizing process grounded in a wide variety of unique experiences generating insights applicable to all human beings. New methodologies would help scholars gain cultural sensitivity and awareness of the impact of power and privilege. While new theories and methodologies alone will not transform the world, they can offer alternative narratives to counter a leadership paradigm that ignores the wide range of experiences constituting the human condition. Perhaps when this happens, we may start imagining how the leadership field can contribute to constructing more democratic, inclusive, and humane social arrangements.

Notes

1 Fassinger, Shullman, and Stevenson (2010) p. 203.
2 Ospina, Foldy, Fairhurst, and Jackson (2017).
3 Evans and Sinclair (2016).
4 United Nations (2017).
5 Dugan (2017) p. 39.
6 Robnett (1996).
7 Ibid. p. 1662.
8 Ibid. p. 1681.
9 Chan and Powell Pruitt (2009) p. 3.
10 Ospina, Foldy, El Hadidy, Dodge, Hofmann-Pinilla and Su (2012).
11 Endres and Weibler (2017).
12 Chin and Trimble (2015) p. 9.
13 Fassinger et al. (2010); Ospina and Foldy (2009).
14 Fassinger et al. (2010).
15 Ospina and Foldy (2009).
16 Fassinger et al. (2010) p. 213.
17 Evans and Sinclair (2016).
18 Ibid. p. 485.
19 Ibid.; Dougan (2017).
20 Kovach (2016).
21 Ibid.

References

Chan, A. and Powell Pruitt, L. 2009. Taking Back the Work: A Cooperative Inquiry into the Work of Leaders of Color in Movement-Building Organizations. New York: Research Center for Leadership in Action, NYU/Wagner.

Chin, J.L. and J.E. Trimble. 2015. Diversity and Leadership. Los Angeles: SAGE Publications.

Dugan, J.P. 2017. Leadership Theory: Cultivating Critical Perspectives. San Francisco: Jossey-Bass.

Endres, S. and J. Weibler. 2017. Towards a three component model of relational social constructionist leadership: A systematic review and critical interpretive synthesis. International Journal of Management Reviews. 19: 214–236.

Evans, M.M. and A. Sinclair. 2016. Navigating the territories of Indigenous leadership: Exploring the experiences and practices of Australian Indigenous arts leaders. Leadership. 12(4): 470–490.

Fassinger R.E., Shullman S.L., and Stevenson, M.R. 2010. Toward an affirmative lesbian, gay, bisexual, and transgender leadership paradigm. American Psychology. 65(3): 201–215

Kovach, M. 2016. Moving forward, pushing back: Indigenous methodologies in the academy. In N.K. Denzin and M.D. Giardina (eds). Qualitative Inquiry Through a Critical Lens. New York: Routledge. pp. 31–39.

Ospina, S.M and Foldy, E.G. 2009. A critical review of race and ethnicity in the leadership literature: Surfacing context, power and the collective dimensions of leadership. The Leadership Quarterly. 20(6): 876–896

Ospina, S.M., Foldy, E.G., El Hadidy, W., Dodge, J., Hofmann-Pinilla A., and Su, C. 2012. Social change leadership as relational leadership. In Uhl-Bien, M. and Ospina S. (eds). Advancing Relational Leadership Research: A Dialogue Among Perspectives. Leadership Horizons Series, Eds. Greenwich, CT: Information Age. pp. 255–302.

Ospina, S.M., E.G. Foldy, G.T. Fairhurst and B. Jackson. 2017. Collective dimensions of leadership: The challenges of connecting theory and method. Human Relations Special Issue Call for Papers, http://www.tavinstitute.org/humanrelations/special_issues/LeadershipCollectiveDimensions.html (Accessed July 2018).

Robnett, B. 1996. African-American women in the Civil Rights Movement, 1954–1965: Gender, leadership, and micromobilization. American Journal of Sociology. 101(6): 1661–1693.

United Nations. www.harmonywithnatureun.org/index.html (Accessed August 2017).

11 Rethinking Relational Leadership

Recognising the Mutual Dynamic Between Leaders and Led

Jackie Ford

Introduction

It has taken a long time for leadership studies to discover its critical possibilities and I want to save fragments of critical leadership studies – most notably, those aspects that speak to the significance of relationships between the leader and led. This chapter seeks to make visible the interdependencies between leader and led, the power and powerlessness within such relations and the damage that happens when leading and following are practised in a real dichotomy – in both positive and negative encounters. I offer a radical reframing of relational leadership thinking through drawing on Jessica Benjamin's psychosocial development of theories of recognition and intersubjectivity.

Many accounts of leadership studies appear to take too lightly, if they treat it at all, the insecurity, anxiety and ambiguity in the lives of leaders and led.[1] Through ignoring these feelings, they actively *create* these feelings. Leaders are told they should be confident, secure and very clear about what they are doing, and why they are doing it, in all circumstances. This is an impossible feat in practice – who could live up to such a paragon? By failing to live up to an over-ambitious norm, leaders can feel themselves to be failures. But in equal measure, there is a risk that control of work processes and conversations may still be regulated by power elites who manipulate organisational discourses through structural and cultural norms that remain embedded in historical traditions. This can in turn have disastrous consequences on followers in organisations – as I illuminate in this chapter.

My research within organisations over the last two decades recognises the significance of interpersonal relationships and the powerful effect that interactions between leaders and led can have on our lives at work. It is impossible to ignore our personal life histories, daily experiences, relationships and interrelationships with others, as leadership, indeed work in general, involves engagement with the multifarious identities of individuals in relation to others.[2] We bring our selves, our psyches, our histories, our idiosyncrasies, our ways of talking and thinking and acting, to these workplace relationships. If we bring all those aspects of the self uncritically to the workplace and are then encouraged to behave as if we are transcendental, homogeneous beings whose impact on others is justified by our positions as leaders, then we may do untold harm to others. Indeed, stories of organisations are besieged with the harm done to the majority by the minority who occupy powerful positions. We need to foster and further develop an approach that enables us to tap into the collective subjectivities of workplaces. This requires a radical rethinking of relational leadership theorising that goes beyond the positive experiences hitherto encompassed within such a tradition. I seek to expose the damaging and oppressive behaviours and relationships that surface in organisational life – even within leader–led encounters in which positive experiences prevail.

This chapter seeks to reframe relational leadership thinking through the lens of Jessica Benjamin's[3] development of the master/slave struggle for recognition. In seeking to develop this understanding, I draw from an intense case study of one manager who I interviewed while she was participating in a leadership development programme. Her working life story is particularly relevant for reframing the relational dynamics of leadership because she divides it into two starkly contrasting periods, a past time when she worked with someone she saw as an excellent, 'romantic' leader, and a present time when she suffers under what she sees as distant, poor, 'absent' leadership. The analysis leads me to argue that both romantic and absent leaders deny her recognition and selfhood. The former swallow her up so that she has no identity other than that of follower, while the latter ignore her and leave her bereft of identity. However, she is not passive in this: she brings her own desires to the relational leadership dynamic. This leads me to challenge unitary, or 'one-size-fits-all' theories of leadership. I conclude by drawing on Benjamin's new theorising of 'the Third' and outline an ethical model of relational leadership recognition in which each party acknowledges that they are flawed human beings who each has a duty of care for the other.

Going beyond the positive projection of relational leadership thinking enables us to examine the murkier aspects of domination and subordination that remain unspoken and under-examined in organisational life. Benjamin draws on Hegel's account of the significance of relational encounters and how selfhood emerges within and through agonistic encounters with an other that grants recognition. This chapter explores such leader/follower relational encounters and how – within the space of that meeting – one party becomes the leader and the other the led (the follower). It offers a new perspective through reframing relational, intersubjective perspectives on leadership. The next section outlines the theoretical location of this chapter, that is, within Benjamin's Hegelian-influenced psychoanalytic theories of the emergence of selves within relational encounters.

Relational Encounters, Recognition and Intersubjectivity

Many theories of subjectivities and identities in management and organisation studies are influenced directly or indirectly by Hegel's thesis on the emergence of the modern Western subject.[4] Summarised in the form of a mythical story known as the master/slave dialectic, it explores how subjectivities emerge through interactions between two parties, one of whom is dominant to a subservient other. It is therefore particularly apposite for exploring the relational leadership dynamic as an encounter in which the leader becomes a leader only through her/his followers recognising them as a leader.

In *The Phenomenology of Spirit*, Hegel[5] outlined a mythical encounter that involves, in brief, a master and a slave, each of whom cannot exist as social beings (become self-conscious) without recognition from the other. This need for recognition from another in order to exist as a subject is foundational to individuated Western selves. However, Hegel argues that the seeking of recognition is dangerous: to become a subject requires recognition from an other, but reaching out to that other carries a risk of annihilation. This is because parties turning to each other for recognition have to go through negation; the individual consciousness has to get out of itself (negate itself) to meet the other consciousness. Each party desires to eliminate the other and so is threatening and can undo or disavow the self.[6] Each reaches out to this dangerous other, so each risks life/identity because only one of the parties can win and earn recognition from the other. Gurevitch[7] illustrates this using the example of a discussion: individual voices struggle to be heard but only one person can speak at any one time if anyone is to be heard. The silenced party is not recognised. Through finding ways of remaining in a relationship of interdependency, albeit one based on inequality, both parties survive and possess a sense of self.

In summary, rather than seeing the subject as a monad, self-sufficient and with an identity that is internally generated, s/he is recognised to be constituted dialectically through agonistic processes of recognition, involving a life and death struggle in which one party may be denied recognition and so can have only an abject identity.

Taylor[8] similarly argued that not recognising or mis-recognising 'can be a form of oppression, imprisoning someone in a false, distorted, reduced mode of being'. Beyond a simple lack of respect, 'it can inflict a grievous wound, saddling people with crippling self-hatred. Due recognition is not just a courtesy we owe to people. It is a vital human need'. This is significant in exploring more radical ways to conceive relational leadership because it emphasises the need for recognition but more fundamentally, it requires mutual recognition – the necessity of recognising as well as being recognised by another.

Benjamin[9] argues that as 'fundamentally social beings' humans crave social stimulation, warmth and affective interchanges from the beginning of life. This can be translated through to organisational life. Individuals throughout their lives continue to have needs associated with emotional exchange and social contact. We are active beings and need the interaction and recognition from others in order to make sense of who we are as well as how we relate to others. Her exploration of the centrality of the concepts of recognition and *intersubjectivity* has what can be perceived as a major contribution to making sense of and providing interpretive potential to studies of leadership relationships in organisations.

The *intersubjective* view is perceived by Benjamin[10] as one in which the individual grows in and through the relationship to other subjects. Most importantly, this perspective observes that the other whom the self meets is also a self, a subject in his or her own right. It assumes that we are able and need to recognise that other subject as different and yet alike, as an other who is capable of sharing similar mental experiences. Thus, the idea of intersubjectivity reorients the conception of the psychic world from a subject's relations to its object towards a subject meeting another subject.

Intersubjectivity describes the existence of a relationship between self and other. It asserts that we are both separate and interrelated beings. It is through *reflexive recognition*[11] by the other that we know ourselves. It is both through the confirming response of others as well as how we find ourselves that is important – and this is why psychoanalytic theory can speak for interpretations of organisational life. It enables the recognition of inter-relationship and reciprocity between individuals, groups and organisations.

Benjamin[12] stresses that this mutuality of recognition is important – that is, the need to recognise others as well as to be recognised by the other. This relationship and inter-relationship is central – to see others as both like us and yet different from us, and to see the interaction and impact of the recognition on our sense of self (or indeed multiple selves). Yet within this, she identifies what she perceives as the paradox of recognition in which the need for acknowledgement by another can turn us back to becoming dependent on the other and may lead to a struggle for control. Tension between the assertion of the self and the need for the other was acknowledged through Hegel's analysis of the core of this paradox and the struggle between the independence and dependence of self-consciousness and its culmination in the master–slave relationship.

From this perspective, if the tenets of various theories of leadership are to be sustained, it requires a radical reframing of the relational dynamics of leadership such that each party should accord the other recognition in such a way as to ensure that each can flourish. However, Hegel (and later Freud) warned about the violence that is integral to recognition, leading to the question of what form of recognition may be ethical in what can be called the leader/follower dialectic. Answers to this question require that we understand how recognition is given in relational leadership encounters: can both parties flourish (such that they can achieve a state of eudaimonia) rather than experience abjection, degradation and melancholy? In other words, there is the potential for the relational dynamics of leadership not only to be positive, as presumed in most theories of leadership, but also destructive.

To understand the struggle for identity within relational leadership encounters, I focus my analysis on the story of one manager, Jane (a pseudonym), who recounts very clearly the experience of working with contrasting types of leaders. She had previously worked with an inspirational leader, and at the time of the interview she was suffering from the effects of absent leadership. I use a model for analysis of the scene of recognition given by Jessica Benjamin,[13] a Hegelian model that illuminates how the desire for recognition works within the psyche and the social. Benjamin uses Pauline Reage's *Story of O* to help understand the experience of dominant and subordinate subjects within the scene of recognition. The *Story of O* is a sadomasochist fantasy that, for Benjamin,[14] exemplifies how one's need for recognition renders one vulnerable to the workings of power in a context in which ethics is absent. It is thus relevant for rethinking the relational leadership dynamic that takes place within a context where organisations bestow power upon leaders but deny it to followers.

The *Story of O* has three major scenes that I will map upon the story of Jane's working life. In the first scene, O gives herself to Rene, with whom she is deeply in love. In the second scene, Rene has passed O to Sir Stephen, a dominant master with whom O subsequently falls in love, and in the final scene O has lost all subjectivity; she exists only as a degraded object. In the first scene of Jane's story, we see her working with someone she identified as an inspirational leader. He left the organisation, leaving her to the mercies of an uncaring leader (Scene Two). At the time of the interview (Scene Three), Jane presented herself as an object devoid of subjectivity.

A Note on Methodology

Jane was a participant in a larger study that I carried out over a decade ago that examined the working lives of managers in the English local government sector that had embarked on an organisation-wide leadership development programme. Full details of the methodology of the larger study are given in Ford.[15] Here I follow Clarke, Hollway and Jefferson, Roseneil, and Smith[16] in focusing on one individual who embodies an entire (organisational) problematic.

Jane is a quietly spoken woman in her mid-fifties. Her early aspirations for a career as a teacher had been shattered by a former economic recession, and she has been employed by the council for 28 years, predominantly in training and human resource management. She looks older than her years, has sunken eyes, a grey pallor and wears loose fitting, nondescript clothes. There was some affinity between Jane and myself as we both had early career experiences in human resource management and we exchanged stories about our earlier careers, but there the similarities ended. Jane's account was one of sheer despair, and as an interviewer I experienced feelings of devastation as we talked, an introjection that Hollway and Jefferson[17] advise requires exploration. What was it that Jane was saying that went beyond the words she spoke? Jane thus stood out from other interviewees, albeit in a deleterious way. She seemed to be telling a story that needed to be explored further.

Jane's interview, like all others in the wider project, used a narrative life history approach.[18] Analysis of the empirical materials started with data reduction through immersion in the transcripts to identify major themes. Following the tenets of narrative theory, those themes were then mapped onto a drama or literary work that explores similar themes, using the insights of the dramatist or his/her interpreters to read the interview participants' experiences in ways that otherwise would not be available.[19] In Jane's case, three major themes emerged: being led by a charismatic leader, being led by absent leaders, and Jane as an object. Benjamin's analysis of the *Story of O* lent itself to a different way of understanding those themes. The methodology therefore takes forward abductive approaches[20] in a way that departs from the linearity that conventionally informs research methodologies. I began with a sense that Jane's haunting of our conversations over the ten or more years since the interview meant she might be telling me more than I had originally heard her say,[21] so I immersed myself in the transcript of her interview to identify what was in it (what themes) that could guide me towards hearing what I otherwise could not hear.[22] I then sought a story that seemed to bear affinities with the newly identified themes, in this case *The Story of O*,[23] and then rewrote Jane's story[24] in the new format. Benjamin's (1988)[25] analysis of *The Story of O* provided a model for better understanding. We turn now to the story of Jane that emerged from this process.

The Story of Jane the Follower

Scene One: The Lovers of Roissy/The Charismatic Leader

We first meet O when she has been taken to a chateau in Roissy by Rene, the man with whom she is deeply in love. Their sexual relationship is sado-masochistic. Benjamin uses O's agreement to being debased by Rene (and subsequently Sir Stephen) to explore how submission works within the dynamic of the encounter in which recognition is given or withheld. This gives insights into why the subordinated or oppressed submit. It is a long way from a chateau in France to a council headquarters in the north of England, and at first sight there is little similarity between Jane's relationship with an inspirational leader and the relationship between O and Rene. However, I will suggest that Jane's absorption in a relationship where she was follower to a charismatic leader means her own subjectivity disappeared beneath her own desire for submission. This suggests that leadership as currently theorised implies that followers should lose themselves in the leader/follower relationship. That is, leadership as currently theorised requires submission in followers, a submission that involves loss of the self. Later I will argue that the recognition of her colleagues is insufficient to grant her recognition, because she craves submission to a leadership that refuses to acknowledge her existence. I subsequently explore how leadership should and could encourage independence rather than submission in followers.

Jane's story begins when she had been transferred to a new role in staff development, which marked a decade she describes as one of the most fulfilling of her career. She remembers it as an exciting time in which she brought in innovative staff development programmes. Her inspiration during these years, from the mid-1970s to the mid-1980s, was a man I call Simon:

> when he worked with me, we had something that was, again, quite powerful that we couldn't explain, but it was some dynamic that really achieved and I think it was what we managed to achieve working together

Here Jane begins by talking about Simon and herself as a team ('when he worked with me'), but goes on to talk with passion and enthusiasm about this seemingly flawless man whom she idealised:

> he was just an incredible person. He had time for everyone, no matter what he was doing, he'd stop and he'd listen, he understood and he showed real care and compassion for everyone – he valued everyone, regardless of who they were. ... he was like a model in terms of how to relate to people.

The power dynamics of the relationship emerge when Jane talks about Simon's influence upon her:

> he planted a lot of things in my mind about what we can actually become as human beings and we're only living a potential of what we could be and he was really influential, I'd say he was a role model.

That is, Simon was the more powerful person in the relationship, someone who took over Jane's mind and who 'made [such] a profound effect on me' that thirty years later, and many years since she last saw him (he left to take up a post elsewhere), she is still searching for his replacement:

> It's something I've never experienced again and I suppose it's one of those things that you always would like to ... to experience again, but it hasn't happened. Never.

The 'dynamic' she recalled earlier therefore appears to refer to some fusing of Jane's identity with that of a charismatic and transformational leader. There is sheer joy in these memories, and grief that she has not been able to repeat such an experience.

This all seems a very long way from *The Story of O*, save that O too merged her identity with a charismatic other.

Rene took O to spend two weeks at Roissy, but at the end of the first week he told her he was leaving and she should stay there for the next seven days. 'But I love you', he told her, 'I love you, don't forget me'. O responded: 'Oh how could I forget him!' What these words disguise is the nature of their relationship while at Roissy. During her first two weeks there, O was subjected to torture, beatings, repeated sexual humiliation and abuse. She grants her lover full permission for sadomasochistic acts, just as she had in their own bedrooms in Paris, and she continued to profess her adulation for Rene. She could not forget him:

> He was the hand that blindfolded her, the whip wielded by the valet Pierre, he was the chain above her head, the unknown man that came down on her and all the voices which gave her orders were his voice.[26]

This seems very different from Jane's relationship with her charismatic leader, but Benjamin's reading of *The Story of O* suggests major similarities, in that both Jane and O have subsumed their own subjectivities within that of the person from whom they crave recognition. Indeed, Benjamin notes[27] that the same desire for recognition fuels both domination and love. Benjamin's thesis concerns the lifelong struggle, originating in infancy, to reconcile one's need for independence with one's need for dependence. Ideally, one balances the two, but where there appears no other option for achieving recognition than submission, then the s/he-who-would-be-a-subject may collude in her/his own submission.[28] This arises because the subject's fear of the psychic pain of loss, abandonment and separation causes her to cling to those who have the power to grant recognition. But where the other does not grant recognition then the subject's selfhood shrivels. That is, when the master refuses recognition, the slave experiences intense pain that 'causes the violent rupture of the self, a profound experience of fragmentation and chaos'.[29] This loss of self-coherence actually creates the master's power, producing for the master a coherent self in which the abjected, subordinated slave can take refuge. Applied to Jane's idealisation of Simon, it is Jane's hero worship that creates what she regards as Simon's charisma. She loses her own self, just as does O, but gains circumscribed access to the more powerful and charismatic self of the idealised leader.

Curiously, after Simon leaves the organisation, all contact between he and Jane is lost. Jane gives no explanation for this. Benjamin's reading of the master/slave dialectic and the *Story of O* suggests such total separation arises because of the dominant partner's need for recognition. S/he cannot receive it from the 'will-less thing' that has no life apart from the (loved) other, and whose extreme dependency has vitiated any sense of a separate reality, and who is therefore in the subject position of the slave and incapable of giving the craved recognition.

Jane started describing her relationship with Simon as a relationship of equals. In this we see perhaps an ideal(ised) leader/follower relationship, such as that expounded in relational leadership theory.[30] That is, each party moves between leader/follower roles and gives and receives recognition as leader/follower. However, Jane's idealisation of Simon (he appears flawless) and her acknowledgement that she had no agency when working with him (he took over her mind) point towards tensions within the leader/follower relationship when one party comes to dominate and the other acquiesces gladly in that submission. We turn now to the second scene, in which Jane laments an absence of leadership, but we start with O, who abases herself totally.

Scene Two: Abandoned

Rene abandons his lover, O, and presents her to Sir Stephen, his stepbrother. Sir Stephen is described as having

> a will of ice and iron which would not be swayed by desire, a will in whose judgement and no matter how moving and submissive she might be, she counted for absolutely nothing. He demands that she obey him without loving him and without his loving her.[31]

O has to abandon herself utterly to Sir Stephen, accepting her status as object even more eagerly than she had with Rene, transcending herself by becoming nothing more than an instrument of his will.[32] Sir Stephen, meanwhile, behaves in such a way as to remain fully independent of his slave.[33] O inexorably loses subjectivity, Benjamin writes, relinquishing 'all sense of difference and separateness in order to remain – at all costs – connected to [the Master]'.[34] She acquiesces so readily because of a desperate desire to be *known*, although there is 'progressively less of O the subject left to be known'.[35]

Just as Rene abandoned O to another master, so Simon abandoned Jane to other leaders when he left during an organisational restructuring. And just as O's subjectivity shrivels, so does Jane's. She had gone from being someone with status, a team of staff and passion for her work, to someone who is marginalised, downgraded, silenced and invisible. Her perspective of the council is of an organisation that no longer places any value on working with people and supporting their development potential. She describes being sidelined and disempowered:

> I was excluded from a lot of arenas and I got told "Oh, erm you can't do this." Meaning "It's not your role or level in the organization to do this", but then, the effect of that long term can be, I start thinking "I can't do this." Meaning: "I haven't got the capability to do it", because I'd been excluded from doing it.

In other words, she receives no recognition of herself as a capable manager, and without that recognition she ceases to be a capable manager. She describes collaborative working relationships with junior managers, but these do not give her the recognition she hungers after, as that can come only from senior managers:

> People at our level in the organization, which is, like, junior to middle management are quite happy to meet and get things done and make

changes and what it is about *them up there*, that they seem unwilling to share information to share ideas, to work cooperatively.

Jane contrasts a hellish present with a heavenly past in which she was recognised by a charismatic and inspirational leader; her colleagues then were 'soul-mates'. Today she works in a leadership vacuum. She depicts the organisation's current senior managers, 'them up there', as macho, self-interested, hierarchical and status-conscious. They have interposed other managers in the hierarchy between herself and them, and so refuse to listen to her and thus have silenced her. Her heart, she says, is no longer in her work. But yet, she shows no agency – she remains in her post, talking about the possibility of looking for a job elsewhere, but never making the necessary moves.

Benjamin's analysis of O's masochistic pleasure in the pain she experiences at the hands of Sir Stephen and his friends is one in which physical pain protects the self from the psychic pain of loss and abandonment. Can it therefore be that Jane finds some sort of pleasure in remaining in her job? So long as the master hurts her, O remains connected to him and the possibility of recognition remains. Could this be the case with Jane, and with others who cling to unhappy working relationships? Benjamin points towards a fundamental operation within the psyche: we cling to that which hurts us for fear of finding something worse (annihilation) if we abandon it. So it is possible to submit to the master's will even while denying that submission: merely remaining physically present in the organisation is a form of submission. But submission to the master's will recognises his power, so 'Submission becomes the "pure" form of recognition, even as violation becomes the "pure" form of assertion'.[36] The first point to note here, therefore, is that by remaining employed by the council, Jane has submitted to the will of 'them up there' – she gets on with her job, feeling that she is achieving little, but still doing it. In this way, she clings to the possibility of somehow gaining that recognition she yearns for. But secondly, even as she laments the absence of direct leadership, she demonstrates its presence, albeit not in a form that she desires. That is, her experiences alert us to the existence of *leaderless followers* or a situation where followers desire to be led but no-one takes up that role. We turn to the final scene in this account in order to tease out the implications of leaderless followership.

STAGE 3: Annihilation/The Interview

At the climax to the tale, O appears as a slave, nude but for an owl-like mask, before a large party of guests who treat her solely as an object:

> But even though they did these things to O, and even though they used her in this way as a model or the subject of a demonstration, not once did anyone ever speak to her directly. Was she then of stone or wax, or

rather some creature from another world and did they think it pointless to speak to her? Or was it that they didn't dare?[37]

On this, Benjamin[38] writes that the master is in danger of becoming the will-less thing he has created unless he separates himself completely, while the slave loses all subjectivity and selfhood. If the necessary tension between subjugation and resistance breaks down, as when the slave becomes so subjugated that s/he has no identity apart from that of the master, then the master must flee from the implications of becoming similarly will-less, such that death (the negation of the self) or abandonment are the only possible outcomes.

Jane turned up for the interview wearing dark and dowdy clothes in which she seemed to fade into the background. Her whole bearing (her low energy levels, quietly spoken voice and generally subdued approach in our discussions) all suggested someone who was working to make herself invisible. The effect on me as interviewer was profound – she felt depressed and lifeless. Jane seemed totally submissive and asking not to be recognised. In this way, Jane resembles O in the final scenes of her story – metaphorically tending towards death, or 'deadness, numbness, the exhaustion of sensation'.[39]

The refusal of the senior managers in the organisation to recognise and value Jane – and even to acknowledge her existence – is further exacerbated by her own acceptance of her lack of subjectivity and her continuing willingness to offer recognition without expecting it in turn, as a complete self-denial. As a consequence, Jane and others placed in the 'follower' subject position in organisational life participate in their own subjugation; they repress their sociability and their social agency and remain as slaves to the organisational master. Leadership research thus needs to take much more account of the ongoing asymmetrical power relationship within relational dynamics of leadership, something I turn to in more detail in the discussion section.

As the absence of mutuality of recognition continues, the unequal complementarity is perpetuated in which the leader plays the master and the follower plays the slave. This sustained lack of subjectivity prevents non-leaders from experiencing the sense of successful destruction and survival that is needed in the interaction of individuals as social beings in organisational life.

Discussion

The *Story of* O and Benjamin's interpretations offer insight into ways in which people submit to others not just out of fear but perhaps also in complicity with their own deepest desires for their own submission. However, the story also alerts us to the desire for submission at the same time as a peculiar contrary position of the craving for recognition, in a search for an elusive spiritual satisfaction. Jane's masochism is part of her search for recognition from this organisation's leaders that have marginalised her, overlooked her for promotion and repeatedly blocked her efforts to speak to more senior leaders within the council. This *other*, the organisation's leaders, has the power for which Jane longs, and through its recognition, she can gain it albeit vicariously. In the *Story of O*, O loses all subjectivity and all opportunity to use her body for action. She is treated merely as an object to be (ab)used. This is how Jane describes her recent working life in the face of numerous restructurings in which her very presence has been marginalised and her voice silenced. Jane described how her initial promising ideals under the guidance of an inspirational leader figure and the developmental and innovative work programmes in the early part of her career in the council became a fading memory. Her passion and energy for those lost times are palpable, and the strong identification that she had at the time with the charismatic leader is a distant dream. She describes how she yearns for the freedom of self-employment and the opportunities she has seen others taking in their subsequent lives beyond the council. However, she seems to be locked in a masochistic hold of a profound inability to express her own desire and agency in the face of the dominant senior leaders of the organisation. She has been abandoned by these very leaders and yet she remains unwilling to let go of the sense of security that her continued employment within this council provides, despite the emotional pain and discomfort that this creates for her. It seems that the more she becomes attached to her current situation, the more she perceives anything else to be a threat to her (fragile) sense of security. She speaks of how former colleagues have moved on from employment at the council and have set up their own businesses, and how much they are thriving in this work. She depicts them as looking years younger since they left their jobs at the council, which is antithetic to her current demeanour and physical appearance and which serves to strengthen the case of her masochistic crusade. Despite the knowledge that her former colleagues have made such a success of their careers outside of the council, she seems to lack the courage to take the steps towards self-employment. In Benjamin's terms, 'the masochist abrogates her will because the exercise of her independence is experienced as dangerous'.[40] Jane's confidence in her abilities over the last decade has been knocked but has locked her into a declining sense of self-worth and an inability to do anything to change her situation. Her four-month absence from work for emotional exhaustion fits the pattern of her submission to the control of the council's senior leaders and their dominance over her. From the halcyon years of working with an inspirational leadership figure (who still denied her recognition), she has fallen into a state of ceasing to exist in the eyes of current leaders. And despite this, she still cannot quite let go.

The relevance of these arguments for radically reframing relational dynamics of leadership is clear. They enable us to better understand the day-to-day workplace experiences of power asymmetries, domination and subordination, voicelessness and inferiority. There is some acknowledge-ment of followers gaining a greater presence in the leadership literature and their role is increasingly evident in contemporary writings on relational leadership, albeit that such focus loiters within positive work encounters that conceal much shadier practices. Despite some recognition of followers in leadership thinking, follower voices remain absent or at the very least marginalised and subsumed in the other of the leader.[41] My concern is that followers submit completely to the power of the leaders in organisational life, whether these leaders are inspirational and charismatic figures or absent figures. Through this complete lack of recognition and total submission to the organisational leadership norms, subjectivity is lost. Furthermore, lead-ership theories that have formed the dominant ways of seeing and under-standing power and control in organisations suggest leaders have become both sacred and institutionalised, divorced from their value-laden founda-tion, to the extent that we assume that they are beyond critique, deconstruc-tion and reformulation.

What is significant is that both the romantic, inspirational leader and the absent leader deny the follower both recognition and subjectivity. The inspi-rational leader subsumes and consumes the follower such that she has no identity of her own and is only recognised as the other to the inspirational leader. The follower's own subjectivity disappears beneath her/his desire for submission. The absent leader ignores her so completely that she is deprived of recognition and identity. As I have argued, followers are not passive in this relationship and at times are both complicit in their loss of subjectivity, even joyful in the state of adulation of the inspirational leader, as well as frustrated at any loss of voice or denial of recognition. This leads me to radi-cally reframe relational leader/follower thinking through active and mutual recognition in which each party acknowledges that they are flawed human beings who each has a duty of care for the other. Through this I seek to develop a theory of the constitution of the identities of leader and follower within the space of the meeting of two subjects, rather than contemporary relational approaches that instigate a desire for submission in which the struggle to maintain the self no longer has to be undertaken. This requires that we explore how leaders and followers find ways to remain in a relation-ship of independence and interdependence, albeit one based on inequality and power asymmetry such that both parties survive and possess a sense of self rather than the submission and loss of self by followers to leaders. The leader/follower relationship is one in which each party should accord the other recognition in such a way as to ensure that each can flourish.

Benjamin's theorising of intersubjectivity and recognition offers potential for understanding experiences of being abjected while at work; it challenges dominant interpretations of relational leadership and provides another criti-cal lens through which the subtleties that make working lives so fraught are entrenched in contemporary presumptions of how to lead and follow. It also provides us with considerable opportunity to explore ways in which leadership thinking could be re-aligned to take account of the significance of recognition. Benjamin's more recent writings develop a position of what she refers to as the 'the Third'. She suggests that recognition is an approach that can be thought of in two ways – firstly as a psychic position in which we are able to explicitly recognise the other as a like subject, and as 'a being we can experience as "another mind" '.[42] It illuminates the potential for balancing the recognition of the leader's needs with the assertion of one's own as an ideal. This entails reconceiving the follower in order to release not only the tendency for ourselves to be complicit in control and submission but also to recognise the parallel tensions involved in our simultaneous desire for freedom and communion with the other. It is this dramatic tension that becomes lost in the ongoing domination by leaders in leadership studies. Without concrete knowledge, empathy and identification with followers and their needs, feelings, circumstances and history, leaders continue to move in the realm of master and slave, as subject and object, untransformed by the other. What is missing from this pairing is the tension of recognising the other as both different and alike. The powerful leader abuses her/his dominant position in the organisation and uses followers to reinforce her/his own status and importance. This leads to a vicious circle in which the more the follower is subjugated the less she is seen as a human subject. The resulting lack of recognition then breeds more of the same and results in the psychic destruction of the follower. The role of the follower in this pairing is no less complicated. The dominated follower whose actions at work are granted no recognition, may, even in the very act of emancipation, remain in love with the ideal of power that has been denied to them and they may in turn seek such powerful trappings as her/his own. The denial of subjectivity to followers means the privilege and power of agency fall to the leader. To halt the cycle of domination, the follower needs to make a difference, and claim her/his subjectivity to be able to survive the destruction of her/his sense of subjectivity.

The second position of recognition is as a process or action, what Benjamin refers to as 'the essence of responsiveness in interaction'.[43] This involves an ongoing process requiring shifts in and out of *thirdness* and which arises without coercion and constraint. The vision of recognition between two subjects (in leaders and followers) gives rise to a new logic – the logic of paradox, of sustaining the tension between contradictory forces of domination, submission, control and communion. It is the acknowledgement that we have a simultaneous and ambiguous need for both recognition and independence: that the other subject is outside of our control and yet we need her. Such acts of recognition, according to Benjamin,[44] confirm that we know each other as individuals that 'my intentions have been understood, I have had an impact on you, that I see and know you, I understand your intentions, your actions affect and matter to me. Further we share feelings, reflect each other's knowing so we have shared awareness'. Such reciprocal relationships allow many different positions that you can move within because they create open space for intersubjective but relational encounters that enable a freeing up of our own minds and emotions which is central to a more emancipatory leader–follower relationship.

Conclusion

This chapter builds on critical leadership scholarship through the powerful psychoanalytic lens of Benjamin's theories of intersubjectivity and recognition to make visible the interdependencies between leader and led; the power and powerlessness within such relations; and the damage that happens when leading and following are practised in a real dichotomy – in both positive and negative encounters. It throws a challenge to the largely positive accounts contained within contemporary relational leadership thinking and exposes the damage that happens when leading and following are practised in either enigmatic or noxious ways. It calls for a radical reframing of relational leadership such that power asymmetries and interdependencies are recognised and acknowledged. Each individual, whether as leader or follower, will experience leadership differently and we know that this relationship will not always be one of equal partnership and communion. I have drawn on Benjamin's earlier notions of recognition[45] and her later appeal for recognition, intersubjectivity and the Third.[46] Domination and submission is a breakdown in equal and mutual human relationships and it is through the notion of the *thirdness* that we are able to move beyond this dyad. Such authorship and agency of both parties is a relationship with some presence of the Third in which each subject is able to express herself with a kind of freedom because there is a space between her and the other person in which she does not feel she is being determined by the other.

To halt the cycle of domination by the leader and ongoing subordination of the follower, the Third enables a movement from the locked-in space of two-ness into the position of the Third in which subjects are able to free up their minds and emotions. The vision of recognition, subjectivity and the Third gives rise to the logic of paradox that requires our simultaneous need for recognition, co-creation and independence: that the other subject is outside of our control and yet we need her. But it goes further than that in allowing an open space that moves away from one living at the expense of the other and into a position of shared, responsible living together.[47] This is the direction in which I suggest that future relational and ethically responsible approaches to leadership theorising need to turn. My plea is to explore an alternative to the traditional relational leadership approach, looking towards one that recognises the potential subject positions of powerful and powerless subjectivities in organisations. In a new era of leadership thinking, I wish to continue the quest for ethical and radically different relational forms – following the Third – and to recognise the inherent dangers of the powerful effects of domination and submission in leadership thinking. It is also clearly beholden on the followers in the leader–follower dyad to ensure that if they suffocate their personal longings for recognition, they will extinguish all hopes for social and moral transformation within the workplace as well.

The refusal of leaders to recognise and value followers – and even to acknowledge their existence – is further exacerbated by followers' acceptance of their lack of subjectivity and their continuing willingness to offer recognition without expecting it in turn, as a complete self-denial. Benjamin describes different types of 'unbearable knowledge': the most intractable being the unbearable knowledge that one is oneself a perpetrator.[48] Renouncing the victim position is a necessary step in the process of recognition. As a consequence, followers participate in their own subjugation; they repress their sociability and their social agency and remain as slaves to the organisational masters. The way forward in an *After Leadership* environment is to radically reframe relational leadership thinking and to rebuild a body of leadership knowledge and practice around *the Third* in which new forms of leadership can be enacted that create workplaces that are more egalitarian and more promising. To paraphrase Benjamin,[49] we need to recognise the mutual dynamic of reciprocal understanding and responsiveness between leaders and led.

Notes

1 Ford and Harding, 2004; Ford, 2006.
2 Ford, Harding and Learmonth, 2008.
3 Benjamin, 1988; 1995.
4 Hegel, 1977; Kenny, 2010.
5 Hegel, 1977.
6 Benjamin, 1988; 2018.
7 Gurevitch, 2001.
8 Taylor, 1994: 25–26.
9 Benjamin, 1988: 17.
10 Benjamin, 1988: 19/20.
11 Benjamin, 1988: 21.
12 Benjamin, 1988: 31.
13 Benjamin, 1988; 1995.
14 Benjamin, 1988: 55.
15 Ford, 2006; 2010.
16 Clarke, 2002; Hollway and Jefferson, 2000; 2001; Roseneil, 2006; and Smith, 2013.
17 Hollway and Jefferson, 2000.
18 Ford, 2006; McAdams, 1993.
19 Gabriel, 2004.
20 Alvesson and Skoldberg, 2009.
21 See also Hollway and Jefferson, 2001; Finlay, 2002.
22 Gabriel, 1999.
23 Reage, 1970.
24 See also Rhodes and Brown, 2005; Rhodes, 2000.
25 Benjamin, 1988.
26 Reage, 1970: 63.
27 Benjamin, 1988: 62.

28 Benjamin, 1998: 59.
29 Benjamin, 1998: 61.
30 See, for example, the many perspectives presented in the edited collection by Uhl-Bien and Ospina, 2012.
31 Reage, 1970: 114.
32 Reage, 1970: 120.
33 Reage, 1970: 121.
34 Benjamin, 1988: 59.
35 Benjamin, 1988: 60.
36 Benjamin, 1988: 62.
37 Reage, 1970: 261.
38 Benjamin, 1988.
39 Benjamin, 1988: 65.
40 Benjamin, 1988: 79.
41 see also Ford and Harding, 2018 for a discussion of follower thinking.
42 Benjamin, 2018: 4.
43 Benjamin, 2018: 3.
44 Benjamin, 2018: 4.
45 Benjamin, 1988; 1995; 1998.
46 Benjamin, 2018.
47 Benjamin, 2018: 20.
48 Benjamin, 2009.
49 Benjamin, 2018.

References

Alvesson, M. and Skoldberg, K. (2009) *Reflexive Methodology: New Vistas for Qualitative Research*. London: Sage.

Benjamin, J. (1988) *The Bonds of Love: Psychoanalysis, Feminism and the Problem of Domination*. New York: Pantheon.

Benjamin, J. (1995) *Like Subjects, Love Objects. Essays on Recognition and Sexual Difference*. New Haven, Yale University Press.

Benjamin, J. (1998) *Shadow of the Other: Intersubjectivity and Gender in Psychoanalysis*. New York: Routledge.

Benjamin, J. (2009) 'Psychoanalytic controversies: A relational psychoanalysis perspective on the necessity of acknowledging failure in order to restore the facilitating and containing features of the intersubjective relationship', *International Journal of Psychoanlaysis*, 90: 441–450.

Benjamin, J. (2018) *Beyond Doer and Done: Recognition Theory, Intersubjectivity and the Third*. London: Routledge.

Clarke, S. (2002) 'Learning from experiences: Psycho-social research methods in the social sciences', *Qualitative Research*, 2(2): 173–194.

Finlay, C. (2002) 'Negotiating the swamp: The opportunity and challenge of reflexivity in research practice', *Qualitative Research*, 2(2): 209–230.

Ford, J. (2006) 'Discourses of leadership: Gender, identity and contradiction in a UK public sector organization', *Leadership*, 2(1): 77–99.

Ford, J. (2010) 'Studying leadership critically: A psychosocial lens on leadership identities', *Leadership*, 6(1): 1–19.

Ford and Harding (2018) 'Followers in leadership theory: Fiction, fantasy and illusion', *Leadership*, 14(1): 3–24.

Ford, J., Harding, N. and Learmonth, M. (2008) *Leadership as Identity: Constructions and Deconstructions*. London: Palgrave Macmillan.

Gabriel, Y. (1999) *Organizations in Depth*. London: Sage Publications.

Gabriel, Y. (2004) 'The narrative veil: Truths and untruths in storytelling', in Gabriel (ed) *Myths, Stories and Organizations*. Oxford: Oxford University Press.

Gurevitch, Z. (2001) 'Dialectical dialogue: The struggle for speech, repressive silence and the shift to multiplicity', *British Journal of Sociology*, 52(1): 87–104.

Hegel, G. (1977) *Phenomenology of Spirit*. Oxford: Oxford University press.

Hollway, W. and Jefferson, T. (2000) *Doing Qualitative Research Differently: Free Association, Narrative and the Interview Method*. London: Sage.

Hollway, W. and Jefferson, T. (2001) 'Free association, narrative analysis and the defended subject: The case of Ivy', *Narrative Inquiry*, 11(1): 103–122.

Kenny, K. (2010) 'Beyond ourselves: Passion and the dark side of identification in an ethical organisation', *Human Relations*, 63(6): 857–873.

McAdams, D. (1993) *The Stories We Live By: Personal Myths and the Making of the Self*. New York: Guilford Press.

Reage, P. (1970) *The Story of O*. England: The Olympia Press.

Rhodes, C. (2000) 'Ghostwriting research: Positioning the researcher in the interview text', *Qualitative Inquiry*, 6(4): 511–525.

Rhodes, C. and Brown, A. (2005) 'Writing responsibly: Narrative fiction and organization studies', *Organization*, 12(4): 505–529.

Roseneil, S. (2006) 'The ambivalences of Angel's "arrangement": A psychosocial lens on the contemporary condition of personal life', *The Sociological Review*, 54(4): 847–869.

Taylor, C. (1994) 'The politics of recognition', in Amy Gutmann (ed) *Multiculturalism: Examining the Politics of Recognition*, 25–73. Princeton, NJ: Princeton University Press.

Uhl-Bien, M. and Ospina, S. (eds) (2012) *Advancing Relational Leadership Research*. Charlotte, NC: Information Age.

12 Post-Leadership Leadership
Mastering The New Liquidity[1]

Stewart Clegg and Miguel Pina e Cunha

Introduction

The world of organisations is in flux: new media generate business innovations, collaborative idea creations, forms of participation, exploitation and criticism. Distinctions between organisations and their environments as objective determinants fade into irrelevance as strategies increasingly focus on creating new environments rather than adapting to existing ones. Traditional forms such as markets and firms are replaced and hybridised by platforms and work is digitalised and informed by "a liquid stream of facts flowing through the web'.[2] The boundaries of the firm thus dissolve: Coase's[3] explanation for the existence of firms is increasingly revisited.

Strategy morphs into a co-produced socio-technical phenomenon where local practices transform globally available resources and professionals move between projects in a world that becomes post-organisational in at least two ways; first, it is one that deviates from the norms of an organisational society premised on Weberian characteristics such as organisational careers, becoming a society where experts use organisations as temporary platforms; second, the organisation, as a specific entity defined by those activities it envelops, is decomposing, fragmenting, reforming and deforming, globally. Control, once vested firmly within organisational pyramids, becomes distributed across a network of actors, including new media and their users.

The private sphere of management control as a peak activity enveloped in a tangible and specifically modernist form of hierarchically dominated bureaucracy is dissolving, which has subsequent implications for the leadership dimensions of the managerial function'. Leadership is becoming dispersed and shared among actors, with the categories of leader and follower blurring, workers becoming globally subcontracted, matrixed and fragmented. Boundaries, choices and control are all shifting in the direction of increasing fluidity and plurality. The times may be changing. Secrecy and boundaries are not what they once were, affecting leaders and leadership, potentially rendering traditional leadership theory obsolete.[4]

We discuss organising in this digital age in terms of a liquidly modern time, whose birth was announced by Zygmunt Bauman. We do so by introducing the notion of liquid times and discussing three liquid themes: liquid selves, liquid organisations and liquid aesthetics. Overall, we defend the hypothesis that if the leadership canon of the last fifty years disappeared, we would witness the construction of a Baumanian theory of liquid leadership.

Bauman and Liquid Organising

The major treatment of Bauman's implications for organisations and for leadership and strategy, implicitly, is to be found in *Liquid Organization: Zygmunt Bauman and Organization Theory*,[5] which characterises Bauman's later work as focusing on three main themes: the *dynamics of modernity*, the *possibilities of radical social change* and the *ethics of compassion* – which they term 'sociological compassion'.

In terms of the *dynamics of modernity*, elements of these themes were anticipated in earlier works, such as the 1993 books on *Modernity and Ambivalence* and *Postmodern Ethics* and the 1998 book on *Work, Consumerism and the New Poor*. In the period before 2000, Bauman's reflections were cast in binary terms, influenced, suggests Jensen,[6] by Tönnies famous distinctions between *Gemeinschaft* (embedded and constraining community) and *Gesellschaft* (disembedded and liberating society), drawing contrasts between 'modernity' and 'postmodernity'.

The apex of modernity, for Bauman,[7] was represented by the death camps that delivered the Holocaust, where the strengths of normal organisation in delivering efficient terminal mass production were exemplified. The thesis has been widely discussed[8] but also criticised by scholars who have argued that the Holocaust was not organised by practices of bureaucracy.[9] The critics, namely du Gay, sought to preserve the ethos of Weberian bureaucracy from what they regarded as its corruption by fascism.

Posing a dualism between modernity and postmodernity, however, is inherently problematic. It leads to a problem of transition: how does one move from one state of existence to the other and how does one know that the transition has occurred? Such historical breaks are the exception rather than the rule, which is not to say that change does not occur, for it surely does, but more continuously, as a process of everyday life and living. The solidities of one time morph slowly into history, into something else, as they die of neglect or are extinguished or replaced. It is these moments of unfolding that are captured by postmodernism as a moment in the unfolding of history.

As Lyotard[10] noted, postmodernism is not the end of modernism, but its birth and rebirth, its constant coming into being. Modernity is a constantly shifting edge, struggles over the meaning of which define both modernism that seeks to condense its meaning and postmodernism that seeks to liquidate rather than consolidate. Still, the idea of a process, of a transition from one state to the other, still accompanies the very idea of there being a dualism, which is why, perhaps, in his later work, Bauman abandons the juxtaposition that served him well in the 1990s for a formulation that better captures this sense of an edge of uncertainty and introduces instead the idea of there being a liquid modernity. Liquid spreads, seeps, leaches and moves by osmosis. Liquid modernity's other is not post but solid: being solid, it does not melt or fade away but becomes a container, here more effectively, there less so, of a liquid edge that is forever spreading beyond its containment. The solid and liquid phases of modernity are implicated together: the one contains but that which it contains is never constrained by the form of the historical container; it shifts shape, it trickles off in new directions and new containers develop to try and restrict its viscosity, to discipline its flows, as it seeks to liquidate its containment.

Bauman distinguishes between solid and liquid modernity. Solid modernity represents the world of conventional organisation and management theory. Its hallmarks are a concern with objective structure, rational strategy and normal equilibrium. It is a world stalked by uncertainty and equivocality – the evils to be minimised and avoided as best as is possible by formulating appropriate strategies and structures: uncertainty as nemesis.[11] Stable bureaucracies, rational systems, orderly routines, formal leadership, and long-range planning – these were the devices used to ward off evils. Even when change was envisaged, it is seen as something the leader is able to control and ought to control, through 'transformational leadership', as if transformation was a smooth process.

The dominance of solid modernity defied much of the post-war era. Large bureaucratic organisations, characterised by rational planning and long-term careers for their cadres, were the norm, in both the state and civil society. But events conspired to unmake this solidity. From the early 1970s onwards, fuelled by the costs of maintaining the US warfare state, initially in Vietnam, the US state began to experience a fiscal crisis as it became more and more indebted due to deficit financing.

The Dynamic Liquids of Modernity

The organisations that flourished from the end of the Second World War through the 1970s, built on the long-range planning that the US Army chiefs of staff engaged in when planning the campaign to defeat Hitler, starting with the Normandy Landings. A natural ecology for leadership was to be found in the very large firms, such as General Motors, that dominated predictable and stable markets that they sought to control through long-range planning. Ironically, at the time that the Soviet bloc engaged in the same practices of long-range planning – the Five Year plans – corporate America, the bastion of private enterprise, sought to do the same, albeit based on corporate as opposed to state planning. In the Soviet case, it was the state that sought to plan; in the American case, it was left to the corporations. In doing so, they were assisted by the facts of post-war corporate life: markets that were largely based in the United States, protected from foreign competition by tariffs, standardisation, regulation, subsidies, price supports and government guarantees. Keynesian demand management was not just a feature of the United States. In Europe, especially in France with its *plannification*, there was a very explicit linking of centralist state and private sector interests by bureaucrats schooled in the Parisian *Grande Écoles*.

Keynesianism was allied with a strong central planning structure in the United Kingdom under the Wilson administrations of the 1960s and 1970s. The state, it was believed, could steer the white heat of technological revolution, a belief that died during the terminal stages of the Callaghan administration when the first fluttering of the new 'monetarism' emerged to assume full bloom in the Thatcher era of the 1980s, as Keynes was dismissed and Hayek became the new point of reference.

After 1980, with the rise of a new economic liberalism under the sponsorship of President Reagan and Prime Minister Thatcher, new competition was unleashed by the joint forces of creative destruction and liberal economic deregulation, liquidating the solidities of the modernist high water mark. The emergence of a new class of managers from the 1980s onward saw them greatly enriched in remuneration relative to all other wage and salary earners, in part by the adoption of agency theory as a strategy in practice widely used in the American corporate world.[12] This new class of managers, often presented as neo-charismatic types, are expected to be able to dramatically shape and reshape their organisations as their environments shift, which presumably justifies their salaries. Peters and Waterman[13] was the fountainhead for this shift to entrepreneurial exhortation, cultural creativity and the narcissism of leadership.

What agency theory added to narcissism was the idea that the corporate organisation is merely an aggregation of individuals contracted as a legal personality, such that the corporate organisation is a fictive collective individual that contracts real individuals to its purposes and is thus, presumably, the principal with whom contracts are entered into. The executives of the legal fiction are thus principals *and* agents. Fama and Jensen define the firm as a nexus of contracts between individuals in which the costs of enforcing contracts that are always incompletely stipulative will be a perennial problem.[14] These contracts are incomplete because of uncertainty that cannot be predicted and covered by contract.

Corporations that were quite obviously social institutions, with organisational employees treated in the way that social democratic citizens would be, with family health care programs, decent wages, salaries and pensions, were being invited to deconstruct. '[T]he "nexus" imagery served as a useful provocation, a lever to bust up the unwieldy and shareholder-hostile conglomerates built up over the prior decades. This was a theory perfectly designed to legitimate a bust-up takeover wave'.[15] Agency theory was an account that spawned in practice on a grand scale what it theorised.

The growth and application of agency theory to practice over the last forty years or so, particularly but not exclusively in the financial sector,[16] has seen agents become rewarded as principals that don't even have to risk their own capital. In tying their agency to that of the principals, they have voted themselves stock options, thus becoming significant principals in their own right. In most companies in the United States, the CEO tends to enjoy a considerable imbalance of power compared to the nominal authority of the board that appoints the CEO and to which they are legally accountable. Hence, the growing control of CEOs in governance on company boards has vested them with an ability to set, up to a point, their own salaries as well as nominate stock options. The discourse of strategy works to legitimate such practices, among many others. Leadership in this context became a proxy for personal enrichment on a scale unprecedented in prior rational-legal organisations as the euthanasia of bureaucracy was accomplished by the triumph of the *rentiers*. Modern organisations were being liquidated.[17]

There were corollaries to these processes of liquidation in terms of organisational changes: careers gave way to project portfolios; leaders gave space to dispersed leadership and self-leadership, that is, the identity of being leader was decentralised and devolved to many but the authority, power and rewards of leadership were more intensively centralised; bureaucracies became leaner as non-core elements of the business were outsourced; and their operations became more global as it was realised that enhanced value could be captured in value chains that probed wide and far into production sites and subcontractors in faraway places. The state also decomposed its bureaucracies in search for more efficient privatisation of those goods and services once taken for granted as within its domain.[18]

In solid modernity, the major container was work and the relations of production that this entailed. Capitalism, however, successful in fulfilling and perpetually expanding material wants and needs, shifted its register inexorably from a productive container defined by relations of production modified by state interventions into the welfare of its labouring citizens to an infinitely plastic container that expanded with the accelerating fetishisation of ever more phenomena, including work itself. Work that had been equated with a lifelong career, in the sense of an unfolding, a linear progression of working, often in the same or very similar organisations, saw its meaning liquefied.

Liquid modernity increasingly replaces citizens with consumers.[19] Whereas solid modernity developed a whole program for citizens around the rights of labour,[20] the relations associated with being employees, having contracts and deploying capital became more fluid, less secure and increasingly unstable. Liquidity was translated in terms of the prevailing political and economic ideologies into increased choice and freedom for the individual. These freedoms dissolved established commitments and senses of obligation and the institutions that supported these, such as mutual societies, trade unions, established religions and political parties. Identities founded in church and chapel, union and community, party allegiance and its tribal oppositions, weakened. The political process became more marketised, with the message becoming more crucial than the message's substance. Universities weakened their collegial bonds and increasingly became sites for the mass production of knowledge workers and specialist boutique ventures for the creation of intellectual property that could be valorised.

The reality of liquid modernity is that the only certainty is change; uncertainty becomes the new norm; instability and insecurity the new order; identity a matter of choice; and choice a matter of improvisational ability and access to the resources available to sustain it. Identity becomes the major arena for struggle: entrepreneurial subjects can propel themselves from being local drug dealers to cosmopolitan hip hop stars, thus setting new norms of identity for others to struggle to emulate or exceed.

Consumption can never be sated when global capital roams. Every day, in every way, new, improved and breakthrough delights for consumption will be tantalisingly available to those that can afford to sample them, disposing of outdated, inferior and unfashionable modes of consumption and of stuff already consumed. Nothing is sacred; nothing is secure; everything can be made redundant, become more liquid – including the leaders of products past. Identity increasingly resides not in being who one is, defined by the old materialities such as work and place, so much as in who and what one might become through the consumption of things in the desire for expressing selfhood. The injunction that by one's work(s) one shall be known is replaced by the exhortation to buy now and become what one might be.

In liquid modernity, life is lived increasingly in public: notions of private life cease to have the same meaning when one's becomings are routinely displayed on Facebook, when one's thoughts are tweeted incessantly, when one's smartphone becomes a McLuhanite extension of one's nervous system by which one creates and consumes content, in which the medium is more constant than the content it produces.[21] Leadership becomes an exercise in external and internal public relations, intended to cope with surveillance.

Leadership in Liquid Times

What does it mean to lead in liquidity? In this section, we discuss liquid selves, liquid organisations and liquid aesthetics as three facets of a post-canonical theory of leadership relations. Leadership changes in liquid spaces, becoming a form of post-leadership leadership.

Liquid Selves

Life lived in public increasingly pervades people's experiences in organisations. It does so in two ways: one is through an enhancement of the panoptical tendencies of solid modernity, where the few exercise surveillance over the many; the other is through the development of new forms of synoptical power, where the many watch each other and the ambitious among them watch the few. The two systems of power combine within liquid modernity.

Organisation studies developed a term to capture this combinatorial effect when it accepted the idea of the 'emotionally intelligent' subject.[22] The emotionally intelligent subject displays emotional competencies,[23] learned capabilities for outstanding work performance. The key competencies are in being liquid about innovation, commitments, adaptability and achievement:[24] each of these is viscous, shifting and redefinable – in a word, liquid. Liquid in the sense of being quick to liquidate not only tasks performed but also how they are performed, where they are performed and with whom they are performed. Liquidity requires autonomy, spontaneity, creativity, adaptability, communicative and relational competence, as well as significant capacities to invest in social and educational capital and a capacity to develop swift trust in switches from project to project, as liquid life in organisations is lived not in a linear career but in a succession of projects experienced in the moment. Being, self and actants are organised in a series of reflexive autopoietic loops, looping round existential angst about the success of the project: managing it on time, on budget, as innovative and in accord with key performance indicators.

The most acute and stubborn worries that haunt liquid leaders are fears of not being in the moment. Organisationally, liquid life is a mess of contradiction: it proposes a series of new beginnings, yet is full of worries about swift and painless endings as this project fails to morph into another, as this contract expires. Liquidly modern leaders (of the self) have to be perpetually constructing and reconstructing themselves; they are forever reassembling the pieces of their own identity, refining themselves day after day.[25] Inadequacy in this new liquidity involves an inability for those who aspire to become leaders to acquire the desired image with the existential doubt always being that theirs is a leadership without appropriate content and compass. Adequacy is having the ability to be simultaneously the plastic subject, sculptor and object of one's self, of becoming both the onlooker of self-work and the teacher of that self, a voyeuristic self, engaged in a process in which watching self watching others watching self becomes the liquid centre of self-existence and leaderly achievement.[26] In short, leaders become strategists of their self to succeed in liquid times. Impression management rules,[27] mediated through the media extensions of the self as LinkedIn, Facebooked, tweeted, and so on. Jensen suggests a prime fear of the liquid organisational member is to be unseen – especially when one occupies a position of visibility, such as that of a leader, an anxiety seen, not least, in the most powerful positional leaders, such as the President of the United States.[28] People engage in self-surveillance and self-discipline, making their self as visible, calculable and evaluable as possible.[29]

Liquid selves are valorised as free selves: free to choose, free to take responsible action for their self, free to construct their own biographies and projections of self. These are all self-centred, even as they project synoptically to others. The chief responsibility owed is to and for one's self.[30] The organisation provides arenas in which scenes may be staged that enable the aesthetic projection of the self. As Clegg and Baumeler[31] suggest, liquidly modern leaders are entrepreneurs of their selves: they must manage with enthusiasm and with passion and expect to share an ethos of immediacy, playfulness, subjectivity and performativity.[32] Between the performance and presentation of self and the reaction of significant others yawns a chasm of uncertainty as the subjects, still of surveillance but now also committed to being passionate, must choose how to present their self in a way that secures their profile as the kinds of subjects they anticipate that their followers and significant others expect them to be.[33] Being in the liquid state is an unfolding project in which constant vigilance and perpetual effort must be expended, with no guarantees that the performance will pay off, as Bauman states.[34] The kind of relationship this leader self forges with its 'followers' presents an interesting paradox: this self-serving self must, simultaneously, appear to *present* itself as acting in the service of others, of being concerned with the needs and interests of others, but this is a matter of appearance only, of the presentation of self, because to remain truly liquid a concrete commitment to acting in accordance with certain values or achieving certain outcomes would act as constraints.

Liquid Organising

The cornerstone of the liquid organisation is an absence of moral concern.[35] Liquid organisations are adiaphoric, that is, subject to *adiaphorization*, '[M]aking certain actions, or certain objects of action, morally neutral or irrelevant – exempt from the categories of phenomena suitable for moral evaluationevaluation'.[36]

Especially, this will be the case in the top management team: while each member may ontologically be a moral subject, the organisation cannot be. This is the essence of leaderly strategies. They may well be formulated within governance structures, rules, guidelines and policies, but are essentially ethically blank in their representations. As Bauman has most recently expressed it: 'Organizations ... serve the process of adiaphorization – of excising large swathes of human behaviour and human habit from the realm of moral evaluation and ethical obligations and thereby rendering them less sensitive to moral impulses'.[37]

Strategic imperatives are seen to flow from this process of adiaphorization: one is not so much responsible for a generalised set of other selves as responsible to the order in which one is employed – its rules, its authorities, its definitions of what is right according to the rules and what the rules make wrong. Necessarily, this invests considerable synoptic power in the hierarchical ordering of judgments and their expression as imperatives designed to manage meaning and transmit bold visions translated into mundane action through vertical command-obedience sequences; simultaneously, it makes of one a specimen subject to the multitude of panoptical powers used to exercise surveillance over one's self at work. Devices such as audit,[38] human resource management,[39] CCTV, and those ubiquitous recordings of customer interactions that call centres suggest may be used for training purposes, are all oriented towards the latter.

The combination of synopticism, panopticism and responsibilisation/ accountability pump and transfer the moral responsibility of the executors of commands upwards, to the command givers.[40] Those that enact, the subordinates, 'are excluded from the authorship of their acts'.[41] Those that command do not enact – that is the responsibility of those subject to the imperative commands: Thus, 'As a consequence, neither bears full, undivided responsibility for their acts. Absolute moral responsibility is thereby "deconstructed"'.[42] There is a myth in the Academy, the Academy of Management that is, that leaders and followers share common interests: to this myth we would respond with an account of exploitation as the necessary bargain entered into between employer and employee where the latter rents their time, creativity, labour and commitment to the control and benefit of the other's goals.

What remains is the ethical pose of the individual subject, only judged according to organisation rules. Responsibility floats and ethics are defined largely in terms of the contracts that leaders have entered into with stockholders, such that, in principle, no leaders can be perceived as a moral subject *qua* organisational membership. Their moral responsibility is to be found in service of organisation strategies, strategies turned towards abstractions of the market and their manifestations in analysis and shared values, not their questioning.

In the past, before modernity became so liquid, this was efficient enough when composed wholly within the envelope of an all-encompassing organisation that organised itself along classical bureaucratic lines, to cultivate virtue. Members were expected to express a vocation, to display character, to respect an ethos. Careers in the service of the organisation and its solid composition as a bureaucracy reinforced a sense of disciplined ethical virtue expressed in deference to routines, rules and rationalities. However, as a result of what Bauman refers to as the 'second managerial revolution',[43] the solid organisation has decomposed. It is not that bureaucracy is being superseded but it is becoming embroiled in complex processes of hybridisation,[44] simultaneously decomposing and recomposing. The notion of post-truth captures the movement.

Decomposition takes us to the world of supply chains and outsourcing, with their avoidance of regulation.[45] Recomposition takes us into the world of new organisational designs. In the former, there are some very familiar politics of surveillance and control; in the latter, there are more innovative developments that centre on the replacement of the central figure of the bureaucrat with that of the project leader and the central life experience of the occupational career followed largely in one organisation being replaced by that of individual's leadership achievements in projects. The politics of the project become the testing ground for elite reproduction.[46]

What is distinctive about leading and working in the contemporary liquid decomposed organisation is that the major mechanism of the career has undergone a substantial change. Careers are increasingly project-based, flowing now like mercury and then reconsolidating in a new plane of activity.[47] The project – whether innovation, research and development, engineering, marketing or whatever, becomes the major vehicle for organisation networks and alliances and developmental tasks within specific organisations – although, increasingly these will involve team members from other organisations. In such hybrid and often unclear situations, conflict and confrontation are inevitable, so managing emotions becomes a crucial skill. Leaders need to create learning environments – via coaching, hands-on teaching and mentoring – to stimulate and develop their employees – and to manage expectations about evolving roles in projects.[48]

If one follows the direction of decomposition, it is clear that in the new margins located on the global peripheries of modernity, in the electronic panopticon of the call centre or the outsourced production line, bureaucracy is alive and well in a particularly centralised, standardised and routinised form. Here the bureaucratisation of the shop floor has proceeded into the heart of the white collar, pink blouse and colourful, indigenously attired digital factory. If, on the other hand, one follows the recomposition route into the upper echelons of leaner and more entrepreneurially oriented organisations, a surprising observation emerges. Leaders are no longer responsible subjects – at least not for performance in all its manifestations: ethical, financial, production, and so on. The more they are able to do less of the work of the organisation the more efficient they become, as well as becoming less responsible. Leadership is hyper-symbolic but increasingly empty of substantive impact when decomposition is widespread. Efficiency is measured in simple terms as value considered only in costs and profits. Responsibility is pushed down and out. Pushed down it is subsidiarised by being constituted as empowerment of the subaltern workforce who become panoptical governors of their employment relations.[49] Pushed out it is outsourced, subcontracted and embedded in a supply chain whose governing mechanism is invariably contractually expressed in financial terms with no special attention to local practices.[50] Should those financial terms be delivered in ways that seem ethically dubious, where people die, become ill, poisoned or incapacitated, in a necrocapitalist variation of capitalism,[51] then the responsibility does not reach the top of the chain: the buck stops where the contract remotely resides. Gains flow upwards through the circuits of power; costs are pushed downwards. Greater responsibilities are no longer attached to higher remuneration: 'Chief executive officers have by now gained a nearly comprehensive insurance against punishment for failure to deliver results, including failures caused by their indolence, incompetence, neglect or downright sloth'.[52]

Leaders self-manage and convince their subordinates to do the same; in doing so they bring to bear all their emotional intelligence and attachment, using digital devices that register their participation in working panoptically as they project their efforts synoptically to all their Linked In network and Facebook 'friends', interpolating work achievements into life lived outside official confines, outside of the office.[53] Those leaders that become most successful are measured by their wealth. As Pfeffer put it, money trumps everything.[54]

The Aesthetics of Liquidity

The truly liquidly modern organisation announces itself to be so at street level and in the disposition of its internal spaces. Not for it are the bland boxes and skyscrapers of solid modernity. There are several ways of being liquidly aesthetic. For early and start-up organisations, it is typical that they will rent a funky, slightly distressed space, perhaps part of an old factory or warehouse, preferably with valid heritage features: the location of design companies such as Advanced Digital Institute in the remains of Salt Mill in Saltaire, Bradford, a World Heritage Site, is typical of a liquidly aesthetic workplace statement. The employees sought are those who Warren terms 'liquid employees'[55] – individuals who choose their jobs as they would a commodity, as a statement, an affirmation, a badge of identity – and the liquid organisation seeks to make the workplace one that offers aesthetic fulfilment and proximity to good transport links and housing. Being in a conventional edge of the city industrial park just doesn't cut it in these terms.

More established liquid organisations will prefer a signature architect, preferably a starchitect. To be a starchitect, the designer must have achieved celebrity and critical acclaim that has transformed them into major figures in the world of architecture, usually indicated by the award of major prizes and the commissioning of landmark buildings. Those that are best known have a name recognition that extends to a degree of fame amongst the general public. To become a starchitect requires some pretensions to the avant-garde – nothing classical or classically modern will do. The essential feature is the aestheticisation of the workplace, whereby 'aspects of objects, places, events, people and experiences of everyday life are made more appealing through the decoration, enhancement or other embellishment of their appearance'.[56] *De rigueur* are highly designed spaces and finishes, coupled with laid back open spaces, bicycle spaces and the provision of quality fit outs in terms of kitchens, cafes, coffee ports, and so on. The occasional sculpture or modern art piece helps also, which an art consultancy can supply on lease; occasional musicians, artists, poets or writers in residence can also help create a suitably funky sense of place.

Hancock suggests that liquid organisations will seek to structure fun, novelty and excitement into the experience of being at work.[57] The work itself becomes liquid – it spills over into downtime, occupies the wakeful creative moments of the organisational members and travels with them as they use their portable digital devices. Above all, the space must be flexible:

it should not be solidified into structures that cannot adapt and change easily. Open spaces, hot desking, bookable meeting rooms, no anchoring in offices – these are all preferred. Of course, the opportunities for both synoptical and panoptical power increase as the visibility and transparency of working conditions increase. Nonetheless, these characteristics signify 'coolness' – the accolade that a liquid organisation and its liquid leaders must express.[58] The contrast is with the constructions of earlier modes of organisation such as factories, modernist towers and desolate warehouse spaces of the industrial park. Aesthetically liquid organisations cannot be authentic if they occupy such spaces. Authenticity has to be signified by style and the style must be cool. The implications for the aesthetics of leadership performance are notorious. The black and white image of Steve Jobs (the bully but visionary leader) in his roll-neck sweater comes to mind, so 'cool' that he could wear something from the 70s and still evoke a sense of being at the cutting edge. The former Uber CEO Travis Kalanick also hardly ever appears to wear a tie, with the absence of a tie in buttoned-down and buttoned-up corporate America sufficient to symbolise the disruptive nature of Uber. Style fuses with substance.

Towards Post-Leadership?

From a liquid perspective, leadership is becoming post-leadership, a process of mutual influence with highly porous borders but also with very clear limits. In the liquid world, leading and following blur, leadership de-materialises and hierarchies apparently give way to organisational landscapes of flatness (see Table 12.1). But the elites are as powerful as ever and

Table 12.1 Organisations in light of solid and fluid modernity

	Solid modernity	Liquid modernity
Organization	• Rational system • Long-term planning • Orderly routines	• Agile organism • Short-term advantages • Dynamic capabilities
Person–organisation relations	• Sense of mutual obligation • Labour contracts • Regulation and uniformity • Long-term careers	• Free selves • Gig economy • i-Deals • Protean careers
Leadership	• Top down • Authoritative • Formal • Gravitas	• Networked, dispersed • Consented • Personal • Collegial
Control	• Panoptical • Hard power • Bureaucratic	• Synoptical • Soft power • Cultural
Society	• Citizenry • Shareholders	• Consumers • Stakeholders

the implicit hierarchies are still there. Everything appears different while the underlying contours of relations of production and administration remain structurally the same.

In liquid modernity, agility prevails. The solid bureaucracies of the past, in which order is an everyday production in explicitly hierarchical spaces,[59] gives way to agile systems rich in expectations of self-leadership. The long-term advantages of the past are replaced with a succession of short-term advantages, as sustainable advantages are an idea of the past in the world of hypercompetition.[60] Orderly routines, founded upon repetition, give way to the preponderance of dynamic capabilities[61] and even routines themselves are rediscovered as incubating change *and* adaptability – recent emphasis being placed on the latter.

Person–organisation relations reflect the trend. The traditional sense of obligation gives way to free selves. Employment is replaced by employability. Labour relations made uniform by labour unions are replaced by i-Deals[62] and frequently by gig work in a gig economy supported by platforms.[63] Apparently, the long-term career is dead as we celebrate the protean career! Leadership, as traditionally devised, founded upon power asymmetries, is seemingly dissolved in cultures sculpted with soft power. Leadership loses its *gravitas* and becomes a form of apparent collegiality, with leaders posing as *primus inter pares*. Leadership seemingly becomes an act of consent rather than a form of coercion, an exercise in articulating an array of stakeholders' rights in such a way that recognises that while all stakeholders are apparently equal, some will always be more equal than others. Some stakeholder issues just have more salience than others; some issues are more meaningful than some others that can be marginalised as largely non-issues.

This liquid world is part fact, part fantasy. Organisations do sometimes appropriate the rhetoric and the logic of liquidity. They move past traditional practices and empower people. But fluidity comes at a price: people are often empowered to align, such that the façade of new organisational designs hides forms of organisational continuity.[64] As Jensen explained, old forms now assume 'many disguises'[65] and power, freed from old pyramid structures, gains a digital edge, a change reflected in the growing interest of organisation theory for the digital.[66] There is more: employability comes with the spectre of unemployment; i-deals dig deeper inequalities; shareholder value creation trumps sustainability; global value chains hide inhumane labour conditions, sometimes close to modern forms of slavery,[67] some of them in highly visible projects such as the Qatar 2022 Football World Cup.[68]

After the leadership of the few, new forms of leadership of the many liquefied the traditional representations, introducing a number of paradoxical effects. Common citizens upgrade their status towards leadership identities and the elites downgrade their's: presidents describe themselves as normal persons and the ordinary folk gain leadership credit. The world of liquid modernity is one of post-leadership: a synoptical space in which everybody's leadership is under the constant surveillance of the multitude of leaders. Leaders are less necessary because (self)leadership is everywhere. The liquid world is a world of leaders free to follow the crowd: leading by watching self watching others watching one's self.

Conclusion

From the perspective of the leaders, they know that they are over the threshold where the golden chains are evident. The largest problem that they must deal with is using the project shape-shifting that goes on outside the threshold as the basis for competitions and tournaments that will decide who of the subaltern may cross the threshold into leadership. Looked at from below, from the perspective of the subaltern, contemporary organisations are shape-shifters, project-based with teams composing and decomposing, locations shifting as projects are completed, key performance indicators changing with projects and one's individual organisational future uncertain.

The hybrid political structure of liquid organising needs both leadership differentiation to ensure a credible competition among various centres of power (individuals and/or subgroups) and unification to ensure a relative consensus on basic values and on the legitimate rules of the internal political arena. Leaders are differentiated from sub-elites who, in turn, are distinguished from the population of knowledge workers, experts and professionals, with regard to values, demographic characteristics and types of aspirations. Beyond everyday concern are the distant global margins where the objects of desire are produced.

Corporate leaders have a direct interest in shaping, grooming and educating selected aspirants, constituting what might be called subjects with an appropriate comportment, etiquette and equipage to qualify as disciplined. Running projects with paradoxical criteria of performativity (on time, on budget, on specification, efficient while delivering innovation) successfully hints, in a weak way, that one has been spotted as someone with potential that the elites wish to test out, to see if the project leader can display certain indispensable characteristics for the leadership elite. Mostly, these characteristics pertain to an ability to accept and work creatively with an existing order and existing rules; thus, they go far beyond merely technical and professional expertise. They are the new way of reinvigorating *habitus* when organisational borders have become porous, careers liquid, and leadership identities contingent.

What the conditions of liquid organisation and leadership offer those ostensibly being led is a great propensity for anomie. Anomie is usually taken to mean a state of normlessness, detachment and non-solidarity created by a mismatch between personal or group standards and wider social standards. The gap occurs because of the lack of social ethics integrating individuals into broader moral sentiments. When behavioural norms of leadership practice spread indifference to the fate of others, when the decomposition of the corporation becomes the norm, when social relations become predominantly digitally mediated, anomie will escalate not only as existing corporate ranks are diminished through increasing culls on membership but also as, in the digital 'sharing' economy, the vast majority of people working become self-employed, precarious and marginal employees or are outsourced subcontractors of the corporate behemoths remaining.[69] The corporation becomes an increasingly remote Kafkaesque citadel that few can breach. When there are few people left to lead and many that feel cast asunder by the leaders of the past and present, through increasingly liquid states and organisations, leadership as an ethical claim to significance and difference tends to be an option with diminishing prospects other than the inflation of rhetoric with which to Trump.

Notes

1 This chapter partly draws on a keynote address prepared by Stewart Clegg for the FORE School of Management, New Delhi Foundation Day International Conference on *Riding the New Tides: Navigating the Future Through Effective People Management*, 24–25 November 2016. The subtitle is from Kelly (2016, p. 73). Miguel Pina e Cunha's contribution was funded by National Funds through FCT – Fundação para a Ciência e Tecnologia under the project Ref. UID/ECO/00124/2013 and by POR Lisboa under the project LISBOA-01-0145-FEDER-007722. We are grateful to the feedback from our editor Suze Wilson. Her feedback was invaluable in improving the text. Her invisible hand is here and there in the chapter.
2 Ibid., p. 279.
3 1937.
4 Fairclough, 2005.
5 Kociatkiewiecz & Kostera, 2014.
6 2014.
7 1989.
8 See Clegg, Courpasson & Phillips, 2006.
9 du Gay, 2000.
10 1993.
11 Tsoukas, 2005.
12 Bower & Paine, 2017.
13 1982.
14 Fama & Jensen, 1983.
15 Davis, 2016a, p. 509.
16 Mallaby, 2010.
17 Davis, 2016a, 2016b.
18 Guillén & Ontiveros, 2012.
19 Nixon & Gabriel, 2016.
20 Abrahamson & Broström, 1980.
21 McLuhan, 1964.
22 Goleman, 1995; Salovey & Mayer, 1990.
23 Goleman, 1998.
24 Clegg & Baumeler, 2014.
25 Bauman, 2005.
26 Clegg & Baumeler, 2014; pp. 51, 52.
27 Goffman, 1959.

28 Jensen, 2014, p. 24.
29 See also Maravelias, 2009.
30 Bauman, 2007, p. 92.
31 2014, p. 38.
32 Hjorth & Kostera, 2007; Bauman, 2008.
33 Jackall, 1988.
34 Bauman, 2000, p. 8.
35 Clegg, Kornberger & Rhodes, 2007.
36 Bauman, 1995, p. 149.
37 2014, p. xvi.
38 Power, 1999.
39 Townley, 1993.
40 Bauman, 2014.
41 Ibid., p. xvi.
42 Ibid.
43 Ibid., 2014, p. xvii.
44 du Gay, 2000; Courpasson & Reed, 2004.
45 Reinecke & Donaghey, 2015.
46 Clegg, 2011; Clegg & Courpasson, 2004.
47 Schein & Van Maanen, 2016.
48 Garvin, 2013.
49 Barker, 1993.
50 Reinecke & Donaghey, 2015.
51 Banerjee, 2008.
52 Bauman, 2014, p. xviii.
53 Clegg & Baumeler, 2010; 2014.
54 2016.
55 2014, p. 71.
56 Ibid.
57 2003.
58 See Lancione & Clegg, 2015.
59 Zhang & Spicer, 2014.
60 D'Aveni, 1995.
61 Eisenhardt & Martin, 2000.
62 Rousseau, Ho & Greenberg, 2006.
63 Spreitzer, Cameron & Garrett, 2017.
64 Pfeffer, 2013.
65 2010, p. 429.
66 Bodrozic & Adler, 2017.
67 Crane, 2013.
68 Reinecke & Ansari, 2016.
69 Clegg, Cunha & Rego, 2016.

References

Abrahamson, B. & Broström, A. (1980). *The Rights of Labor*. Beverly Hills, CA: Sage.
Barker, J.R. (1993). Tightening the iron cage: Concertive control in self-managing teams. *Administrative Science Quarterly*, 38, 408–437.
Banerjee, B.S. (2008). Necrocapitalism. *Organization Studies*, 29(12), 1541–1563.
Bauman, Z. (1989). *In Search of Politics*. Palo Alto, CA: Stanford University Press.
Bauman, Z. (1995). *Life in Fragments: Essays in Postmodern Morality*. Oxford: Blackwell.

Bauman, Z. (2000). *Liquid Modernity*. Cambridge: Polity Press.

Bauman, Z. (2005). *Liquid Life*. Cambridge: Polity.

Bauman, Z. (2007). *Liquid Times: Living in an Age of Uncertainty*. Cambridge: Polity.

Bauman, Z. (2008). Organization for liquid-modern times? Unpublished paper provided by the author.

Bauman, Z. (2014). Preface. In J. Kociatkiewicz, J. & M. Kostera (Eds.), *Liquid Organization: Zygmunt Bauman and Organization Theory* (pp. xiv–xix). London: Routledge.

Bodrozic, Z. & Adler, P.S. (2018). The evolution of management models: A neo-Schumpeterian theory. *Administrative Science Quarterly*, 63(1), 85–129.

Bower, J. & Paine, L.S. (2017). The error at the heart of corporate leadership. *Harvard Business Review*, May–June, 50–60.

Clegg, S.R. (2011). The futures of bureaucracy? *Insights* 4(1), www.dur.ac.uk/ias/insights//.

Clegg, S.R. & Baumeler, C. (2010). Essai: From iron cages to liquid modernity in organization analysis. *Organization Studies*, 31(12), 1713–1733.

Clegg, S. & Baumeler, C. (2014). Liquid modernity, the owl of Minerva and technologies of the emotional self. In J. Kociatkiewicz & M. Kostera (Eds.), *Liquid Organization: Zygmunt Bauman and Organization Theory* (pp. 35–57). London: Routledge.

Clegg, S.R. & Courpasson, D. (2004). Political hybrids: Tocquevillean views on project organizations. *Journal of Management Studies*, 41(4), 525–547.

Clegg, S.R., Courpasson, D. & Phillips, N. (2006). *Power and Organizations*. Thousand Oaks, CA: Sage.

Clegg, S., Cunha, M.P. & Rego, A. (2016). Explaining suicide in organizations. Durkheim revisited. *Business & Society Review*, 121(3), 391–414.

Clegg, S.R., M. Kornberger & Rhodes, C. (2007). Business ethics as practice. *British Journal of Management*, 18, 107–122.

Coase, R.H. (1937). The nature of the firm. *Economica*, 4, 386–405.

Courpasson, D. & Reed, M. (2004). Introduction: Bureaucracy in the age of enterprise. *Organization*, 11(1), 5–12.

Crane, A. (2013). Modern slavery as a management practice: Exploring the conditions and capabilities for human exploitation. *Academy of Management Review*, 38(1), 49–69.

D'Aveni, R.A. (1995). Coping with hipercompetition: Utilizing the new 7-S's framework. *Academy of Management Executive*, 9(3), 45–57.

Davis, G.F. (2016a). What might replace the modern corporation? Uberization and the web page enterprise. *Seattle University Law Review*, 39, 501–515.

Davis, G.F. (2016b). *The Vanishing American Corporation*. Oakland, CA: Berrett-Koehler.

du Gay, P. (2000). *In Praise of Bureaucracy: Weber, Organization, Ethics*. London: Sage.

Eisenhardt, K.M. & Martin, J.L. (2000). Dynamic capabilities: What are they? *Strategic Management Journal*, 21, 1105–1121.

Fairtlough, G. (2005). *The Three Ways of Getting Things Done: Hierarchy, Heterarchy and Responsible Autonomy*. Greenways, UK: Triarchy Press.

Fama E.F. & Jensen, M.C. (1983). Agency problems and residual claims. *Journal of Law and Economics*, 26, 327–349.

Garvin, D.A. (2013). How Google sold its engineers on management. *Harvard Business Review*, December, 74–82.

Goffman, E. (1959). *The Presentation of Self in Everyday life* Harmondsworth, UK: Penguin.

Goleman, D. (1995). *Emotional Intelligence: Why it Can Matter More Than IQ*. New York: Bantam Books.

Goleman, D. (1998). *Working with Emotional Intelligence*. New York: Bantam Books.

Guillén, M. & Ontiveros, E. (2012). *Global Turning Points: Understanding the Challenges for Business in the 21st Century*. Cambridge: Cambridge University Press.

Hjorth, D. & Kostera, M. (Eds.) (2007). *Entrepreneurship and the Experience Economy*. Copenhagen: Copenhagen Business School Press.

Jackall, R. (1988). *Moral Mazes: The World of Corporate Managers*. New York: Oxford University Press.

Jensen, T. (2010). Beyond good and evil: The adiaphoric company. *Journal of Business Ethics*, 96(3), 425–434.

Jensen, T. (2014). On adiaphoric organizations and adiaphoric organizational members. In J. Kociatkiewicz & M. Kostera (Eds.), *Liquid Organization: Zygmunt Bauman and Organization Theory* (pp. 13–34). London: Routledge.

Kelly, K. (2016). *The Inevitable: Understanding the 12 Technological Forces that will Shape our Future*. New York: Viking.

Kociatkiewicz, J. & Kostera, M. (Eds.) (2014). *Liquid Organization: Zygmunt Bauman and Organization Theory*. London: Routledge.

Lancione, M. & Clegg, S.R. (2015). The lightness of management learning. *Management Learning*, 46(3), 280–298.

Lyotard, J-F. (1993). *Toward the Postmodern*. Atlantic Highlands, NJ: Humanities Press.

McLuhan, M. (1964). *Understanding Media: The Extensions of Man*. Cambridge, MA: MIT Press.

Mallaby, S. (2010). *More Money than God: Hedge Funds and the Making of a New Elite*. London: Bloomsbury.

Maravelias, C. (2009). Make your presence known! Post-bureaucracy, HRM and the fear of being unseen. *Personnel Review*, 38(4), 349–365.

Nixon, E. & Gabriel, Y. (2016). 'So much choice and no choice at all': A social-psychoanalytic interpretation of consumerism as a source of pollution. *Marketing Theory*, 16(1), 39–56.

Pfeffer, J. (2013). You're still the same: Why theories of power hold over time and across contexts. *Academy of Management Perspectives*, 27(4), 269–280.

Power, M. (1999). *The Audit Society: Rituals of Verification*. London: Sage.

Reinecke, J. & Ansari, S. (2016). Taming wicked problems: The role of framing in the construction of corporate social responsibility. *Journal of Management Studies*, 53(3), 299–329.

Reinecke, J. & Donaghey, J. (2015). After Rana Plaza: Building coalitional power for labour rights between unions and (consumption-based) social movement organisations. *Organization*, 22(5), 720–740.

Rousseau, D.M., Ho, V.T. & Greenberg, J. (2006). I-deals: Idiosyncratic terms in employment relationships. *Academy of Management Review*, 31, 977–994.

Salovey, P. & Mayer, J.D. (1990). Emotional intelligence. *Imagination, Cognition, and Personality*, 9(3), 185–211.

Schein, E.H. & Van Maanen, J. (2016). Career anchors and job/role planning: Tools for career and talent management. *Organizational Dynamics*, 45(3), 165–173.

Spreitzer, G., Cameron, L. & Garrett, L. (2017). Alternative work arrangements: Two images of the new world of work. *Annual Review of Organizational Psychology and Organizational Behavior*, 4, 473–499.

Townley, B. (1993). Foucault, power/knowledge and its relevance for human resource management. *Academy of Management Review*, 18(3), 518–545.

Tsoukas, H. (2005). *Complex Knowledge*. Oxford: Oxford University Press.

Zhang, Z. & Spicer, A. (2014). 'Leader, you first': The everyday production of hierarchical space in a Chinese bureaucracy. *Human Relations*, 67(6), 739–762.

Part III
Discarding, Deconstructing, Starting Again

13 Imagining Organisation With and Without Leadership

Suze Wilson

Introduction

It may be that only when directly confronted by radically different alternatives to what we normally take for granted that we recognise quite how limiting, and even arbitrary, is our sense of reality and truth. Consider, for example, the following:

> Animals are divided into (a) belonging to the emperor, (b) embalmed, (c) tame, (d) sucking pigs, (e) sirens, (f) fabulous, (g) stray dogs, (h) included in the present classification, (i) frenzied, (j) innumerable, (k) drawn with a very fine camelhair brush, (l) *et cetera,* (m) having just broken the water pitcher, (n) that from a long way off look like flies.
>
> (Borges, quoted in Foucault, 1994, p. xv)

How might we respond to this seemingly bizarre approach to categorising the animal world? Foucault proposes that '(i)n the wonderment of this taxonomy, the thing we apprehend in one great leap, the thing that, by means of the fable, is demonstrated as the exotic charm of another system of thought, is the limitation of our own, the stark impossibility of thinking *that*' (1994, p. xv). Drawing on this insight, the thought experiments offered here contemplate, firstly, the character of organisations if the modern canon of leadership knowledge was simply wiped from our collective memories and then, secondly, what a turn to medieval understandings of leadership might bring to contemporary organisation.

The use of fanciful thought experiments is, of course, at odds with expectations that organisational scholars focus on topical issues and deploy rigorous scientific methods.[1] Curiosity-driven efforts, or work that is simply out of step with key trends in a field, is likely considered less relevant when positivist empiricism, Kuhnian normal science and a concern to sustain the marketability of university education and research prevail.[2] But such musings, improbable though they may be, have critical potential to expose and challenge taken-for-granted assumptions – and to offer fresh visions of what might be possible.

By imagining today's organisation without the plethora of theories, concepts and practices generated via modern leadership studies, there is potential to envisage a different 'system of thought', as Foucault encourages. However, as contemporary management and leadership thought are both products of modernity and modern science, the epistemological break likely remains fairly modest if all we do is remove that which sees leadership as a distinctive capacity or practice from our frame of thinking. By turning to medieval leadership thought, however, there is scope to explore ideas founded in a system of thought that is at a considerable remove from our own. This, potentially, increases our chances of exposing the limitations of current knowledge. It may also reacquaint us with lost and forgotten ideas, which we can then look to adapt to contemporary concerns.

The first scenario posed here – modern organisation *sans* leadership – is, of course, largely unthinkable because it has become ubiquitous to assume and assert the desirability, inevitability, impact and sheer necessity of leadership as a life force for organisational success.[3] Since the late 1970s, talk of 'leadership' has progressively colonised territory previously deemed the purview of 'administrators' or 'managers' while, simultaneously, claiming much greater potency of impact. As a consequence, our understanding of leadership these days routinely positions 'leaders' and leadership practices as the key to unlocking 'excellence' in employee motivation, satisfaction, commitment and performance; to forming and successfully achieving inspirational visions and innovative, adaptive strategies; and to addressing wicked, complex and ambiguous challenges and crises.[4] As part of this shift, the knowledge, practices and individuals seen as 'management' have been relegated in value in leadership texts, deemed incapable or less effective in addressing such concerns. The effort is made, in many leadership studies, to position it as something fundamentally different to management, and to claim that 'leaders' possess distinctive capacities that 'managers' lack. Via this framing, management is positioned as effective for routine, concrete matters but lacking the 'x factor' in relation to people, strategy and difficult challenges that is claimed by and for leadership.[5] Leaders, Bennis famously told us, are those who 'do the right thing', while managers merely 'do things right'. As part of all this, it is also taken for granted that modern, scientific knowledge is vital to developing better data, theory and practice, both in the realm of leadership and of management.[6]

However, what if, in a flash of light, modern leadership knowledge suddenly disappeared and we were left with two possibilities: organisation without leadership, reliant on *management* theory and practice or, alternatively, organisation where insights about *leadership* were drawn from the efforts of medieval-era scholars. By imagining organisations absent the knowledge developed by modern leadership studies, we can move some way towards disrupting dominant assumptions; however, this shift does remain bounded by the modernist perspectives that are infused in management thought. A turn to medieval thought, therefore, potentially provides a greater level of disruption to what is currently taken for granted. As we explore these different scenarios, we might also well ask, under which might organisational life become more tame, frenzied or fabulous?

Imagining Organisation Without Leadership: Is the End of the World Nigh?

The first thought experiment is that of organisation shaped by *management* ideas, such as those we would find featured in a standard 'introduction to management' textbook but absent the chapter on leadership.[7] Would employees lack motivation, satisfaction, commitment and perform at a lesser level without leadership? Would inspirational visions and innovative, adaptive strategies be impossible, if we were reliant only on managerial knowledge? Would wicked, complex and ambiguous challenges and crises be beyond our capacity to address?

In contemplating organisation with management and without leadership, it is worth noting firstly that despite the alleged importance of leadership, and the hype that we now live in a post-industrial era, the legacy of Henri Fayol and Frederick Taylor continue to inform much organisational practice, often complemented by what Max Weber would readily recognise as elements of what he called the bureaucratic form.[8] Weber's notion of legitimate authority still lends credibility to a hierarchical basis for decision making on which even recent forms of organisation design mostly still rest. Taylor's interest in defining, measuring and organising tasks, equipment and labour in ways that seek to optimise outputs for the least amount of inputs still remains central to much organisational practice. As Taylor proposed, the conception of work principally still falls to management, while its execution falls to labour. As Fayol commended, it remains commonplace to find managerial attention directed to issues of planning, organising, commanding,[9] coordinating and controlling, these being understood as key means of securing efficient and effective organisation. Fayol's administrative principles also directly inform or underpin common practices such as: the division of work into specialised roles; defining job holders' authority and responsibility; structures which provide for unity of command and a scalar chain; expectations to subordinate individual interests to team, unit or organisational interests; efforts to assure unity of direction, discipline and orderliness; and a concern with esprit de corps.

These 'classical' modern foundations of management thus still provide much that brings to organisational functioning a concern to use reason and logic in decision making; organise authority relations hierarchically; seek orderliness and efficiency in how tasks are completed; engage in goal-directed action; plan ahead; align employees' efforts towards managerially sanctioned purposes and direction; provide clarity as to expectations; and foster co-operative workplace relations and strong morale. As a minimum, these managerial practices seem geared towards ensuring that organisation can be sustained absent leadership. Indeed, 'leadership' as now commonly understood is wholly or largely absent from these approaches to organising work.

That said, the subsequent refocussing of managerial thought and practice initiated by the likes of Mary Parker Follett and Elton Mayo, and the vast array of subsequent developments that are broadly concerned with organisational behaviour issues, such as psycho-social needs and dynamics, employee motivation, team dynamics and manager–employee relations, encourage a strong focus by managers on emotional and relational factors, thereby counter-balancing the heavily rationalist tenor of classical management thought.[10] When the classical tradition in management thought is combined with the organisational behaviour tradition, managerial attention is directed towards both facts and feelings, to both efficiency and to harmonious relations. By drawing on these, organisational life thus need not be bereft of the emotional, relational elements that are often seen as distinctive features of leadership. Granted, the intense follower loyalty often attributed to leadership may be missing from the equation – however, so too are the problematic dependency relations and passivity which critical scholars have shown are often implied by the notion of followership.[11]

What, then, of inspirational visions and the formation and implementation of innovative, adaptive strategies, which some have sought to position as distinctive attributes of leaders? Here, knowledge developed by the fields of strategic management and change management has much to say. Its principal governing assumption is that those in managerial roles, by virtue of their position, can and should engage in strategic and change management, meaning it does not depend on notions of leadership as a distinctive practice or capability to proceed.[12] In recent years, strategic and change management have also come to treat creativity, innovation and issues of organisational purpose, values and culture as central concerns, meaning this managerial knowledge offers much that can aid in forging visions that people will find inspiring and strategies that are innovative and adaptive.[13]

Meanwhile, the focus given to issues of organisational culture means it is now orthodox management practice to seek to shape organisational culture, instil shared values and engage in meaningful, two-way communication to secure stakeholder buy-in, both as part of ongoing operations and as part of strategic and change management efforts.[14] To this we may further add that the fields of project management and risk management offer disciplined, routinised means of managing organisational change and innovation.[15] Overall, then, these literatures indicate that there is much that management theory and practice has to offer in enabling organisations to formulate and change visions, cultures and strategies in ways that have potential to garner active stakeholder support, even if leadership, as a concept or a practice, were to be removed.

In sum, then, there seems to be no compelling reason to believe that managerial practices are incapable of generating inspiring visions and innovative, adaptive strategies and to hold that these matters are the exclusive domain of leadership. Moreover, if leadership is removed from our frame of reference, it may be that it is the substantive *ideas* generated through such managerial processes that will attract attention and support, rather than the *leader*, as is so often the case now, which is arguably a more sustainable state of affairs. The tenor of these managerial efforts may well lack the rather glamourous, emotional punch and intense symbolism tied up in notions of visionary or transformational leadership, through which a somewhat frenzied desire to take on the changes promoted by the leader is said to be triggered.[16] However, this also likely facilitates a greater focus on matters of substance rather than matters of style, and a greater reliance on reason rather than emotion in decision making, both of which seem rather helpful given what is normally at stake is the organisation's capacity to survive in a changing environment.

But what of the truly tough challenges – those that are wicked, complex or ambiguous? Surely leadership is essential for these? Perhaps. However, complexity theory, the managerial concept of bounded rationality, systems thinking, modelling techniques derived from operations research and literature on team problem solving all offer ways of engaging constructively, critically and creatively with wicked, complex or ambiguous challenges. Importantly, these perspectives also tend to direct our attention to what kinds of practices, processes, methods or data we need to address such challenges. In contrast, if leadership is returned to the picture, the risk is that we are drawn back to a focus on the individual characteristics of those who we wishfully hope can save us from ourselves.

Overall, the romantic mysticism that so often attaches itself to understandings of leadership, and the resources this offers for building a leader identity as one imbued with rare and special abilities, upon whom others may depend, may be what we lose in organisation without leadership. Yet it is not immediately clear that this constitutes a retrograde step, given the evidence that managers struggle to live up to the fantasy of the all-knowing, infallible leader and, as a result, suffer from a sense of existential failure which likely undermines their capacity to act.[17] A manager identity, as commonly understood, also seems to offer less scope to indulge in narcissistic and hubristic tendencies than does the typically more heroic cast given to a leader identity. Meanwhile, employees no longer positioned as followers may also be less inclined to dependency on a leader and have greater clarity as to the exchange basis of the employment relationship and, hence, its limits. This in turn may encourage employees to look to other aspects of their lives as potential sources of wish-fulfilment, rather than to the leader-manager, providing a limit to the extent to which our workplace identity colonises the private/personal domain.

What also becomes evident from the foregoing is, I suggest, the distorted and distorting character of contemporary understandings of leadership. Such grand claims are made for leadership. Such extensive efforts are made to mark it out as distinctive and special, as being more potent, more creative and more humane than management. Yet when we drain leadership thought out of our minds, we see that, in reality, management is extremely potent, can be creative and can be practiced in humane ways. Even given its instrumentality, management without leadership doesn't imply a soulless corporation any more than does a corporation with both leadership and management. The gloss may be gone, but the substantive capacity to elicit positive engagement from people, form visionary goals and adaptive strategies and tackle wicked, complex and ambiguous challenges is not lost to us.

That said, the ineffable value of leadership that may make it worth resurrecting in a different form rests, I suggest, in its potential to be positioned as that which is founded in a *duty to serve* the interests of all members of the organisational community. This framing carries with it the radical potential of constituting leadership as a distinctive contribution that sits in a state of ongoing tension with management, whose role is ultimately limited to serving the interests of owners. To advance this potential, however, I suggest we might again largely sidestep the modern canon of leadership science and explore what medieval scholars have to offer.

Creating the Future From the Past: Imagining Medieval Leadership in a Modern Age

There is a dreadful violence I am inflicting on medieval leadership thought here, uprooting it from its context and pulling only selectively from its otherwise holistic nature. Such is the use we often make of history, rather than valuing it for its own sake, on its own terms. With this plea for forgiveness from our ancestors, then, I want to firstly offer a very brief overview of the general character of medieval leadership thought, before identifying aspects that seem to have potential to foster leadership of ethical and/or practical value for the world in which we now live.

Medieval leadership knowledge was, almost entirely, built around the person of the king or prince. Thus, in its original context, it offers an account of leadership that is masculinist, hierarchical, inherited, non-democratic, absolute in its powers, expecting of loyalty and compliance, elitist and reliant on the belief that the leader/prince/king was chosen by God.[18] To a modern, critically oriented readership this won't appear as a promising basis from which to proceed – although we might also note that these ideas are not that distant from contemporary realities in many instances! It is hardly a stretch, for example, to suggest that leadership in the Trump corporation, like many others, is masculinist, hierarchical, inherited, non-democratic, absolute in its powers, expecting of loyalty and compliance and elitist. No doubt God is also often positioned as a supporter of this state of affairs, even if not formally a member of the CEO appointment committee. However, what should be obvious, I hope, is that these are features of medieval leadership thought and practice that I think are best left in the past (as I wish we could do with Trump himself and all that he represents, for that matter).

So what is worth resurrecting or adapting, to help address our needs? Perhaps in recognition of the extensive powers held by medieval monarchs, and the often reckless manner in which such powers were exercised, medieval leadership scholars were extremely concerned with questions of duty, service and character. The quid pro quo, it seems, for paying obeisance to claims of the leader's God-given right to rule appears in the conceptualisation of leadership as a duty, an obligation, one which ought to be directed towards serving the interests of the whole community, not the leader's own interests, and in a sustainable manner.

This way of thinking has, I suggest, radical potential, providing a basis for re-imagining leadership as a practice whose ethical foundations lie in a commitment and sense of obligation towards the group, organisation or community one ostensibly leads. To fulfil these obligations, without a return to paternalism, implies an inclusive and long-term approach and a focus on promoting organisational strategies, policies and practices that take into account the interests of all stakeholders. These understandings offer an entirely different proposition than we find today, where leadership is typically constituted as a career move that gives rise to the right to advance one's vision for the future, rather than as an obligation to serve others.[19]

There is extensive commentary in medieval leadership texts that extols the lifelong, deeply felt and serious-minded nature of this duty to serve others. Sacrifice of the leader's personal needs and wishes was routinely recommended as the price to be paid for the privilege of leading. Character virtues such as prudence, clemency, modesty, diligence, a commitment to lifelong learning, a willingness to seek and listen to expert counsel, a distrust of flattery and a concern with ensuring justice, are all matters advocated by medieval leadership scholars. If these behaviours were to become commonplace amongst today's organisational leaders, substantive changes that benefit the majority of people would be the result.

A turn to medieval thought also offers potential to reconstitute the relationship between leadership and management. Presently, a formal leadership role will normally carry the same *fiduciary* duty as that placed on management – indeed the possibility that *leadership might imply obligations that conflict with those of management* is likely never even considered, such is the extent to which leadership these days is constituted as something to be used by managers to serve business interests. Essentially, when push comes to shove, today leaders are expected to act as would managers, serving the interests of shareholders. However, conceptualising leadership as a duty to serve the long-term interests of the whole organisational community would, in some instances, place leadership in direct conflict with management. In these situations, leadership as reimagined here implies bringing a different perspective to the debate, one that is not captured by, or reducible to, what best serves shareholder interests. How a manager who seeks to also engage in leadership reconciles this tension becomes an overtly ethico-political dilemma to be grappled with. Such situations are likely uncomfortable to contend with, but better some discomfort than the pretence that organisational decisions are somehow free of ethical and political considerations.

Leadership that is grounded in a sense of duty to serve others' interests has several other key implications. It de-legitimates the careerism now routinely encouraged of leaders. It provides a basis for challenging the privileges and 'perks' routinely attached to leadership roles. And, it facilitates critique of short-term or shareholder-centric decision making as constituting poor leadership. Overall, the current conflation of leadership with managerial interests becomes much more difficult by this account, and there exists a clearer and ethically grounded basis for distinguishing between leadership and management. Perhaps surprisingly, then, a turn to aspects of medieval thought that focus on a concern with duty and service offers the potential to 'raise the bar' for what constitutes good leadership today. Equally, a turn to the knowledge developed to help tame the power of kings and princes could, if applied as posed here, see leadership as a force for taming managerial power, through promoting greater consideration of the long-term interests of all organisational stakeholders. Now wouldn't that create a frenzy?

Conclusion

Foucault advocates that we 'make thought groan', testing the foundations on which that which seems real, natural and good depend, and finding and then seeking to breach the limits of what is presently constituted as *thinkable*. What arises from such efforts may, from a certain perspective, amount to nonsense or merely wishful thinking. Yet what is clear is that the precise form and functioning of leadership is not stable and enduring. What we ask of it varies across time and place. What is held to constitute the truth about leadership is continually changing, and not simply due to the processes of scientific discovery. Rather, the truth about leadership is always under construction as different claims are made about it and for it. The claims provoked by scenarios explored here test the value presently attributed to leadership (and management) and explore what medieval knowledge may offer us in thinking about leadership today. Their true value, however, may lie in the extent to which they elicit a greater awareness of the limited focus of contemporary understandings of leadership and, from this, help sustain the search for new and more fabulous ways of thinking about leadership.

Notes

1 Alvesson, Gabriel & Paulson (2017).
2 Alvesson (2017).
3 Wilson (2016).
4 For example, see Bass & Riggio (2005) or Bennis & Nanus (1985).

5 Ford & Harding (2007).
6 See, for example, DuBrin (2016) or Northouse (2013).
7 For example, Robbins et al. (2015) or Samson & Daft (2014).
8 Shafritz, Ott & Jang (2015); Knights & Willmott (2017); Du Gay (2001); Taylor (2012); Rodrigues (2001).
9 This 'command' element might arguably be understood as showing that Fayol did see the necessity of a (directive) form of leadership which management alone cannot offer, thereby undermining the credibility of my argument. However, as directive behaviours are now normally seen by leadership scholars as falling in the domain of management, while 'influence' is the currency of leadership, that is how I have interpreted Fayol's position.
10 Knights & Willmott (Eds.) (2017).
11 Harding (2015); Tourish (2013); Wilson (2016).
12 Dess, McNamara & Eisner (2016); McCalman, Paton & Siebert (2016); Pearce & Robinson (2011).
13 Angwin, Cummings & Smith (2011); Bilton & Cummings (2010); Szczepańska-Woszczyna (2018).
14 For example, Schein (2010). While there is often talk of 'leadership' in such texts, the presumed distinctiveness of 'management' and 'leadership' so evident in leadership studies is far less emphasised and the expectation that mangers undertake activities labelled as 'leadership' means it is fundamentally being conceptualised as an element of the managerial role, not something distinctive in its own right.
15 Kerzner (2017); Pritchard (2015).
16 For example, Bass (1985); Burns (1977).
17 Ford, Harding & Learmonth (2008).
18 See Wilson (2016) for more on medieval leadership thought.
19 Greenleaf's servant leadership is an obvious exception to this; however, the proposition here, I suggest, goes further because of its simultaneous problematisation of management.

References

Alvesson, M. (2017). Waiting for Godot: Eight major problems in the odd field of leadership studies. *Leadership*. doi:10.1177/1742715017736707.
Alvesson, M., Gabriel, Y. & Paulson, R. (2017). *Return to Meaning: A Social Science With Something to Say*. Oxford, UK: Oxford University Press.
Angwin, D., Cummings, S. & Smith, C. (2011). *The Strategy Pathfinder: Core Concepts and Live Cases* (2nd edition). Chichester, UK: John Wiley & Sons.
Bass, B. M. (1985). *Leadership and Performance Beyond Expectations*. New York, NY: Free Press.
Bass, B. M. & Riggio, R. E. (2005). *Transformational Leadership* (2nd edition). Mahwah, NJ: Lawrence Erlbaum Associates.
Bennis, W. & Nanus, B. (1985). *Leaders: The Strategies for Taking Charge*. New York, NY: Harper & Row.
Bilton, C. & Cummings, S. (2010). *Creative Strategy: Reconnecting Business and Innovation*. Chichester, UK: John Wiley & Sons.
Burns, J. M. (1977). *Leadership*. New York, NY: Harper & Row.
Dess, G., McNamara, G. & Eisner, A. B. (2016). *Strategic Management: Creating Competitive Advantages* (8th edition). New York, NY: McGraw-Hill.
DuBrin, A. J. (2016). *Leadership: Research Findings, Practice, and Skills* (8th edition). Boston, MA: Cengage Learning.

Du Gay, P. (2001). *In Praise of Bureaucracy.* London, UK: Sage.

Ford, J. & Harding, N. (2007). Move over management: We are all leaders now. *Management Learning,* 38(5), 475–493.

Ford, J., Harding, N. & Learmonth, M. (2008). *Leadership as Identity: Constructions and Deconstructions.* Basingstoke, UK: Palgrave Macmillan.

Foucault, M. (1994). *The Order of Things: An Archaeology of the Human Sciences.* New York, NY: Vintage Books.

Harding, N. (2015). Studying followers. In B. Carroll, J. Ford & S. Taylor (Eds.), *Leadership: Contemporary Critical Perspectives* (pp. 150–166). London, UK: Sage.

Kerzner, H. (2017). *Project Management: A Systems Approach to Planning, Scheduling, and Controlling* (12th edition). Hoboken, NY: Wiley.

Knights, D. & Willmott, H. (2017a). Organisation, structure and design. In D. Knights & H. Willmott (Eds.), *Introducing Organisational Behaviour and Management* (3rd edition, pp. 240–295). Andover, UK: Cengage Learning.

Knights, D. & Willmott, H. (Eds.) (2017b). *Introducing Organisational Behaviour and Management* (3rd edition). London, UK: Cengage Learning EMEA.

McCalman, J., Paton, R. & Siebert, S. (2016). *Change Management: A Guide to Effective Implementation* (4th edition). Los Angeles, CA: Sage.

Northhouse, P. (2013). *Leadership: Theory and Practice* (6th edition). Los Angeles, CA: Sage.

Pearce, J. A. & Robinson, R. B. (2011). *Strategic Management: Formulation, Implementation, and Control* (12th edition). New York, NY: McGraw-Hill/Irwin.

Pritchard, C. L. (2015). *Risk Management: Concepts and Guidance* (5th edition). Boca Ratan, FL: CRC Press.

Robbins, S. P., Bergman, R., Stagg, I. & Coulter, M. K. (2015). *Management* (7th edition). Melbourne, Vic: Pearson Australia.

Rodrigues, C. A. (2001). Fayol's 14 principles of management then and now: A framework for managing today's organisations effectively. *Management Decision,* 39(10), 880–889.

Samson, D. & Daft, R. L. (2014). *Management* (5th edition). South Melbourne, Vic: Cengage Learning.

Schein, E. H. (2010). *Organisational Culture and Leadership* (4th edition). San Francisco, CA: Jossey-Bass.

Shafritz, J. M., Ott, J. S. & Jang, Y. S. (2015). *Classics of Organisation Theory* (8th edition). Boston, MA: Cengage Learning.

Szczepańska-Woszczyna, K. (2018). Strategy, corporate culture, structure and operational processes as the context for the innovativeness of an organisation. *Foundations of Management,* 10(1), 1–12.

Taylor, F. W. (2012). *The Principles of Scientific Management.* Auckland, NZ: The Floating Press.

Tourish, D. (2013). *The Dark Side of Transformational Leadership: A Critical Perspective.* New York, NY: Routledge.

Wilson, S. (2016). *Thinking Differently About Leadership: A Critical History of Leadership Studies.* Cheltenham, UK: Edward Elgar.

14 Can We Be Done With Leadership?

Martin Parker

The anarchist art critic Herbert Read, in an essay published during the Second World War entitled 'The Cult of Leadership', suggested that there was a close link between the idea of leadership and a fascist politics. He proposes that the alternative to the glorification of leadership is 'collective responsibility', in which members of the 'body politic' are differentiated according to their function, but socially equal. Even those 'whose function is to co-ordinate others' are really just one part of that functioning whole, no more or less important than all the other parts.

> These are the organizers, the administrators and the managers who are essential to a complicated industrial society; but I see no reason why the co-ordinator should be more highly placed or more highly paid than the originator, the creator, the worker. The manager owes his present status and prestige, not to the nature of his work, but to his immediate control of the instruments of production. In any natural society he would be as unobtrusive as a railway signal-man in his box.
>
> (Read 1963: 67)

In the 70 years since Read's essay, management has gone from being a cult to becoming a fully sanctified religion. The single largest subject studied at universities in the global north is business and management and the number of business schools continues to expand, standing at 13 thousand in 2011 (Parker 2018:12). The management consulting industry extracts fees from the public and private sector which, as of 2016, were estimated to be worth $250 billion (Consultancy UK 2017). If we add the management books, academic journals and magazines, training companies, professional associations and lobby groups, then we have a gigantic industry that legitimates and profits from selling the idea that more 'management' is always the answer, whatever the problem. It is, I believe, the largest sustained public relations campaign for any occupation, and one that has justified the idea that every organisation needs management, managers and special parking spaces for the signal-man.

But management – as cadre, practice and form of knowledge – is not value neutral. It can be questioned on the grounds of its necessary commitment to hierarchical social relations, the inequalities of status and reward it produces, as well as its foundational assumptions about disparities in the distributions of knowledge and expertise (Parker 2002). Only some people can be managers because most people are more equal than others. In capitalist societies, ideas about management are also now deeply entangled with the idea that only managers understand markets, and that the job of the manager is to maximise profits and minimise costs (including wages), as well as externalising whatever costs are possible (including taxation and environmental damage). The idea of management normalises and naturalises a particular set of functional relations and hides the alternatives in its shadow. It is easier to imagine the end of the world than the end of management.

Leadership, on the other hand, is a much more dangerous idea.

If management describes a set of organised relations between people, knowledge and money that are specific to the last few hundred years, then embedded in the idea of leadership is a much wider claim, one that suggests the necessary subordination of many to the will of a few. This is not just a claim about a specific form of organisation in a particular place and time, but about the conditions for any form of organisation. It assumes that asymmetries of information and power are required, whether we are discussing the political arrangements of states, the hierarchies of corporations or the coordination of universities. Once the concept of leadership has been conjured, its manifestations are found everywhere – in the kinship arrangements of tribal societies, the relationship of angels to god, the social structure of chimpanzees, or the decision making of armies, sports teams and orchestras. It is a viral idea, a meme that contains enough truth to make it seem generalisable, and enough implied importance to make people want to be able to understand the alchemy that produces it.

Just as the grey-suited science of 1950s administration was replaced by the jet-setting excitement of strategic management, so is management now being positioned as a form of organising that needs an infusion of leadership to make it sexy. Not all managers are leaders, we are told, because some managers are more equal than others. The idea of leadership neatly trumps other forms of hierarchy because it contains an implied anthropology, a diagnosis of the human condition. It suggests that most of us are members of the herd, and just want to follow by someone who is bright of eye or wears a nice hat. It's not at all surprising that those in power want to convince us, and themselves, that this is the case. Neither is it surprising that the business school sells these sorts of ideas to people who want to become powerful themselves, who want to look in the mirror and see a leader, not just an anxious sweaty blob of a human being.

There is a more general problem here too. The concept of leadership gets in the way of thinking generously about the idea of 'organisation' because it implies that human beings can only come together in particular patterns, usually pyramidal ones. This just isn't correct, historically or spatially. Organising is a general capacity for clever monkeys like us, and it is a term that includes leadership and management but isn't reducible to them. Rather, we might say that leadership and management are specific forms of organisation, interesting enough in their own way, but not forms that express timeless truths about human nature, or that are the outcome of a particular historical trajectory.

There are lots of other forms of actually existing organisation that do not assume leadership or the prerogatives of the manager's right to manage: producer co-ops, communes, local exchange trading systems, community interest companies, industrial democracies, partnerships, open source organising, collectives, worker self-management, intentional communities, bartering, feminist separatist groups, the social economy, community currencies, complementary currencies, bioregionalism, self-provisioning, slow food, civil society, transition towns, time banks, gift relations, the commons, community benefit trusts, craft production, horizontalism, community energy, prefigurative democracy, permaculture, appropriate technology, communitarianism, credit unions, ecovillages, consumer co-ops, the sharing economy, mutualism, peer-to-peer finance, fair trade, social enterprise, bartering and many more (Parker et al. 2007, 2014).

Now we can debate the merits of all these forms and others, but it is really important to keep this variety in mind when thinking about leadership because these 'alternatives' (or perhaps better, just different forms, since alternative assumes a dominant form) are all forms of organisation that, to a greater or lesser degree and in different ways, problematise ideas of hierarchy and authority. Varieties of feminism, socialism and communism, ecodemocratic and deep green thinking and, of course, anarchism, all share this suspicion of ceding individual or collective decisions to distant others, whether styled as rulers, experts or leaders. They don't assume that their members or participants lack capacity, and they don't assume that a cadre of special people are required to make organising happen, as if, left to their own devices, people would just fuck things up, idiots that they are.

It is important to be clear about the 'function' of leadership here because, as Herbert Read notes, a division of labour does not necessarily imply hierarchy at all. Leadership is a particular form of the division of labour; it is not integral to it. Some sort of separation of tasks is one of the features of complex organising, just as different parts of a body or machine perform distinct functions, but there is no necessary implication that the brain is more important than the liver, or the steering wheel more important than the brakes. If these functional analogies are pursued, we might think about leadership as the coordination or communication function, but even then we do not need to assume a hierarchical relationship between nodes. Leadership, in other words, could be distributed across a network, a feature of feedback systems which govern the behaviours of component parts. But this is pretty much the same as saying that there is no leadership, but instead that the arrangement is self-organising. Just because a concept exists doesn't mean that it is always helpful, or that we can always find a referent for it in the world. We can easily be bewitched by words.

But none of what I have said should encourage us to think that we could have done with leadership. It would be nice to be able to claim this, with an outburst of horizontal outrage, and demand that the arrogance of leadership be quashed. I'm not going to do it though, first because there is a logical asymmetry in any argument that relies on the idea of variety, that deploys a pluralist ontology, and then tries to deny that one particular form is not itself part of that variety. I don't want to, but I have to acknowledge that leadership is a form of organisation, just as fascism is a form of organisation. But just as all organisation is not necessarily fascist, so does organising not necessarily involve leadership. Organisation is the umbrella term here, and it contains multitudes.

Choices about different forms of organisation are political, in the sense that all organising is politics made durable, the sedimentation of assumptions about who owns, controls and benefits. I am assuming here that to call something 'political' is to suggest that it could be a matter for contestation, that the world could be arranged otherwise, and hence that there are decisions that could be made visible and struggled over. To push towards the generalisation of politics in this way is therefore to push against the idea that organising has to have a particular shape, for reasons of human nature, functional necessity or economic efficiency. To move something into the realm of the political, and away from some sort of determinism, is to insist that there are choices being made, even in domains that appear frozen into particular forms by what the Brazilian social theorist Roberto Unger calls 'false necessity' (2004). It is to suggest that that which appears solid can be made fluid, and that inevitability is actually just a lack of imagination.

There is a second reason why we can't have done with leadership, and this book is an ironic testament to it, with its 'after' perhaps better read not as hopeful chronology (as I would like), but an attempt to pin down something evasive that refuses to be captured. The idea of leadership is everywhere and nowhere, ubiquitous and vague, entirely generalised and almost meaningless. As with management, this is a form of organising that is being continually told and sold, in hagiographic biographies of transformational leaders and entrepreneurs, in the output of the business school and the offerings of management consultants, and in a North Atlantic culture that bellows that success and celebrity are individual qualities, rewards for extraordinary personal characteristics. The sheer noise and universality of these assumptions means that the concept has become an article of common sense, one that is hard to challenge because it is everywhere, embedded into a socio-economic order that valorises the success of a few in order to disguise the powerlessness of the many.

A few thousand words in an academic book will not change all that, but it might serve to remind some what is at stake when we naturalise the idea that the many must be governed by the few. However benign, however transparent, however distributed, however relational, however transactional, the very idea of leadership is predicated on the idea that the autonomy of most people must be restricted in order that organisation can happen. That is why Herbert Read regarded it to be related to fascism, and why the strident cult of leadership should be contrasted with the blossoming variety of actually existing forms of organisation. We might not be able to be done with leadership but should keep trying to put the signal-man back in his box.

References

Consultancy UK (2017) 'Consulting Industry Global' http://www.consultancy.uk/consulting-industry/global, accessed 6/3/17.
Parker, M (2002) *Against Management: Organization in the Age of Managerialism.* Oxford: Polity.
Parker, M (2018) *Shut Down the Business School.* London: Pluto Books.
Parker, M, Fournier, V and Reedy, P (2007) *The Dictionary of Alternatives: Utopianism and Organization.* London: Zed Books.
Parker, M, Cheney, G, Fournier, V and Land, C (eds) (2014) *The Companion to Alternative Organization.* London: Routledge.
Read, H (1963/2002) 'The cult of leadership'. In *To Hell with Culture, and Other Essays on Art and Society.* London: Routledge, 48–69.
Unger, R (2004) *False Necessity: Anti-Neccessitarian Social Theory in the Service of Radical Democracy.* London: Verso.

15 After Hierarchy
Building a New World in the Shell of the Old

Neil Sutherland

Part I – In Which We Meet Our Protagonist and Learn of Their Faith in Hierarchical Organisation

Before 'it' happened, I remember the feeling of reading texts that framed hierarchy as a dirty concept – something outdated and outmoded, and something that crushed the human spirit and reduced innovation and satisfaction at work. I never understood these critiques on a philosophical level, and certainly knew that the alternative of free and open dialogue through decentralised relationships would never work in the real world and would likely descend into chaos.

Fundamentally, this belief was born from my view of human nature. According to social Darwinists, humans are innately competitive beings; from Thomas Huxley's claim that life is like a 'gladiator's show'[1] to other discussions of selfishness and greed as baseline personality attributes,[2] all argue that competition remains an instinctual drive that leads to evolution and progress through continual betterment and one-upmanship. In the contemporary world, various managerial team-building games see groups pitted against each other and given the choice to act collaboratively or in self-interest. Whilst not entirely confirmatory, researchers regularly find that people act in competitive ways when left to their own devices and wish to avoid being in 'last place' at all costs, ultimately noting that self-interest *can* be of benefit.[3]

This view of human nature had also assumed a central position within contemporary forms of management. In viewing humans as inherently selfish and competitive, we could not afford to fully trust them to fulfil tasks to the best of their abilities. In turn, leaders adopted a sceptical and critical view of their followers: keeping check of what they were up to (through overt or covert means), influencing their thoughts and actions and ensuring that they toed the line.[4] This sort of asymmetrical power relation was a defining feature of the modern organisation – from the factory to the open-plan Google office – that was dominated by a belief that some form of hierarchy is necessary to achieve effective goals. Leaders were the active agents, and followers were the 'blank slates' marked by their 'susceptibility to leadership behaviours and styles'.[5]

Granted, there were always some issues to contend with. Many lambasted more traditional hierarchical organisational structures as monolithic and overly bureaucratic. They told us that formal chains of command led to a slow and inefficient beast and that leaders did not draw on the creativity of those who occupy positions further away from the apex.[6] These people were reduced to the position of Josef K in Kafka's 'The Trial' – unable to impact upon an organisation and alienated from the fruits of their labour. Elsewhere, others were keen to note that hierarchy encourages, rather than curbs, the less salubrious side of humanity, such as greed and insensitivity. I would not have necessarily disagreed with this statement, but always thought: are these same characteristics and traits not also present when human beings enter into more collective and non-hierarchical structures? Do we not see individuals acting in their own self-interest even though they claim to be acting on behalf of the 'collective'? Selfishness is omnipresent – it is not created through hierarchy – and may in fact be channelled most effectively through a pyramid structure. Writing on similar issues, Jaques[7] tells us:

35 years of research have convinced me that managerial hierarchy is the most efficient, the hardiest, and in fact the most natural structure ever devised for organisations. Properly structured hierarchy can release energy and creativity, rationalise productivity and actually improve morale.

Indeed, it was my firm belief that hierarchy enables humans to reach their potential. Discussing bureaucratic hierarchical organisations, Erich Fromm notes that it allows subordinates to be 'free from freedom'.[8] That is, when responsibility is taken from their shoulders, they reach a state of liberation where they are not expected to make decisions or take accountability for performance and actions. Fromm tells us that through increasing order and predictability, hierarchy can help to reduce uncertainty and conflict. Most famously, this was popularised and operationalised by Frederik Taylor and his principles of scientific management, in which he sang the praises of breaking jobs down into constituent parts and distributing tasks to individual workers. In this way, they could become specialised experts and would be free from the strains of really 'thinking' about their work. Thinking can cause confusion, misinterpretation and, ultimately, error. This was solidified through training courses and textbooks that taught leaders to act as a parental figure; to give clear direction and monitor progress; to be responsible for an overall vision and to see it through; to ensure the conflict and organisational politics were reduced; and to act in as 'authentic' a way as possible – to influence others, but not be influenced in return.[9] This in turn created happier, more relaxed (and certainly more unquestioning and productive) followers. Within capitalistic organisations governed by the bottom line, a reduction of resistance, uncertainty, conflict and dissent should be praised.

Part II – In Which the Catastrophe Strikes and The Ghosts Come Knocking

And then ... .Suddenly it was gone. The catastrophe. It wiped my slate clean. I felt it happen – like files being permanently deleted – and somehow knew that it had happened to everybody. Those beliefs that seemed so sturdy and true had started to fade away to nothingness. The knowledge that hierarchy was fundamental, natural and liberating suddenly blurred and faded. Too terrified to see the terrible state that our society would be in once all security had vanished, I cocooned myself in my bedroom, drew the curtains and waited. I could not imagine the chaos that would await me if I left. I spent many sleepless nights trying to remember my former self. I would mentally chase down past constructs and stories to try to grasp them, but alas, each time I caught up they disappeared in a puff of air.

Then, one night I was visited by three ghosts (clichéd, I know), who were embroiled in some debate. As they rose up the stairs, I heard one voice speaking quickly and excitedly:

> by anarchist spirit, I mean that deeply human sentiment, which aims at the good of all, freedom and justice for all, solidarity and love among the people; which is not an exclusive characteristic only of self-declared anarchists, but inspires all people who have a generous heart and an open mind.[10]

I cleared my throat, and the three looked around at me. They saw the fear and confusion in my eyes, and the speaker introduced himself as Errico Malatesta, and the others as Mikael Bakunin and Peter Kropotkin. They informed me that they were debating the fundamental nature of humankind and that I was welcome to participate. Still feeling empty and unsure, I politely declined, whilst remaining curious about hearing more from these philosophers. Sensing my hesitance, Bakunin then rose to the air: 'Mankind has allowed itself to be governed long enough', he yelled, 'the origin of its unhappiness does not reside in this or that form of government, but in the very *principle* and fact of government, whatever kind it may be'.[11] There was a moment of silence before he continued in a quieter voice, 'I recognise no infallible authority, even in special questions, consequently whatever respect I may have for the honesty and the sincerity of such an individual, I have no absolute faith in any person'.[12]

This triggered a response in me, and for a moment I felt as though I were my past self again. Before I could stop, I heard myself blurting out: 'But surely, we need some kind of structure in our lives, somebody to answer to? It is how humans have evolved over time! Hierarchical authority gives us some freedom, No? It is a form of kindness'.

The ghosts all looked at each other, all brimming with responses. Kropotkin began by drawing out a simple point: 'Where there is authority

... there is no freedom'.[13] 'Correct!' called Bakunin, 'when the people are being beaten with a stick, they are not much happier if it is called "the people's stick". If there is a state, then there is domination, and in turn there is slavery'.[14] Malatesta held up his finger and leaned in to offer a clarification: 'Anarchists generally make use of the word "state" to mean all the collection of institutions, political, legislative, judicial, military, financial, and so on, by means of which management of their own affairs are taken from the people and confided to certain individuals, and these, whether by usurpation or delegation, are invested with the right to make laws over and for all, and to constrain the public to respect them'.[15] Unable to contain himself, Bakunin – channelling an old friend, Pierre-Joseph Proudhon – exclaimed: 'Whoever lays his hand on me to govern me is a usurper and tyrant, and I declare him my enemy!'[16]

The other ghosts nodded, and Kropotkin continued, 'But it is not enough to destroy... We must also know how to build! And it is owing to not having thought about it that the masses have always been led astray in all their revolutions. After having demolished, they abandoned the care of reconstruction to the middle-class people who possessed a more-or-less precise conception of what they wished to realise, and who consequently reconstituted authority to their own advantage'.[17] Malatesta picked up on this line of enquiry: 'Indeed, organisation, far from creating authority, is the only cure for it and the only means whereby each of us will get used to taking an active and conscious part in collective work, and cease being passive instruments in the hands of leaders'.[18]

As the night progressed, the ghosts were animated. Amongst other things, they discussed the notion that capitalism had corrupted the human spirit through rewarding selfishness, competition and greed, thus exacerbating these qualities in humans, and making them appear as if they were natural. Fundamentally, however, they argued against seeing this as innate, and noted that just because people act this way in capitalist society, it does not reflect their *essential* nature. True liberation and development was something that could only happen through mutual aid and collaboration. As the sun started peeping through the drawn curtains, Kropotkin summarised a point by stating: 'Don't compete ... competition is always injurious to species, and you have plenty of resources to avoid it'.[19]

My head was swimming in new information. I could feel my brain rushing but my eyes starting to glaze over. These ideas sounded so idyllic and utopian, and although I could start to see how they might also have some basis in action, I was still unsure of what this would look like in a practical sense. As the ghosts began to fade away, Bakunin drew closer so I could see the wisps of his beard glittering in the light. 'Remember', he said, 'by striving to do the impossible, man has always achieved what is possible. Those who have cautiously done no more than they believed possible have never taken a single step forward'.[20]

Part III – In Which A New World Is Imagined

When the last wisp had faded, I collapsed onto my bed. I felt conflicted about viewing the outside world. I was still concerned that I might see the very worst of people, where in lieu of single leaders there would be unrestrained conflict and misery. On the other hand, the ghosts had set up the image of a beautiful and free world where humans constantly collaborated and treated each other with respect. When I finally left my room, blinking in the sunlight, I was surprised to find that in reality, this new world all looked quite ... well ... normal. It felt logical and rational, and somewhat mundane. It reminded me of how I would have organised and behaved at a dinner party amongst friends. I wandered through the streets for some time and saw small clusters of people sitting around in circles throughout the landscape. I hesitated close to one of them and was beckoned over. A young woman waved and said 'You're probably overwhelmed by all of this. It's a lot to take in ... a lot has changed since the world you knew. Why don't you come and watch how we do things? We're going to be in a meeting for a couple of hours now, see what you pick up'. The meeting, it turned out, was based on sorting out some trading relations with another group. They were gathering to discuss some of the finer details and offered to introduce me to several lessons that guided how they interacted and made decisions.

First up was a brief rundown of 'consensus decision making', understood as the now established alternative to more adversarial and binary processes (where individuals may 'vote through' proposals instead of deliberating, with a majority determining the position of the entire group).[21] Whilst this form of majority rule may have had the advantage of being able to produce a prompt and clear decision, it apparently allowed no space for challenge, negotiation and compromise, as explained by one meeting goer:

> It's just ... if we accept the idea that the 'majority' of people support an idea, what about those that don't? What can they do about it? It's disempowering. There's no room for discussion, and normally you'll only be voting on idea A or B anyway. What about idea C?

In these consensus processes, emphasis was placed on dialogue, discussion and deliberation amongst participants, and rather than accepting the notion that one side should win and the other lose, instead, 'win-win' solutions were sought out. This process inherently encouraged direct democracy, where every member had the opportunity to engage in some form of meaning-making and leadership, either by suggesting and defending ideas or by preventing changes that they find unacceptable.[22] This helped ensure equality in that every member could contribute and have their opinions and uncertainties taken into account, but could also result in surprising and creative solutions, where *new* ideas emerged as a result of negotiation and discussion.[23] Furthermore, it may also be seen that this environment also helped to prevent any individual from taking too much of a permanent leading role, as active decisions were the product of *collective* deliberation. More hierarchical decision-making processes (such as majority rule) did not always offer such opportunities and were therefore more susceptible to being overtaken by specific individuals. Another attendee remarked:

> That's the thing with consensus decision making. Because you all get a say, it's harder for one person to dominate everything. I mean ... it does happen ... but the focus is on the 'we', not the 'I'. We are all working together in this, and the best way to go forward is to have everybody on the same page ... with the same opportunities. It's all about equality of opportunity.

After this introduction, I found myself in two minds. On one hand, this seemed like an effective and meaningful way of interacting with humans during decision making – and it felt more alive than any other meeting I had attended. However, on the other hand, I still had that niggling sense that although the overly hierarchical aspects of the society had gone, was it not a utopian idea that everybody would always behave, follow the rules and get on with each other?

As we continued on, I started to find part of the answer in the way that friendship and collegiality was prized. More than simple politeness, the emphasis on friendship seemed to form a crucial part of encouraging equality, making sure that everybody had a chance to participate, and relationships of dominance/subservience were not formed. The group went one step further than this, however:

> We're all friends, of course. But I don't really challenge my 'friends' much, I don't tell them to check their privilege, I don't tell them to watch their space ... I think to use the word 'friend' is a bit of a cop-out here. We aren't afraid at calling each other out in our meetings. In a way, I guess that means we're ... more than friends. It's something harsher but more productive.

What was being articulated here is a kind of 'critical friendship', broadly defined as 'a trusted person who asks provocative questions, provides data for examination through an alternative lens, and offers critique as a friend'.[24] More specifically, critical friendship involves not being unconditionally positive, but happens through the meeting of unconditional support and unconditional critique.[25] Indeed, consensus processes opened up a space that allowed for critical friendship where members would constantly keep each other 'in check' through 'calling out' people if they stepped out of line. When prompted on this, one man told me:

> We all got the potential within us to mess up. When it's you doing it, you can't always see it – maybe you talk too much, maybe you silence

somebody else, maybe you say something offensive – so you need to be made aware of it. I have no problem with being called out, or calling people out.

One particularly common reason for calling out was related to leadership. That is, if others felt that one person was monopolising floor time, or becoming too much of a permanently influential figure, it would be raised. Because of this, it was also not unusual for particularly vocal members to *self*-censor if they felt that they were taking too much of a leading role, and open up the floor for others to speak in order to reinforce the notion that leadership and meaning-making should be a collective process. For example, towards the end of my time with the group, one member noted:

> Well, I've got a few ideas brewing, but I'm aware that I've spoken a lot in the last couple of meetings about what we could be up to. It might be good to hear from anybody else to get our juices flowing ... I don't want to be the only one who says stuff.

However, whilst critical friendship was understood as something that all members should aspire to in their everyday interactions, in some cases, friendship would get in the way of criticality. Therefore, each meeting had a formal 'facilitator' – an individual who assisted with the coordination of decision making in a non-authoritarian way, by making sure that discussions remained on-track; that the overarching goals were always in sight; that everybody had an equal say; that the meeting ran to time; that there were no unresolved issues; and that an acceptable level of consensus was reached. Importantly, the facilitator was not considered as part of the discussion, but more an objective outsider.[26] By stepping back, the facilitator was able to provide some perspective by asking big-picture questions, linking together proposals and suggesting possible courses for action and areas for negotiation/compromise.[27] Through doing this, the group not only ensured that there was always one person who acted as a 'spotter' and critical friend, but also in turn built a culture where this kind of behaviour was treated as the status quo.

As the session drew to a close and the hum of post-meeting chatter increased, I reflected on how trust, openness and a questioning culture were now deemed of central importance for enacting non-hierarchical organisation. Of course, all of this required *every* member to voluntarily participate in such underpinnings; to agree to listen; to challenge and to be challenged; to constructively critique; and to always act in a reflexive and reflective manner. However, through achieving this, individuals and collectives become re-skilled in the attributes of behaving in a collaborative way, which leads to a considerably more creative and (literally) more humane environment.

Part IV – In Which We Learn to Resist Human Nature

Some months have now passed since the catastrophe. If you would have told me beforehand that I would spend my days making decisions *with* other people rather than *for* them, I would have branded you a liar and a fool. But now I find it hard to empathise with my former self. Normality to me is getting as many opinions as possible on a topic; it is being able to admit that I am wrong; it is being able to both stand *up* and stand *down*; it is being able to speak and to listen. I am a more reflective person now, but still often find myself grappling with the issue of nature and cooperation. When I read through the life's work of the ghosts who visited me on that fateful night, much of the discussion centres on the understanding that humans do have an essential nature that is cooperative and good. There is something inherently appealing about this idea, although I was still not convinced, and wondered if the reality is more complex.

In fact, through observing and participating in radically reimagined activities, it would appear that selfishness and a competitive spirit have *not* completely gone away with the abolishment of hierarchy. That is, some element of asymmetry still remains. In some situations, there are individuals who seem to be coming forward and being positioned as more permanent and stable leaders. Some have louder voices or are more effusive with their hand gestures. Some look more attractive or more like the other group members ('prototypical', I hear it mentioned). Others are able-bodied, white and male. In one way, shape or form, all of these individuals carry a certain form of 'cultural capital',[28] and it is evident that when they speak a majority of people pay more attention to them than others. A (admittedly, wordy) poster is stuck to the wall in a meeting room, and in the early weeks of my new journey I squinted to read the following:

> Everywhere we turn in capitalist society is hierarchical organisation. The habits and perspectives that accompany such a social arrangement do not automatically disappear as one enters the gates of the revolutionary movement. Without explicitly renouncing anarchist politics, people often begin to drift into modes of behaviour that are decidedly authoritarian.[29]

I felt a tap on my shoulder and a woman addressed me: 'It's a warning to ourselves', she smiled, 'We're naturally fallible beings and no matter how hard we try, there are some ugly elements of ourselves that remain'. She paused – sensing my confusion – and then continued: 'the thing is, we recognise that it exists, but we're putting into practice various processes that can help us learn about and curb those elements of ourselves. We've seen what can happen when we work together, and we know how much it can bring out in individuals and the collective. We're battling ourselves, but we're winning'.

Thus, it turns out that our old bedfellows – selfishness, competition and greed – may remain as spectres at the feast forever more, taunting us and jumping out when we least expect it. My critical self then asks: if these elements remain *even* in the absence of formal hierarchy, why should we resist and be concerned in trying to organise in collective ways? Why not accept that our nature defines our path in life? The answer comes back to what nature leads to if left unchecked; it comes back to the destructive nature of unfettered individualistic leadership. Before the catastrophe, we were starting to realise how the blind belief in the 'power of one' could result in damaging implications. Increasingly tumultuous global landscapes, non-democratic decision making and narcissistic world leaders were receiving more public attention and being framed as unsustainable, yet inevitable. The populous found themselves between a rock and a hard place as they were simultaneously dissatisfied and worried about the lack of engagement coming from hierarchical social relationships, yet also unable to see any other way of organising. Our old friends Gemmill and Oakley expanded on this, assuming a psychodynamic perspective to argue that people were simply afraid of making their own decisions or taking initiative: it filled them with anxiety and fear of failure.[30] Instead, humans would rather 'willingly submit themselves to spoon-feeding, preferring safe and easy security to the possible pains and uncertainty of learning by their own efforts and mistakes'. Despite all of their destructive potential, individual leaders served to repress these uncomfortable emotions and acted as a slate upon which anxiety could be projected.

As I look around the world now, I am filled with an immense pride, but also wonder if this same result would have been possible without the catastrophe and if humans could have anticipated it by themselves dismantling hierarchy. Indeed, it was only ever a social construction (that is, created and morphed by the human mind), and could have always been challenged and questioned. Whilst we may not be able to change how our brains are wired towards competition in the short term and accept that these traits will long form a part of our collective unconscious, we always have the ability to question how we utilise those parts of ourselves. The conversion for me was made simpler by the catastrophe but would have been entirely possible beforehand. With hard work, understanding and reflection, the job is still to generate more and more sophisticated methods for keeping our selfish selves at bay. In a sense, this is quite a thrilling prospect: knowing that humans are constantly battling their inner pull provides me with a great deal of respect for our action, reflexivity and resilience.

Notes

1 Huxley (1888).
2 Hobbes (1651[2005]); Christiansen, F. and Loeschcke, V. 'Evolution and Competition', republished in Wohrmann and Jain (1990).
3 Kuziemko et al. (2014); Plotkin (2014).

4 For discussions of the role of leadership in corporate culture, see Alvesson and Willmott (2002) and/or Willmott (1993).
5 Collinson (2011).
6 Grey (2009).
7 Jaques (1990).
8 Fromm (1994).
9 Ford et al. (2008).
10 Malatesta (1922).
11 Bakunin (1882a).
12 Bakunin (1882b).
13 Notation written on black banners carried at Peter Kropotkin's funeral.
14 Bakunin (1873).
15 Malatesta (1891).
16 Proudhon (1840).
17 Kropotkin (1922).
18 Malatesta (1897).
19 Kropotkin (1922).
20 Attributed to Bakunin in *Novaresio* (1996).
21 Graeber (2010).
22 Maeckelbergh (2009).
23 Maeckelbergh (2011).
24 Baskerville and Goldblatt (2009).
25 MacBeath '"I didn't know he was ill": The role and value of the critical friend', in Stoll et al. (1998).
26 Graeber (2009).
27 Cornell (2011).
28 Bourdieu and Passeron (1977) 'Cultural Reproduction and Social Reproduction', in Brown (2011).
29 Prolecat (2004).
30 Gemmill and Oakley (1992).

References

Alvesson, M. and Willmott, H. (2002) 'Identity regulation as organisational control: Producing the appropriate individual'. *Journal of Management Studies*, 39(5): 619–644.

Bakunin, M. (1882a) *God and the State*. London: Dover Publications.

Bakunin, M. (1882b) *What is Authority?* Dieu et l'etat.

Bakunin, M. (1873) *Statism and Anarchy*. Cambridge, MA: Cambridge University Press.

Baskerville, D. and Goldblatt, H. (2009) 'Learning to be a critical friend: From professional indifference through challenge to unguarded conversations'. *Cambridge Journal of Education*, 39(2): 205–221.

Brown, R. (2011) *Knowledge, Education and Cultural Change*. London: Tavistock.

Collinson, D. (2011) 'Critical leadership studies', in: Bryman, A. Collinson, D. Grint, K. Jackson, B. and Uhl-Bien, M. (Eds) *The Sage Handbook of Leadership*, London: Sage publications: 181–194.

Cornell, A. (2011) *Oppose and Propose: Lessons from Movement for a New Society*. San Francisco, CA: AK Press.

Ford, J., Harding, N. and Learmonth, M. (2008) *Leadership as Identity: Constructions and Deconstructions*. London: Palgrave.

Fromm, E. (1994) *Escape from Freedom*. New York, NY: Henry Holt and Company.

Gemmill, G. and Oakley, J. (1992) 'Leadership: An alienating social myth?' *Human Relations*, 45(2): 113–129.

Graeber, D. (2009) *Direct Action: An Ethnography*. Thousand Oaks, CA: AK Press.

Graeber, D. (2010) 'The rebirth of anarchism in North America'. *Historia*, 8(21): 124–146.

Grey, C. (2009) *A Very Short, Fairly Interesting and Reasonably Cheap Book about Studying Organisations*. Thousand Oaks, CA: Sage.

Hobbes, T. (1651[2005]) *Leviathan Volume 1*. London: Continuum.

Huxley, T. (1888) 'The struggle for existence in human society' *Science*, 1: 15–17.

Jaques, R. (1990) 'In praise of hierarchy'. Harvard Business Review, January–February: 1–8.

Kropotkin, P. (1922) *Mutual Aid: A Factor of Evolution*. San Francisco, CA: AK Press.

Kuziemko, I., Buell, R. Reich, T. and Norton, M. (2014) 'Last-place aversion: Evidence and distributive implications'. *The Quarterly Journal of Economics*, 129(1): 105–149.

Maeckelbergh, M. (2009) *The Will of the Many: How the Alterglobalisation Movement is Changing the Face of Democracy*. London: Pluto Press.

Maeckelbergh, M. (2011) 'The unimaginable: My night of violence at the hands of the Belgian police', Available online: http://plutopress.wordpress.com/2010/10/22/the-unimaginable-my-night-of-violence-at-the-hands-of-the-belgian-police/ [Accessed 4 May 2017].

Malatesta, E. (1891) *Anarchy*. London: Chadwyck-Healey Incorporated.

Malatesta, E. (1897) 'Anarchism and Organisation' Unpublished Manuscript.

Malatesta, E. (1922) *Umanita Nova*.

Novaresio, P. (1996) *The Explorers: From the Ancient World to the Present*. New York: Stewart, Tabori and Chang.

Plotkin, J. (2014) 'The collapse of cooperation in evolving games'. *PNAS*, 111(49): 17558–17563.

Prolecat (2004) 'Towards more effective political organisations'. *The Dawn*, 4: 12–16.

Proudhon, P. (1840) *What is Property? An Inquiry Into the Principle of Right and of Government*. Open Library: BR Tucker.

Stoll, L. and Myers, K. (1998) *No Quick Fixes: Perspectives on Schools in Difficulty*. London: Falmer: 118–132.

Willmott, H. (1993) 'Strength is ignorance, slavery is freedom: Managing culture in modern organisations'. *Journal of Management Studies*, 30(4): 515–552.

Wohrmann, K. and Jain, S. (Eds) (1990) *Population Biology and Evolution*. Berlin: Springer: 367–339.

16 The Last Leaders

Donna Ladkin

Initially, we blamed them for everything. But then we realised that doing so was symptomatic of what had led to The Collapse in the first place. No, we had to take responsibility for what had happened. That was just one of the lessons we learned from the last leaders, but it was probably the most important.

The small cracks in our beliefs – about our leaders and what they should do for us, about the way the world worked – became chasms as everything we had taken for granted for so long began to disintegrate. Although we'd had intimations of the things to come, none of us had imagined the weather would become so unpredictable, so fast. The last leaders kept telling us it was part of a natural cycle, that the only way out was a technological fix. They continued pouring money into seeding clouds, building turbines to cool us down and fortifying sea defences – long after the absurdity of their efforts became clear. Millions either drowned in the sudden floods that washed across the planet or burned as once verdant meadows became deserts, almost overnight.

And then of course the food shortages started. We had thought that the shortfall of avocados and brazil nuts were 'middle-class problems' when they began to occur in 2017. But when the rice crops were decimated by hurricanes in China and America's great mid-West bread basket became a dustbowl, grain shortages hit us all. One spring the bees, upon whom we had always relied for free pollinating services, just didn't appear. The catastrophic colony collapse that the 'tree huggers' had been predicting actually occurred. That put a swift end to any fruit that was still eking out of the earth. Before long the emaciated cattle who roamed the lands that had once been rain forest had to be slaughtered. Still, as we had so long ago lost the urge for self-reliance, we turned to the leaders, fervently believing that just as they told us, they would 'sort things out', make everything 'great' again.

The last leaders introduced rationing plans, centralised the distribution of water and measured rainfall and temperature spikes; in other words, they offered bureaucratic solutions in response to apocalyptic events. When those did not work, they distracted us by instigating ever more deadly wars.

They told us it was 'the only way', that salvaging even a vestige of our former way of life necessitated completely destroying others'. But those we attacked found ways of striking back. Suicide bombings became daily events. We lived in constant fear of chemical warfare. Any sense of control quickly spiralled away. For all the lack of food and basic necessities of life, the supply of bombs, bullets, grenades, missiles, armoured vehicles and deadly submarines never ran out. Leaders throughout the world had stockpiled weapons of every kind. In the aftermath of it all, the few of us remaining have wondered about the sickness of mind that enabled us to continue to look to them for salvation.

Our Mistakes

In hindsight, it became clear that we had failed to make a number of key distinctions when choosing who would best lead us. Firstly, we had mistaken the proclivity to dominate for the ability to lead. Just because someone appeared strong and certain, we thought they would take care of us. It was too late before we realised that the tendency to dominate was often coupled with self-centredness. No matter what these leaders said about their wanting to 'reach out' to common folk, their actions betrayed only self-service and greed. Their dominance was used to trample others, especially those they sensed were weak.

We also mistook our enemy. Our leaders told us it was those who were different from us, those with different skin colours or those who worshipped in other ways. They told us we should be frightened of them – suspicious and ungenerous. They spent billions on walls to keep them out and surveillance to track their moves. But in fact it was the leaders themselves who squandered our inheritance. It was they who trumpeted self-serving untruths and stole our very way of life from us. Although we now know we were responsible for allowing them to do so, we also see that they were the true enemy, not those poorer than ourselves.

We believed them when they reduced complex relationships to simple memes. We longed for the straightforwardness they offered, mistaking minimalism for clarity and strength. When they told us that meeting our energy needs necessitated destroying wilderness and desecrating sacred lands, we laughed in the face of those who proposed alternatives. The web of life was too complicated a story to understand, we wanted solutions that were as quick as the internet and reducible to 120 characters.

The most important distinction we failed to make was where the power in our relationship lay. We believed it was all in their hands when actually we were always much more powerful than we suspected. We added to the myth of their unquestioned authority by building fantasies of their superhuman abilities: the talent of foreseeing the future, insight into what was 'best' for us, the capacity to dominate Nature Herself. All along, the power was ours – the actual power, the ability to say 'no' to the craziness, even as it was pedalled as truth. Who were they, we must ask, that they were able to mesmerise us even when the cost of our fascination was our own demise?

Who Were They?

They were men who sprouted up around the globe like pernicious weeds during those decades of confusion and collapse. The context of fear can't be overlooked – as the world became unpredictable on every level we looked for answers outside ourselves. Assuredly, they told us they would make it better, that they understood what was going on, and could solve our problems. Their body language was expansive, their smiles fixed, their promises irresistible.

Perhaps none of them had been set on evil at the start. But even during their early days they committed the sin of believing they knew what was best for everyone else. They failed to question the interests that underpinned their beliefs, or the life circumstances and privilege which skewed their view. Their self-centeredness was, in retrospect, thinly veiled by the rhetoric of connection. These were 'boy men', never really tested in the theatre of life, never having had to account for their own faults and foibles. There was something attractive about their naïve simplicity. Perhaps we longed to believe that Peter Pan could solve our problems.

Importantly, we failed to spot the factions and collusions that supported them behind the scenes. It was only later that we learned that these leaders were actually frontmen, the face of more sinister forces which, in addition to our endorsement, kept them in place. It was these un-named and unknown others that pulled their strings, and ours as well. They were the arms manufacturers, the heads of petrol companies, and the bankers and media moguls who were only interested in maintaining a status quo in which they prospered, even if it cost the planet. Because they were faceless and unacknowledged, their ploy was foolproof; they were assured of policies that supported their lifestyles, without bearing the brunt of any public comeback or upbraid. The extent of smoke and mirrors that held it all in place was astonishing, and few of us suspected the entire picture.

Perhaps part of the reason for our ignorance was what had happened to notions of 'truth' in the lead-up to The Collapse. Indeed 'truth', or any semblance of it, became one of the first victims of the last leaders' policies. Informed by scholars who had read Foucault, they understood the relationship between truth and power and stockpiled their own power reserves by creating 'alternative facts' and alluding to their own, secret access to 'the way things actually worked'. Those who contradicted them were discredited or labelled 'expert', a term which provoked jeers and condescension from the rest of us. The media played their role, consolidating leaders' declarations through sheer dint of exposure. Their watchword for quality became 'number of hits' and the extent to which items 'went viral', rather than the veracity of anything reported. Innuendo and uncertainty fed our anxiety.

No one knew what to believe any more. Society atomised. It is as simple as that – we detonated in ways not even the most lethal bombs could achieve. How had we come to this?

Who Were We?

We had become lazy. We idolised 'youthfulness', going to extreme measures to obfuscate any evidence of 'growing up'. We had become enamoured by distraction and fed ourselves on a constant diet of Facebook, Twitter, Tinder, Instagram, Netflix and YouTube. We wanted everything instantaneously and our attention span resembled that of gnats. We sought titillation rather than intellectual pursuit. In hindsight, we had degenerated into populations of sitting ducks, ready to be colonised by anyone who promised ease, simplicity and a return to some idealised notion of 'the good ole days'.

Indeed 'nostalgia' was endemic in the years just preceding The Collapse. Any intimation of 'the good ole days' attracted us like flies to dead meat. Everyone conveniently forgot that even in the halcyon times of the 1950s, there were dug-out shelters in people's backyards and ears were always half-cocked for the sound of the attack sirens. Any other rendering of those perfect memories was rejected culturally (although it is said that some groups did exist in which people spoke freely of different memories). For the most part, however, we believed it was possible to live pain-free lives and sought to achieve this state without question. If we felt any discomfort we searched for someone else to 'fix it', allowing our internal wisdom to flounder.

Perhaps that was our fatal flaw: the tendency to fantasise that anyone could make things better, that it was possible, indeed desirable, to pass that responsibility to someone else. When these loud-mouthed, boisterous men began to declare that they could make everything better, we longed to believe them without question. And in a cycle that was indeed vicious, all of our capacities for curiosity, persistence and criticality evaporated as we used these faculties less and less. It is a terrible thing to see human beings reduced to automatons. The Collapse was a material disaster, all of our societies, structures and cultures obliterated. But what happened in the lead-up to it was even worse: it was a squandering of human spirit, the destruction of any potential for personal agency. We didn't learn that exchanging rants on Facebook made no impact until it was far too late. We traded our birth right as humans for the fantasy of someone who would 'make it all better'. We called these people our 'leaders' and longed for them to ease the collective distress that tormented us.

We learned the hard way that this fantasy was not possible, and not even desirable. Between the food shortages, the wars and the extreme weather events, it became clear that no matter what these last leaders said, they could not fix anything. Although the banding together of small groups of men, women and children was initially labelled 'civil unrest', we learned it was the only way to survive. Once the infra-structure collapsed and the internet was obliterated, we could look nowhere but to ourselves for answers. There have of course been rumours about the last leaders and what happened to them in the end. It is thought that one of them was eaten by a crocodile in Florida as the bayou waters flooded his golf course there. Another was said to have been wrestled to his death by a roaming Siberian bear. In the East, one was said to have detonated himself in the blazing glory of a nuclear missile test. Although we now understand that the blame for what happened cannot rest with them, none of us wish them well.

How We Live Now

The aftermath of The Collapse has not been easy. There are few of us left, and the planet is not the hospitable place it once was. It's been especially hard to learn to take responsibility again. It's difficult to rely on ourselves and one another for our collective security, but we have learned that it is the only way. We live in small nomadic communities. There is no place on the planet (that we have found yet, anyway) that can support human life for any extended period of time. We have to keep moving to find the small plants and animals we can eat, and the places that have not been devastated by the weather. Any place we find that is habitable only remains that way for a short time, as violent storms and hurricane-strength winds are the reality of our lives as the earth tries to regain her balance.

We have banned leadership: both the idea of it and its practice. We encourage initiative taking and agency, but those who develop any kind of following are temporarily ostracised from the community. This is not to punish initiative takers, but instead to rehabilitate those who would follow. Without the influence of those who initiate, individuals are forced to look to themselves, to find their own answers and act on them. It is that kind of self-reliance we now encourage, and we guard against fantasies and interactions which encourage seeking guidance and answers from others.

We govern ourselves through councils, in which every person from the age of six onwards contributes. Everyone is expected to have a view and intelligence about how we might collectively survive. Even the smallest child knows where berries grow. We have no time for distractions anymore; there is no television, no internet, no film. Interestingly, we don't miss these things very much. We do gather and make time to dance, and tell stories and share food. The Collapse was dreadful, but in its wake we have learned just how precious our human lives are, and the things that truly make us happy. We have learned to be sensitive to one another. It is the only way.

Truth is based on what is best for those of us who are the worst off, those of us still suffering from disease, or suffering the aftermath of trauma. We have also learned to welcome strangers and to truly value diverse thought. In order to survive, we have come to understand how vital 'the other' is: she will have knowledge that we have forgotten; he might be able to solve a problem we have yet to encounter. Those of us who are left seem to have experienced a shift of consciousness in which rather than assuming threat, we understand how strangers enrich our lives.

The legacy of the last leaders is that we have learned that in order to survive, we need one another, rather than a 'leader'. They also taught us the behaviours to avoid: self-aggrandisement is discouraged, we do not ignore those poorer than ourselves, we do not engender fear and, importantly, we accept uncertainty as the well-spring of everything creative. Leadership, we have come to understand, was an idea, like that of slavery, or the quest for perpetual youth which was of another time. We never want to make it possible for a few individuals' insanity to destroy so much again. We are not fearful. We have survived the end of days; we know we can carry on. Critically, we will do so without the fantasy of leadership to guide us.

17 Conclusion

Brigid Carroll, Josh Firth and Suze Wilson

Having reached this point in the book, our hope is that you have found much that has enabled and provoked a questioning and rethinking of your most dearly held assumptions and beliefs about leadership. Our ambition, certainly, is that 'leadership' has been reconstituted in your mind as something different than it was before you read this book. In all likelihood, you will have reached this concluding chapter with the expectation that we will attempt to now review all the key insights that we think the book offers and identify next steps. While we will highlight some common themes, before doing that we want to turn back to our engagement with MacIntyre one more time. The reason for doing so relates to a particular feature of MacIntyre's 'A Disquieting Suggestion' to which we haven't yet alluded: his imaginary post-apocalyptic world was not in fact imaginary but, rather, the current state of his chosen subject and field – morality. We quote this admission here:

> What is the point of constructing this imaginary world inhabited by fictitious pseudo-scientists and real, genuine philosophy? The hypothesis which I wish to advance is that in the actual world which we inhabit the language of morality is in the same state of grave disorder as the language of natural science in the imaginary world which I described. What we possess, if this view is true, are the fragments of a conceptual scheme, parts which now lack these contexts from which their significance derived. We possess indeed simulacra of morality, we continue to use many of the key expressions. But we have – very largely, if not entirely – lost our comprehension, both theoretical and practical, of morality.[1]

The question we therefore now ask at the end of this book is whether the same can be said of leadership studies?

MacIntyre makes it clear that this is far from an easy question to answer. The very ability to detect the kind of 'grave disorder' he speaks of is generally hidden from scholars and from scholarly analysis and he reminds us that both inhabitants of imaginary and real worlds are not necessarily in a position to recognise and acknowledge the kind of catastrophe he has outlined. He speculates that if such a catastrophe had happened, then we would not necessarily recall specific events or even a pattern of decline or fall, and that the academic privileging of a 'value-neutral viewpoint'[2] in any case renders decline and disorder invisible. What we might be able to track is a succession of schools of thought – what we often refer to as the canon – providing successive changes in focus and assumptions without a language or narrative that makes sense of those. This succession of alternative schools and theories without meaning 'in-between' he calls 'symptoms of the disaster' and posits that a prolonging of this pattern creates a schism between the curriculum and 'the real world and its fate'.[3]

At a first glance, it does seem an easy leap to apply such a diagnosis to leadership studies. Any student of leadership can rattle through a canon of half a dozen schools of thinking (trait, behavioural, contingency, charismatic, transformational, authentic) that all overlap, replicate core assumptions and compensate for the deficits in the others. Beyond this mainstream of thinking we then find collective, distributed, relational, post-heroic and critical schools of thought, circulating amongst entirely different communities of scholars. By and large, there is little interaction between mainstream and alternative perspectives.

What is clear, then, is that the leadership studies field is comprised of 'fragments of a conceptual scheme'. These fragments, moreover, are often decontextualised due to the use of research methods that aspire to formulate universal truths about leadership, meaning their actual significance for the real world is also often lacking. A prime example of this are issues of ethics and power. While these appear in both mainstream and alternative schools of thought, acting as sources of friction and contestation, they remain disturbingly and stubbornly on the periphery of the leadership construct despite their pivotal, real-world importance. Overall, there is no shortage of MacIntyre's 'symptoms of the disaster' evident in the leadership field.

We note also the tyranny of a 'value-neutral viewpoint' in leadership studies, something that every chapter in this book without exception seeks to expose, dispel and reimagine. That one can *claim* to research and write about how leadership operates clinically, distanced from the effects or consequences of such leadership, is both well established and indeed often expected in our field. Leadership research also remains dominated by models, frameworks and assessments, or what we could call the technicalities and technologies of leadership that, albeit surrounded by anecdotes and illustrative examples, appear to presume that history, purpose, culture, relationships and context at best are variables or case study background information and at worst have no significance at all.

As evidential and prescriptive connections to performance and results remain the Holy Grail for many researchers, we find repeated references to change and transformation. In contrast, attention to issues of emancipation, justice, status quo breaking and systemic, structural reform sits at the outer edges of the field, is marginalised and thus has marginal theoretical and practical impact. Yet if these issues are taken seriously – as we argue they need to be if leadership studies is to be of relevance in addressing real-world problems – then the dominant approach taken in the field can be likened to an emperor with no clothes; a fancy and sparkling rhetoric that legitimates 'business as usual', positional and authoritative direction and the relentless pursuit of doing the same thing faster, managerially smarter, and with less resource.

If the current state of leadership studies, then, is a field comprised of conceptual fragments whose real-world significance is at best unclear and at worst of no real relevance in helping to address the pressing problems facing humanity, these problems arising in part from the misplaced effort to produce technocratic value-free knowledge in relation to a phenomenon that is laden with ethical, political and symbolic meaning and impact, then what does this book contribute to addressing these concerns? While we can't speak for our readers' experience, we highlight next just *some* of the questions, propositions and metaphors that the conceptual explorations offered here have surfaced and the possibilities glimmered from the speculative thought that is the heart of this book. While we do not directly mention by name every chapter or author, we firmly believe that each offers something unique and deserving of consideration. Here, then, we merely highlight some common themes that we have taken from what this book offers.

After Leadership abounds with old stories that leadership studies needs to be reminded of and new ones that it needs to acquaint itself with. In terms of old stories, we find ourselves surrounded by the ghosts of three anarchists in Neil Sutherland's chapter (Chapter 15) debating 'the fundamental nature of humankind' and then by the characters of Platonic myths in Jonathan Gosling's and Peter Case's chapter (Chapter 9) in exploring patterns of death and rebirth to untangle agency and myth. Both chapters remind us that in order not to operate at the level of transactions and functions, leadership needs to be in active dialogue with philosophical thinking. At the other edge of the spectrum we meet *The Terminator* franchise in Nancy Harding's chapter (Chapter 8), where the population seek protection (at often significant cost) from leaders of faceless and inhumane corporations, while Marian Iszatt-White's engagement with robot-human interaction (Chapter 4), helps us see what it means to be human in a world where, at the very least, humans share agency with technology and, at the most, potentially lose the ability to lead such technologies. If we, as a scholarly leadership community, are to engage with MacIntyre's oft-quoted premise, 'I can only answer the question "What am I to do?" if I can answer the prior question "Of what story or stories do I find myself a part?"', then this book abounds with old and new stories that frame alternative leadership possibilities and questions that must be engaged with.

We also find the seeds of a new language for a new leadership epoch. From Stewart Clegg's and Miguel Pina e Cunha's chapter (Chapter 12) we gain the word 'liquid' and the notion of liquid selves, liquid organisations and liquid aesthetics to help us locate leadership in unabashedly public, adiaphoric and creatively flexing spaces and times. Helena Liu's chapter (Chapter 7) offers us 'whiteness' and a battery of associated processes – normalisation, solipsism and ontological expansiveness – to give us a literacy to redo and abolish a white supremacy at the very core of the leadership construct. Sonia Ospina's chapter (Chapter 10) gives us 'social location' in order to ground intersecting identities, the framing of experience and the dynamics of power in leadership acts and 'commons' to signify a space where people come together to do interconnected work with common purpose and perseverance through conflict and difference. *After Leadership,* in short, reminds us that we have a plethora of words for individual, heroic and managerially orientated activity but a dearth of ones that enable leadership to move beyond leader-centric and authoritative boundaries.

One dimension of leadership studies that the book brings to the fore is its inherently interdisciplinary nature. Once we were proud of its roots and connections across multiple fields but in recent decades there has been a palpable sense of a retreat into psychology and management theory. *After Leadership* puts leadership into dialogue with archaeology, cartography, classical mythology, philosophy, critical race studies, media and cultural studies, anarchism and political theory, French literature and medieval history. Such intertwining with other fields creates richness, depth, expansiveness, surprise, novelty and new directions. Leadership needs to escape what can be a straitjacket of the business school canon, one that seems to cause a hard 'to spot and stop' slippage into instrumentality, reductionism and functionalism. Leadership studies needs to constantly replenish itself with new edges, new questions, new metaphors, new narratives and new concepts. *After Leadership* speaks to the adventures leadership can undertake by connecting itself with diverse ways of knowing, thinking and being.

Any book titled *After Leadership* is bound to raise questions about whether leadership can and should survive, and if so, in what form. Those are questions to which we don't want to dictate an answer, seeing them as matters for each reader to ask and answer for themselves. However, we suggest the following may help in the process of grappling with those questions. Firstly, we note that the majority of our authors don't flinch from the significant change needed in leadership theory and practice to make it worth saving. There are other concepts and practices to which we can turn if leadership scholars and practitioners resist addressing the concerns raised here – such as collaboration, consensus, activism, mobilisation and even organisation – so *After Leadership* isn't willing to accept its survival at any cost. Further, the unsettling ease with which many authors have exposed the oft-presumed 'specialness' of leadership to be nothing more than hubris or hype reveals a real need for leadership scholarship to continue to wrestle with the distinctive character of what leadership can offer organisations and society – and this book has offered an array of diverse and surprising springboards for this work.

We note also something that might be considered incidental, but we instinctively think is not, and that is the passion, energy and commitment to researching and writing on leadership that all these chapters share. Even the most critical of authors and the most direct of polemics have a strength of voice and affective connection to the leadership construct. We see little evidence of indifference or neutrality – and experience tells us that if it is a construct that can still inspire frustration, rage, care and even desire then it is a construct with some life yet. Equally, however, we note that this reaction seems tied to the potential for leadership, both theory and practice, to subordinate, pacify and disempower as strongly as any of its more redeeming qualities. For us, this speaks to an important tension at the heart of our field, one which is stirred up as we continue to redefine and rebuild leadership from the inside, holding on and letting go all at once.

We have never seen this book as one motivated or shaped by a pessimistic stance. It certainly has doubt, perplexity, critique of fondly held 'truths' and uncertainty, but our spirits don't sink with the feeling that *After Leadership* had turned its back and given up on a construct, a field or a practice that certainly has not escaped the baggage of its history, nor lived into the promise of an emancipatory social process. We could certainly glimpse in these pages a future where leadership doesn't survive as a meaningful construct or practice, or where it morphs into another construct, discourse or practice. However, the need to connect across individual, collective and system boundaries, to break through established practices, and to engage with challenges that unlock a new humanity and future seems to have undeniable power for the authors in this book. We end as MacIntyre ended 'A Disquieting Suggestion', with a firm sense that angst, despair and pessimism are beside the point and a contemporary indulgence that we can't afford, regardless of whether leadership or something else is the vehicle for a collective effort to challenge the status quo and build a better world.

> Do not however suppose that the conclusion to be drawn will turn out to be one of despair. Angst is an intermittently fashionable emotion and the misreading of some existentialist texts has turned despair itself into a kind of psychological nostrum. But if we are indeed in as bad a state as I take us to be, pessimism too will turn out to be one more cultural luxury that we shall have to dispense with in order to survive in these hard times.[4]

Notes

1 MacIntyre, 1981, p. 2.
2 Ibid., p. 4.
3 Ibid.
4 Ibid., p. 5.

Reference

MacIntyre, A. C. (1981). *After Virtue: A Study in Moral Theory.* Notre Dame, IN: University of Notre Dame Press.

Index

Printed in the United States
by Baker & Taylor Publisher Services